Reconnecting Consumers, Producers and Food

Cultures of Consumption Series

Series Editor: Frank Trentmann

ISSN 1744-5876

Previously Published

The Making of the Consumer
Knowledge, Power and Identity in the Modern World
Edited by Frank Trentmann

Consuming Cultures, Global Perspectives
Historical Trajectories, Transnational Exchanges
Edited by John Brewer and Frank Trentmann

Fashion's World Cities
Edited by Christopher Breward and David Gilbert

The Khat Controversy
Stimulating the Debate on Drugs
David Anderson, Susan Beckerleg, Degol Hailu and Axel Klein

The Design of Everyday Life
Elizabeth Shove, Matthew Watson, Jack Ingram and Martin Hand

Food and Globalization
Consumption, Markets and Politics in the Modern World
Edited by Alexander Nützenadel and Frank Trentmann

Forthcoming Titles

Governing Consumption
New Spaces of Consumer Politics
Clive Barnett, Nick Clarke, Paul Cloke and Alice Malpass

Reconnecting Consumers, Producers and Food

Exploring Alternatives

MOYA KNEAFSEY, ROSIE COX,
LEWIS HOLLOWAY,
ELIZABETH DOWLER,
LAURA VENN
and
HELENA TUOMAINEN

Oxford • New York

English edition
First published in 2008 by
Berg
Editorial offices:
First Floor, Angel Court, 81 St Clements Street, Oxford OX4 1AW , UK
175 Fifth Avenue, New York, NY 10010, USA

Berg is the imprint of Oxford International Publishers Ltd.

Library of Congress Cataloging-in-Publication Data
A catalogue record for this book is available from the Library of Congress.

British Library Cataloguing-in-Publication Data
A catalogue record for this book is available from the British Library.

ISBN 978 1 84520 252 1 (Cloth)
978 1 84520 253 8 (Paper)

Typeset by JS Typesetting Ltd, Porthcawl, Mid Glamorgan
Printed in the United Kingdom by Biddles Ltd, King's Lynn

www.bergpublishers.com

Contents

Tables and Illustrations

Acknowledgements

This book is based primarily on research conducted during a project funded by the Economic and Social Research Council and the Arts and Humanities Research Council (Ref: RES-143–25–005), which ran from 2003 to 2006, as part of their joint Cultures of Consumption Research Programme. This book presents the key findings of our research, but also reflects a distillation of our wider thinking and post-project reflections in the context of a fast moving field of study.

Many people have helped us during the course of the research. Without extended co-operation from the producers, growers and scheme managers whose endeavours form a central focus of this book, we could never have completed our project: so, to Paul and Doreen Robinson, Andy and Tish Jeffery, Peter and Liz Scott, Veronica Barry, David Straker, Pam Bochel and Manuela Cozzi, we are enormously grateful. We are also indebted to the many people who attended our workshops, agreed to be interviewed, took photographs of their food, and even let us into their homes to find out about their food habits! We are especially grateful to Graham Noble, of Moray, Scotland, for donating his photograph of the beautiful EarthShare box of vegetables for the front cover of our book, and Barbara Taylor, also of Moray, for the photograph used in Chapter 6. For assisting with various stages of the research we would like to thank Dr Jane Ricketts Hein, Dr Kate Mahoney and Mr Mark Donnarumma.

We also want to acknowledge the members of our Consultation Panel, who met with us during the course of our research, and provided invaluable advice and critique:

Ann Baldridge and Dr Tom Macmillan (both of the Food Ethics Council), Helen Barber (Co-operatives UK), Joy Carey (Soil Association), Naomi Diamond (f3), Sue Dibb (formerly of the National Consumer Council, now at the Sustainable Development Commission), Chris Firth (formerly of the Henry Doubleday Research Association), Dr Jill Hopkinson (Church of England National Rural Officer), Jamie Inglis (Advantage West Midlands),

Dr Tim Marsh (National Heart Forum, formerly of the Women's Institute), James Pavitt (formerly of the National Advisory for Farmers' Markets), Paul Sander-Jackson (New Economics Foundation, formerly Somerset Food Links/Food Links UK), Chris Thomas (Sustainability Co-ordinator, Coventry City Council) and John Turner (Farm). We also want to thank the National Consumer Council, for hosting our final dissemination event, as well as the delegates who attended. Their contributions helped us greatly in thinking through the implications of our research as we drew to the end of the project.

For their insightful comments on the draft manuscript of this book, we are extremely grateful to Professor Frank Trentmann, Professor David Goodman (who both also provided key critical comments at various stages of our research) and Dr Mike Goodman. Any faults and errors are entirely our own. For help in preparing the manuscript and undertaking additional research, we appreciate the excellent work of Ms Rachel Peak; and for designing the map, we thank Mr Stuart Gill, the cartographer at Coventry University. Each of us would also like to thank colleagues in our respective departments at Coventry, Birkbeck, Hull and Warwick for the intellectual and moral support they have provided at key moments during the research and writing of this book. And of course, we are grateful to our publishers, Berg, for their patience and understanding as deadlines came and went.

Finally, the six authors whose collective work is represented in these pages, would each like to acknowledge the love and care shown by their spouses, partners, childminders, friends and families; care which in countless practical, and often mundane daily ways, has helped to make this book possible.

CHAPTER I

Contextualizing 'Alternative' Food Relationships

INTRODUCTION

We live at a time when serious socio-economic, ethical and environmental problems associated with food regularly cause concern. Many people – consumers, producers, campaigners and policy-makers – are said to worry about the ways in which food is provisioned for a whole variety of interlinked reasons. Alongside the rapid technological changes associated with processes of industrialization and globalization in food production, processing and retailing, insistent critiques of the structures and relationships of food provision are now gathering momentum. There is a growing recognition that the very values underpinning contemporary food supply arrangements are in need of critical scrutiny (Food and Agriculture Organization 2001). In other words, to what extent and how do we value food, its production, its distribution and its consumption?

Indeed, some of the key ethical questions of our time relate to food. For example, how can we address food inequalities, and the challenge of the so-called 'obesity epidemic'? How can trade relations be structured more fairly, especially for small-scale food producers and growers? How much should consumers know (or be told, or want to know) about their food, and to what extent should they be 'trusted' or 'empowered' to choose the 'healthiest', 'fairest' and most ecologically benign foods? To what extent can scientists, processors, retailers and governments be 'trusted' to tell the whole story about food? How far should the environment be degraded, or animals have to suffer to produce food people want to buy? Such questions are, of course, addressing highly complex issues, but the point is, answering them requires an explicit evaluation and prioritization of values, which in turn can only be achieved through critical reflection on what societies and individuals are really prepared – and enabled – to care for. In this book, we aim to contribute to such an appraisal of the value of food, by examining some of the diverse ways in which consumers and producers are actively involved in building food relationships and practices which they regard as better suited to meeting their everyday needs, sustaining their lifestyles, addressing their anxieties and satisfying their own, as well as more widespread, daily ethical dilemmas.

Within this broad context, this book provides a detailed and empirically grounded analysis of the activities of food producers and consumers involved in the creation of 'alternatives' to the current dominant models of food provision. In the United Kingdom, there is now growing evidence that different people in all sorts of different places are actively engaging with some of these fundamental questions about our relationship with food: from inner city residents creating vegetable gardens from reclaimed wastelands, to neighbours in remote rural locations sharing agricultural risks and responsibilities. In a variety of locations, producers and consumers alike are working to construct new and ethically significant food relationships and practices, which they see as helping to address concerns about health, social justice, animal welfare and the environment. For example, markets for local, organic, and fairly traded foods are continuing to expand, and not only among the higher income consumer groups. The Institute for Grocery Distribution (IGD) (2005a) suggests that 70 per cent of British consumers want to buy local food and 49 per cent want to buy more of it than they do now. In 2005 retail sales of organic products were worth an estimated £1.6 billion, an increase of 30 per cent on the previous year (Soil Association 2006), and the retail value of products carrying the Fairtrade Mark rose from £16.7 million in 1998 to over £195 million in 2005 (Fairtrade Foundation 2007).

Evidence also suggests that not only are people increasingly interested in the origins and ethical and health properties of their food, but they are also prepared to buy direct from producers through a variety of different channels. This is said to engender more trust in food provenance, support local businesses and enhance pleasure in food purchase and use (Sage 2003; Kirwan 2004). The first farmers' market in Britain was launched in Bath in 1997. By 2006, farmers' markets were being held in 550 locations around the United Kingdom, with a combined turnover of £220 million (National Farmers' Retail & Markets Association 2006; Soil Association 2006). There are also several hundred organic vegetable 'box schemes' now operating in the United Kingdom, which provide produce direct from the grower to the purchaser, and are thought to have combined sales in excess of £100 million per year (Soil Association 2007). Sales through independent shops, farm shops, farmers' markets and box schemes in total increased by 32 per cent from 2004–5 (Soil Association 2006). Large retailers are also keen to build on these trends. So, for example, Waitrose advertisements currently focus on British and local sourcing, and other major supermarkets promote local and regional quality produce (e.g. Tesco's 'Finest' and Sainsbury's 'Taste the Difference' ranges). 2007 also saw the arrival in West London of the American Whole Foods Market, a farmers' co-operative which began in Texas, and which now sells organic and 'green' products in 190 stores in the United States, Canada and United Kingdom, and in 2006 had a turnover of £3.2 billion (Renton 2007).

Through detailed explorations of six 'alternatives' to predominant food supply arrangements, this book examines the identities, motives and practices of people actively involved in trying to produce and consume food in ways which allow them to address a variety of societal and individual concerns about food. Their efforts, we argue, are integral to the construction of a practical critique of current food structures. Recognizing the multidimensionality of 'alternative' food relationships, we move beyond the emphasis on economic imperatives for producers to 'connect' with the market, and examine the ethical, emotional and reflexive spaces of 'reconnection'. In so doing, we engage with themes of care, love, pleasure, anxiety, choice and convenience, and show how these elements are spoken of, and experienced by, a range of producers and consumers. And we argue that the motives and practices of those involved, can be understood within the context of a broad framework of care for close and distant 'others' (variously defined), which in turn provides discursive and material expressions of 'reconnection' with the potential to radically realign producer and consumer relationships through food.

CONTEXTUALIZING PRODUCER, CONSUMER AND FOOD 'RECONNECTION'

Food is currently the subject of much debate and controversy in the United Kingdom.[1] Celebrity chefs are omnipresent, cookery programmes are screened on television in abundance, there has been a renaissance in 'British' ingredients and cuisine, and books on cooking, diets and health regimes proliferate. Despite all this, consumers are often accused of having 'lost' their cooking skills and knowledge about food origins, preparation and nutritional values. Food is abundant, of consistent quality and often cheap, and yet it can also cause anxiety and illness. Food provides essential nourishment for health, and yet the over-consumption of saturated fats, salt and refined sugars, and the under-consumption of vitamins and minerals, particularly those found in vegetables and fruits, threatens the lives and health of millions in 'developed' and 'developing' economies (Popkin 1999; World Health Organization/Food and Agriculture Organization 2003; World Health Organization 2007).

Barely a week passes by without a 'scare' concerning particular ingredients or production methods, often involving a supermarket accused of deceiving consumers about where products come from, and how they are made. Recent examples include concerns about residues of pesticides and veterinary medicines found in certain foods, plus fears about salmonella, BSE, *E. coli* 0157, genetically modified foods, foot and mouth disease, dioxins in animal feeds, toxic cooking oil and Sudan I, a potentially carcinogenic food dye (Morgan et al. 2006). We could also add avian influenza and the existence of PCBs in farmed salmon to the list, plus the 297 food additives permitted in non-organic food, which have been linked to heart disease, osteoporosis, migraines and hyperactivity (Soil Association 2005a). There are also concerns about the level of salt hidden in everyday products such as cereals, bread and meat, where consumers might not expect to find it (Scientific Advisory Committee on Nutrition (SACN) 2003). Salt is an important determinant of high blood pressure, which is a contributory factor in over 170,000 deaths per year in England (SACN 2003).

Not only are there fears about what is in food, but also what is missing from it; so, for example, evidence is emerging of lower levels of trace minerals, secondary nutrients (e.g. antioxidants) and vitamins found in conventionally produced fruit and vegetables compared to organic produce (Soil Association 2005a). Thus, Felicity Lawrence, in her best-selling *Not on the Label*, argues that '[P]aradoxically, as we have become more affluent as a nation, we have also become more anxious about our food and how it is produced' (2004: xiii). Those concerned with the environment, meanwhile, point to the damage caused to wildlife, soils, water and climate by the current methods used to grow, process, package and transport food (see, for example, Sustain 2001; Defra 2002a; Soil Association 2005a, 2005b), whilst others draw attention to the living conditions experienced by intensively produced livestock, such as factory farmed chickens.

These concerns are no longer new. Indeed, food panics have recurred cyclically throughout modern history (e.g. Cobbett 1979 [1822]). Writing about food choice in the 1990s, Murcott (1998a: 1) described that decade as one which saw 'a veritable explosion of international public concern about food'. Almost ten years after the end of the Economic and Social Research Council's programme on the Nation's Diet, anxieties about food on the part of the public have not disappeared. If anything, they have intensified and proliferated. The government responded to this erosion of consumer confidence in the food supply chain and its regulation by establishing the independent Food Standards Agency (FSA) in 2000 (Morgan et al. 2006), while retailers have launched a raft of new labelling schemes, product ranges, and environmental initiatives in order to secure consumer trust. Yet, despite government and retailer strategies to reassure consumers, critiques of the food system from various perspectives are gaining coherence and momentum. For instance, at the time of writing, the Strategy Unit in the Cabinet Office is reviewing the whole food system and the challenges it poses to government and citizens alike (Strategy Unit 2008).

We argue that the problems briefly outlined here are attributable, at least partly, to the disconnection of consumers from food, in the sense that many consumers know very little about where much of their food comes from, what it is made of, how it is produced, and by whom. And in response to this situation, we suggest that there is evidence of attempts by both consumers and producers, to try to 'reconnect' with each other, and with food, through engagement in more direct relationships. Just how and why people – whether producers or purchasers – become enrolled into these relationships, and why they matter, forms the main focus of this book.

In the rest of this chapter, we provide a more detailed context for our research and analysis. First, we establish what we mean by 'disconnection', and explore its implications for producers and consumers; this enables us to 'flesh out' some of the introductory points made above and provides a sense of some of the key motivations driving contemporary urges to 'reconnect' producers, consumers and food. Crucially, we want to establish that discourses and practices of 'reconnection' have emerged *in relationship with*, rather than simply 'in opposition to', discourses and practices of 'disconnection' in the food system. Second, we introduce six examples of 'reconnection' between food producers and consumers. These examples provide the empirical data upon which our analysis is based, and form the focus of subsequent chapters in the book.

A 'DISCONNECTED' FOOD SYSTEM? EVIDENCE AND IMPLICATIONS

It could be argued that rather than being disconnected, the contemporary food system is more connected than ever. Farming is now generally viewed as part of a wider, vertically integrated agro-industrial food system, in which the production sector is contractually linked upstream to input suppliers, and downstream to processing, distribution and retail industries (Ilbery

2005). Large agribusinesses, or food chain 'clusters' (Hendrickson and Heffernan 2002) manipulate land, technical knowledge, chemical inputs, machinery and processing facilities, export and distribution systems. Thus, for example, in 2002 just five global companies dominated the seed industry (Hendrickson and Heffernan 2002).

The larger retailers are also more connected than ever to other actors in the food chain. They contract farmers to grow crops or raise livestock to meet their exact specifications, and they contract processors to produce goods that carry the retailers' own label (Millstone and Lang 2006). Consumers are also increasingly connected to these political economic networks, in that, although the variety of foods available has grown enormously, they have in fact arguably less and less choice about where to buy food. According to Simms (2007: 92), the four largest supermarket chains in Britain now control 75 per cent of the grocery market and, as he points out of the market leader, 'if all its current plans are allowed to come to fruition, Tesco will double its size at home. According to insider City analysis …, Tesco is set to end up taking £1 in every £4 spent by United Kingdom shoppers.' (The figure currently stands at about £1 in every £8, and this is not exclusively expenditure on food but also includes other goods and services.) Consumers therefore have more 'choice' of commodity range, but less choice of retailer. Additionally, because of retailer size and scale of operation, most are unable to stock produce from very small and/or 'local' producers, so reducing customer access to these products. With their ability to conduct extensive market research and track expenditure linked to socio-demographic indicators in considerable detail from various forms of 'loyalty' cards, retailers also hold sophisticated and closely guarded information about consumers' buying habits and preferences; such knowledge remains privileged, outside the public domain, and is used to manage the system to competitive advantage. Not least, the information enables retailers to develop new products and services (extending into banking, insurance and so on) with which to 'connect' ever more completely with their customers.

In this book, we argue that, in fact, it is these very trends that are contributing to the 'disconnection' of consumers from their food and its production. The idea of 'disconnection' refers not only to structures and relationships within the food system, but also to perceptions and feelings about the food system. 'Disconnection' evokes the perceived and actual separation of food production from food consumption. This is most notable in the sense that, as we said above, most consumers in developed market economies do not know where (or how) much of their food is produced. This state of affairs is hardly new. As Trentmann (2007) notes, the lengthening of food chains is associated with processes of globalization dating back to the seventeenth century, when in Holland, for example, about one third of peoples' food came from afar. By 1913, food made up 27 per cent of world exports (according to O'Rourke 2003, cited in Trentmann 2007) and was firmly entrenched in the global economy. The increased geographical and technological distances involved in production–consumption networks mean that food origins and conditions of production are often 'dis-placed' (Cook and Crang 1996). Indeed, as Cook, Crang and Thorpe point out, 'the practical possibility of a complete knowledge of food provision systems has to be questioned. The distance food travels to get to our plates and the sheer complexity of the food system, inevitably means that the biographies of the foods we eat are rather opaque to us' (Cook et al. 1998: 164). Moreover, many consumers do not want to know where their food comes from or how it is made, and place trust in governments, regulatory systems and retailers to provide food that is safe to eat.

'Disconnection' in the food system is an outcome (but by no means an end result) of the complex interplay of several major processes, including farm industrialization, the growth of food processor and retail power, the contested governance of international trade and changing consumer lifestyles, expectations and practices. This state of affairs has a number of interlinked implications for producers, consumers and food itself.[2] In the following sections, we examine these implications, and thus begin to demonstrate the ways in which 'disconnecting' trends in the food system are opening up co-evolving spaces of 'reconnection', as producers and consumers seek more sustainable, healthy and equitable models of food provision.

The Implications of 'Disconnection' for Producers

The term 'producer' is used here to refer mainly to farmers, those who grow crops and raise livestock. During the transition to an industrialized, technologically driven system for the mass production and distribution of food, it is generally recognized that there has been a shift in power, away from farmers and growers, and towards processors and retailers (Tansey and Worsley 1995; Millstone and Lang 2006). One important indicator of this is that farmers in general have experienced a fall in income as processors and retailers have become more adept at capturing the value added to raw materials. The Soil Association (2007) reports a 61 per cent decline in the total income from farming in Britain and a 39 per cent decline in the average income per person (in real terms) employed in agriculture from 1973 to 2004. The Department for Environment, Food and Rural Affairs (Defra)

(2006) reports that at the beginning of the 1950s, agriculture accounted for 5 per cent of GDP and broadly 6 per cent of employment, whereas in 2006 the figures stand at broadly 0.7 per cent and 2 per cent (although the share of employment is higher in rural areas, at 4 per cent for England). The total labour force in agriculture fell by 16,000 between 2002 and 2006 and over half of the labour force now works on a part-time basis (Defra 2006). Less money goes back to rural spaces and communities, and the growers of food – once centrally located in social, symbolic and economic terms – have thus been kicked sideways in pursuit of what Hendrickson and Heffernan (2002: 359) describe as the 'elegant vision' known as the 'bottom line'.

The shift in power away from farmers and towards food retailers and processors has also meant that many smaller farmers have been unable to find markets for their produce. They are unable to produce the volumes and consistencies of quality required by supermarkets, while at the same time the number of different outlets (retail markets, independent greengrocers or butchers) has fallen. Still others, notably in the dairy industry, have been unable to survive on the meagre profit margins squeezed down by supermarket contracts. The power shifts in the food system are not only reflected in terms of the reduction in farmer incomes and the disappearance of many smaller farms. There are those who argue that, as they have been enrolled into relationships with large processors and retailers, farmers have lost much of their autonomy and have had less use for traditional and inherited knowledges about land and livestock (Pretty 2002). In an agriculture dependent on chemicals to maintain soil fertility, control pests and promote growth in animals, farmers have become 'disconnected' from traditional knowledge-practices about how to achieve these ends. In their scathing attack on productivist agriculture and its associated values, Bové and Dufour (2005) write fiercely of the loss of agricultural knowledge and the resultant de-skilling of farmers in France. Writing about the response to epizootic outbreaks, they note that 'As they watch the bonfires and the killing, farmers are made to realize the full extent of the transformation that has been forced on them; from being producers of food and foodstuffs ... they have become manufacturers of raw materials, of merchandising pure and simple, which is a violation of their original role' (2005: 49). Although Bové and Dufour's writing is polemical, it captures the passion evoked in discussions about what has happened to farmers and farming. The language of violation and force is significant; it reflects a common feeling in farming communities that the changes that have happened have not been at their behest. Farmers often represent themselves – and are represented as – victims of a fast changing, highly competitive, globalized food system in which they have little power. Thus, according to Bové and Dufour, the basic elements of the farmers' job have been 'stripped out'; 'the connection between the act of production, which consists of giving life, and the social act of eating and appreciating the value of our daily bread' (2005: 49) has gone. In their view, this loss of knowledge has implications not just for farmers, but for society more broadly, in that the value of food has been downgraded. We would suggest that rather than a complete loss of farming knowledge, it is more accurate to refer to complex entanglements of 'traditional', lay or tacit knowledges with 'new' scientific knowledges (Holloway 2005). Nevertheless, the changing role of farmers in agriculture, rural life and wider society cannot be denied (see, for example, Halfacree 1999).

In a similar vein to Bové and Dufour, Pretty (2002) also argues that, in the industrial age, changes that have occurred in peoples' relationship with food production amount to a loss of connection with cultures and natures of food and place. He writes passionately that, through the industrialization of agriculture, 'we have … allowed ourselves to become disconnected from nature' (2002: xiv) and the result is that we tend not to notice when it is damaged. Moreover:

> As food has become a commodity, most of us no longer feel a link to the place of production and its associated culture. Yet agricultural and food systems, with their associated nature and landscapes, are a common heritage and thus, also, a form of common property. They are shaped by us all and so in some way are part of us all, too. (2002: 2)

For Pretty, the link between people and the places and cultures of food production has been broken through the implementation of agricultural productivism, and the gradual exclusion of the poor through enclosures and the privatization of common properties. In England, such processes date back to the seventeenth century and were accelerated by acts of parliament in the early eighteenth century. In developing countries, dispossession through enclosures has also happened and continues to do so, causing conflict, exclusion and poverty. Pretty argues that this literal 'disconnection' from the land has resulted in a loss of traditional knowledges, memories and stories associated with nature. This has implications not only for the food producers, but for people more generally because, for Pretty, this loss of a relationship with nature is ultimately de-humanizing: 'For all of our time, we have shaped nature, and it has shaped us, and we are an emergent property of this relationship. We cannot suddenly act as if we are separate. If we do so, we simply recreate the wasteland inside of ourselves' (2002: 10). He argues that in order to address this loss, it is necessary to 'reconnect' whole food systems, a point which we return to in more depth in the following chapter.

In the United Kingdom, it is recognized that farmers have experienced high levels of stress, depression and even suicide: since 1993 the proportion of deaths from suicide for both farmers and farm workers has been consistently higher than the rate for all workers (Defra 2007); the Farm Crisis Network has reported an increase in requests for help from farmers and their families who are facing economic difficulties which are often exacerbated by the solitary nature of the work and the sense of isolation that this can engender (see www.farmcrisisnetwork.org.uk). The human costs of 'disconnection' for producers in the food system should not be underestimated; that some farmers and growers are now attempting to 'reconnect' with consumers as a strategy to redress these problems is one theme of our book, particularly in Chapter 4, where we discuss the identities, motives and practices of six producers engaged in different types of 'reconnection'.

The Implications of 'Disconnection' for Consumers

It is important to clarify our general stance towards the concept of 'the consumer', a term which is increasingly confusing. Economists use it to refer to those who expend cash; nutritionists and health professionals mean those who eat food; the retail sector refers to 'customers', and people seldom employ the word of themselves (cf. Barnett et al. 2005a). Although Barnett and his colleagues are not writing specifically about food consumption, the points they make in the following extract apply:

> a great deal of the consumption people do is not undertaken by them as 'consumers' at all. Much of it is embedded in practices where they are being parents, caring partners, football fans, good friends. Some consumption is used to sustain these sorts of relationships: giving gifts, buying school lunches, getting hold of this season's new strip. But quite a lot of consumption is done as the background to these activities, embedded in all sorts of infrastructures over which people have little or no direct influence as 'consumers' (Barnett et al. 2006, no page reference)

Food consumers are often the focus for both public policy and private markets, as those who need to be persuaded to 'act differently' – to buy and use different or new commodities, in order to be healthier, work harder, live actively longer, do less damage to the environment, or, alternatively, keep global capitalist food markets functioning. As noted by Cook et al. (1998) discussions about the nature of the consumer often polarise between the neo-liberal notion of the 'sovereign' consumer and the consumer as 'dupe'. The former, in the British political context at least, is increasingly elided with the idea of the demanding 'citizen-consumer'. This figure is knowledgeable, holds high expectations and is sophisticated at negotiating and manipulating a complex and often contradictory array of information concerning different products and services. The latter figure is confused, overwhelmed by information, anxious and malleable. Cook and colleagues, among others, call for an 'escape [from] the blunt dichotomy between either a knowledgeable, and hence powerful, or ignorant, and hence manipulated, consumer' (1998: 166). A second dichotomous positioning contrasts 'consumers' as individualistic, possibly hedonistic and dominated by informed 'choice' for personal, largely material ends, with 'citizens' as expressing more collective interests, privileging the public as well as, or even rather than, private good (Gabriel and Lang 2006; Clarke et al. 2007; Soper 2007a). The latter also transmutes into/appears as the 'conscientious' or 'ethical' consumer who has a long history (Trentmann 2006), but is much sought after by contemporary politicians and others as a means of addressing the ills of 'over-consumption' – poor health, inequalities and environmental degradation. Thus there is potential for 'connecting the politics of consumption with the practices of being a discerning, choosey consumer [which] embeds altruistic, humanitarian, solidaristic and environmental commitments into the rhythms and routines of everyday life' (Clarke et al. 2007: 233). Whatever the realities, there is nevertheless, a good case for simply recognizing consumers primarily as *people*, with all the complexity and sometimes contradictory identities, motives, thoughts and practices this implies, and not simply as entities defined only by their consumption. Some of these complexities are brought into relief when we examine two major consequences of 'disconnection' for consumers, namely: food-related anxieties and inequalities in access to healthy food.

Anxieties   Anxiety about food (its safety, security of access, reliability as a source of goodness) chimes with what several authors have described as the emergence of an 'age of anxiety', associated with long-term processes of modernization (May 1950; Dunant and Porter 1996). While people can develop personal strategies or 'security patterns' for dealing with fears, '*in anxiety it is this security pattern itself which is threatened*' (May 1950: 191, emphasis in original). In other words, individuals feel powerless to influence economic conditions, environmental damage and so on (Dunant and Porter 1996). A common theme in these accounts is that paradoxically, it seems that increasing knowledge about something can produce even more anxiety as the individual becomes more aware of the things to be anxious about (Midgley 1996; Mulgan 1996). Anxiety is enhanced by a lack of trust in science and government (Beck 1992). In research with over 800 consumers, Duffy et al. (2005) found that consumers did not really trust *anybody* to give them impartial and objective information about food.

One reason anxiety and trust relating to food are so powerful is precisely because, as Fischler (1988) argues, the very act of eating is linked with the process of 'incorporation': food crosses the barrier between the 'outside' world, and the 'inside' world of the body. We thus incorporate all or some of the food's properties; in other words, 'we become what we eat' (Fischler 1988: 279). Consequently, it is vital to identify, know and trust foods in both the literal and figurative sense, for 'if we do not know what we eat, how can we know what we are?' (1988: 282). For Fischler, the source of the problem is 'the omnivore's paradox', which refers to the 'tension between the two poles of neophobia (prudence, fear of the unknown, resistance to change) and neophilia (the tendency to explore, the need for change, novelty, variety)' (1988: 278). Such anxiety, we argue, can be attributed in no small way to the 'disconnection' of food consumers from producers. In part, this is the anxiety of food being 'untrue' or contaminated – not what it purports to be, and thus what we incorporate is neither what we 'know' nor wholly trustworthy. This fear is not new: Rappaport (2006) for instance, usefully reminds us that anxieties about adulteration – in this case of packet tea – date back to at least the mid-Victorian era. Burnett (1989: 93), in his lengthy discussion of food adulteration, clearly links the risk of adulteration and the 'distancing' of consumers and producers. Fischler (1988) also argues that instead of regulating the 'anxiety of the paradox', modern society tends to aggravate it.

This is because, as we discuss above in relation to producers, modern production processes are highly complex, and the ways in which food is grown and processed have become ever more opaque to the consumer. Much of our food thus comes from 'elsewhere.' For the individual consumer this has paradoxical effects: on the one hand, there is a wider range of possible foods available, including exotic ones; on the other, food in the industrial world has become homogenized to the extent that 'modern food has become in the eyes of the eater an 'unidentified edible object', devoid of origin or history, with no respectable past – in short, without identity' (Fischler 1988: 289). Fischler contends that 'the growing demand for symbols of nature could be interpreted in terms of a response to, a reaction against, the increasingly serious problem we have in *identifying* our food' (Fischler 1980:

945). He argues that a shift is taking place in what Western culture perceives to belong to the categories of purity and pollution. Whereas traditionally, raw foodstuffs had to be 'civilized' or 'tamed' through processing in order to become fit for consumption, this 'industrial purification' appears no longer to guarantee symbolic purity. Instead, it breeds 'symbolic danger' in the form of chemicals or trace elements. His argument is that this is why, as a consequence, people start preferring 'natural' or 'organic' food.

The 'disconnected' ways in which contemporary consumers learn about their food are also anxiety inducing (a similar point is made by Bové and Dufour 2005: 4–5). Arguably, in contemporary industrial societies, consumers learn about food through 'scares' reported by the media, which they cannot judge or assess, partly because of their remoteness from the processes of food production. These food 'scares' are often referred to by critics as an inevitable result of the 'stretched out', industrialized food system, such that the emphasis on productivity has resulted in practices which in many instances help to nurture and spread biological threats to human health. When a food crisis hits the headlines, the knowledge gained is often fragmented, framed so as to be sensational or frightening, and presented in isolation from scientific, traditional or practice-based knowledge forms.

Whilst a focus on anxiety may paint a dismal picture of the state of being a consumer, it is also important to recognize that although anxiety can be debilitating, it can also be productive for those who respond with attempts to change themselves, or their environments to counter their anxieties (Levitt 1980; May 1996). As Midgley (1996: 49) notes, 'anxiety has a function'; it can be associated with collective action, creativity, energy, and with alternative visions of how things might be done. In these terms, anxieties about society and the environment might be associated with radical or utopian visions for better futures.

Inequalities in Access to Healthy Food   While the nation may be more affluent, and food more plentiful than ever before, the socially and geographically uneven experience of diet-related ill-health continues to cause concern, since coming to the fore in policy and research agendas during the 1990s (Acheson 1998; Dowler et al. 2007). While there is no agreed definition of 'adequate access' to healthy food (O'Neill 2005), the term 'food poverty' is widely used to describe the inability to acquire or consume a sufficient quantity of food in socially acceptable ways, or the uncertainty that one will be able to do so (Dowler et al. 2001b).

Current arrangements of food supply mean that poorer consumers in some locations are literally disconnected from food, not least due to geographies of food retail. Large supermarkets, for instance, have tended to be located in higher income areas, or out of town where they are only accessible by car. In recent years the penetration of town centres by smaller 'quick use' versions of the main retailers, has nevertheless tended to continue the geographical isolation of those poorer communities located in peri-urban and suburban estates. In combination with a 'compliant' planning system, this has created 'geographies of plenty and scarcity' (Marsden et al. 2000b: 36). Although the concept of 'food deserts' has been subject to critique (Wrigley 2002; Dowler et al. 2007), it is still the case that those consumers constrained by 'mobility restrictions' – notably women, the elderly and disabled – are in some places unable to access supermarkets (Westlake 1993; Wrigley 1998; Dowler et al. 2007). It is also the case that smaller shops in many districts have either closed down (Guy 1996) or are considerably more expensive (Acheson 1998). Dowler and Caraher (2003) found that the corner stores on which some groups of poorer consumers depend charge from 6 to 13 per cent more for a nutritionally adequate diet than large supermarkets. Research in Staffordshire revealed that products from local shops were, on average, 37 per cent more expensive than the equivalent items from a supermarket (O'Neill 2005). Moreover, a 'healthy' diet could be up to 88 per cent more expensive and local food outlets were found to have a 'disproportionate amount of shelf space devoted to foods high in fats, sugar and salt, and their fresh food is more likely to have detectable pesticide residues' (O'Neill 2005: 1). Lower income groups thus tend to depend more heavily on cheap meat products, full-cream milk, fats, sugars and preserves, with a relatively low intake of vegetables, fruit and wholemeal bread (Lang and Heasman 2004). They are also more likely to buy economy brand ranges which have been shown to contain higher levels of salt, fat and sugar than standard equivalents (National Consumer Council 2006).

Low-income consumers are thus constrained in their ability to choose healthy food. Dowler and Caraher (2003) argue that, since the nineteenth century, when Victorian covered food markets were seen as public health initiatives to bring wholesome food to the workers, responsibility for food provision in the United Kingdom has shifted from the State to the individual. In other words, and in common with many other industrial countries such as the USA and Australia, there has been a transition of food (along with other public health utilities such as water, sewage and housing) from the realm of common goods to that of consumerism and commodity culture. Marsden et al. (2000b) explore the relationship between the State, corporate retailers, individuals and the provision of food supply, quality and choice further. Their argument is that the food legislation of the early 1990s (i.e. The

Food Safety Act 1990 and the Department of Health White Paper 1992) introduced a switch in public policy, to shift responsibility for delivering consumer rights and choices on behalf of the State, to the retailers. Whereas early post-war policy was shaped by a sense that there was a 'collective consumer interest, whose choice was largely determined by government' (2000b: 47), the contemporary period is characterized by the privatization of choice. This has also been seen in public health: critics of the most recent White Paper *Choosing Health* (Department of Health 2004) argue that it puts the responsibility for maintaining personal health back on to individuals (see Hunter, 2005, among many). So, too, within food, choice of that which is appropriate for health in terms of safety, avoidance of chronic disease and long-term well-being is back within the individual's remit. Indeed, 'health' is widely used as a marketing tool, as well as other aspects of desirability: 'now it is the corporate retailers who play a central role in promoting to individualised consumers their vision of quality and diversity of consumption' (Marsden et al. 2000b: 47). Within this context, the consumer is given the 'right' or 'freedom' to choose, as well as the 'responsibility' to 'get it right'. The government ensures that basic standards of food safety are established and, above this, the retailers then create additional choices based on their different guarantees of food quality.

Inequalities are exacerbated by the current structure of food supply, whereby the vast majority of food is sold by just a few large retailers. As noted by Marsden et al. (2000b), rights are usually held by all members of a society. In contrast, freedom to consume is highly differentiated, and for some is unlikely to exist. In a country with some of the highest rates of child poverty in the industrialized world (Burchardt et al. 2002), sections of the population are literally disconnected from access to healthy and affordable food, partly because of the geographical isolation described above, which for those on low incomes remains a barrier because of the cost of transport. In addition, such households lack sufficient money to engage with the contemporary food market in such a way as to appeal to the major retailers. In 2005–6 there were nearly 13 million individuals living in homes with incomes below the Government's main poverty threshold (defined as 60 per cent of the median household income after deducting housing costs). This was 1 million fewer than in 1996–7, but was still almost double the number twenty years ago (New Policy Institute 2007). As shown above, people who are short of food also tend to eat food that is less healthy. Moreover, food is often sacrificed when other fixed costs have to be met, such as utility bills or debt repayment. It has been estimated that 4 million people in the United Kingdom cannot afford a healthy diet and one in five parents and one in ten children regularly go hungry because they do not have enough money for food (NCH 2004). Low-income consumers experience a higher incidence of premature and low birth-weight babies, heart disease, stroke and some cancers in adults. Dowler and Caraher (2003: 63) argue that a key principle of food security – namely the idea that people should be 'free from fear and anxiety about being able to eat healthily, or even at all' – is being undermined. In addition, '[A]ccess to food – that is, the shops or markets people can reach, what they can buy, how much of it and at what cost – is governed by decisions in which few ordinary citizens play any part' (2003: 58).

To sum up, then, we have argued that the implications of 'disconnection' for consumers are twofold: first, 'disconnection' can result in food-related anxiety; second, it contributes to inequalities in access to healthy food. These two factors in turn are helping to stoke the growing consumer interest in food and its origins, and when combined with an increasing awareness of the environmental and ethical implications of food consumption, they are creating a powerful mix of motives for some kind of 'reconnection' with the people and places associated with food production. Thus, discourses and practices of 'reconnection' are co-evolving with discourses and practices of 'disconnection'. In our research we engaged with six different forms of 'reconnection', and at this point we now want to introduce these in order to set the scene for our unfolding analysis.

INTRODUCING SIX EXAMPLES OF 'RECONNECTION'

Over a period of three years (2004–2007) we worked with six food businesses and initiatives that allowed direct contact of some kind between producers and consumers. These six examples were selected from a purpose-built database of 'alternative' food initiatives. The selection process was also informed by an extensive literature review, plus stakeholder consultation (for a full discussion of database construction and the stakeholder panel, see Appendix I). Taking the nature of producer–consumer relationships as our starting point, we devised a typology of 'reconnection', into which our database entries could be fitted. It can be seen from Table I.I that our typology differentiates schemes according to the relative 'connectedness' of food consumers to the act of food production, but what they all have in common is a direct relationship between producers and consumers. Using this three-way typology, six illustrative 'case studies' were selected, and these

Table 1.1 Typology of Producer–Consumer 'Reconnection'

Type of producer–consumer relationship	Examples	Illustrative case studies
Producers as consumers Food is grown or produced by those who consume it. Often promote healthy lifestyles. Extent of commercial orientation varies. Produce is usually sold on a local level but may be targeted at specific groups, e.g. low incomes, ethnic minorities.	Community gardens, community co-ops and allotments	Salop Drive Market Garden, West Midlands, England
Producer–Consumer Partnerships The risks and rewards of farming are shared – to varying degrees – due to subscription or share arrangements.	Community Supported Agriculture Schemes (CSA)	EarthShare Community Supported Agriculture, Moray, Scotland
Direct Sell Farmers or producers cut out middlemen and sell direct to consumers. Can be direct face to face or over the Internet.	Farm shops, farmers' markets, box schemes, adoption schemes	Waterland organic box scheme, Cambridgeshire, England Farrington's Farm Shop, Somerset, England Moorland Farm (direct retail and farmers' market stall), Somerset, England Adopt-a-Sheep, Abruzzo National Park, Italy

are listed in the final column of Table 1.1. We selected more examples from the 'direct sell' category because the database indicated that these are the most common type of 'alternative' food arrangement, involving the largest number of consumers. The six cases are situated in contrasting geographical locations, as shown in Figure 1.1. We should clarify at this stage that we see our case studies as 'instrumental' rather than representative. Our aim is to use particular examples to suggest 'fuzzy generalizations' or possibilities and to open debate rather than to make claims for truth (see Cousin 2005). As Stake (1995: 43, quoted in Cousin 2005: 426) has argued: '[T]he function of research is not necessarily to map and conquer the world but to sophisticate the beholding of it' and it is in this spirit that we present the case studies in this book (see also DeLind and Ferguson 1999).

For each case, we conducted an in-depth interview with each producer or manager, and a follow-up interview approximately one year later. We held two rounds of consumer workshops, involving eighty-nine consumers across the five schemes based in the United Kingdom, plus forty-four in-depth consumer interviews and thirty-two follow-up telephone interviews. We also conducted detailed household research with six households with different socio-economic and demographic characteristics. Questionnaires and an online discussion were used to engage with 'Adopt a sheep' consumers in different locations around the world. Our research methods

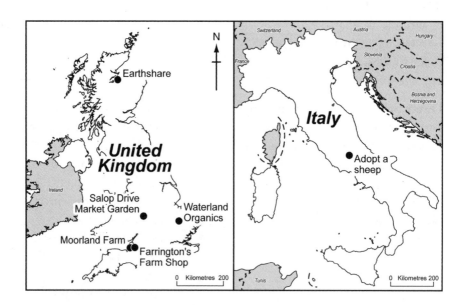

Figure 1.1 Map of the case study locations.

are described in full detail in Appendix 1. For now, we want to provide a very brief introduction to the cases we investigated. We gained permission to identify our 'case studies' and the producers/growers/managers who were interviewed for the research. Aliases for consumer respondent names have been used throughout.

Salop Drive Market Garden is located in the heart of an inner city housing estate in the English West Midlands and delivers bags of fruit and vegetables to about seventy nearby households. EarthShare Community Supported Agriculture is located in the district of Nairn, north-east Scotland and serves around 200 households. Waterland organic box scheme is located just outside Cambridge and delivers boxes to around 100 households. Farrington's farm shop sells a range of home-made, locally and internationally sourced products to over 8,000 consumers in Somerset. Moorland Farm Direct is also located in Somerset and sells direct to consumers through a farm shop and stalls at farmers' markets. Finally, 'Adopt a sheep', located in the mountainous Abruzzo region of Italy allows consumers to adopt individual sheep and receive their milk and wool products through the post. These six examples of 'alternative' food arrangements are discussed in detail in Chapter 3, but in order to begin building a sense of the kinds of places these examples are located in, we summarise some key economic indicators (see Table 1.2).

It can be seen from Table 1.2 that the local authority of Sandwell has by far the highest population density and the lowest life expectancy of all the locations. The proportion of the population suffering from long-term illness is higher than the other locations and above the English average. Evidence from a number of sources indicates that access to healthy food within walking distance is a significant issue for many low-income households in the area (Dowler et al. 2001a). Sandwell is more ethnically diverse than any of the other locations and has lower than average house prices. The percentage of households without a car is higher than in the other areas, educational indicators are lower and total household income is lower. All the other locations have above average life expectancy, and the three other English locations have above average household incomes. The Scottish ward of Nairn, where EarthShare is located, however, has household incomes below the Scottish average, has lower than average house prices, and a lower than average proportion of car owning households. These general features show that while some of the places accord with the usual perception that 'alternative' food outlets cater to middle-class, well-educated and relatively affluent consumers, others challenge this stereotype. Salop Drive is the most obvious example, but it is notable that Sedgemoor, the ward within which

Table 1.2 Socio-economic indicators of scheme locations

Scheme	Salop Drive	Waterland Organics	Farrington's	Moorland	–	EarthShare	–
Local authority	Sandwell	East Cambridgeshire	Bath & Northeast Somerset	Sedgemoor	English average	Nairn	Scottish average
Population density (people per hectare) (2001)	33.06	1.12	4.89	1.88	3.77	0.27[1]	0.65[1]
Life expectancy (2002–2004)							
Male	74.1	77.8	78.4	77.6	76.6	75.2[2]	73.4[2]
Female	79.2	82.3	82.8	82.2	80.9	80.4[2]	78.7[2]
Population suffering from long-term limiting illness (%) (2001)	21.7	15.2	15.9	18.9	17.9	18.4	20.3
Proportion of occupants classified as non-white (%) (2004)	21.5	3.6	4.3	2.1	10.5	–	–
Proportion of local authority housing (%) (2005)	26.5	0	0	9.8	9.8	21[3]	27.2[3]
Average house price (£) (2005)	116,848	198,799	242,872	174,177	192,274	144,539	147,936

Scheme	Salop Drive	Waterland Organics	Farrington's	Moorland	—	EarthShare	—
Percentage of households without a car or van (2001)	42.46	14.78	22.04	22.04	26.84	25[4]	34[4]
Percentage of pupils achieving 5 GCSEs at grade C or above (2004–2005)	47	62	64	52	56	183[5]	172[5]
Total household income (£ per week) at ward level (2001–2002)	430	780	630	540	526[6]	560[7]	575[7]
Deprivation value[8]	0.9	0.2	0.35	0.325	—	—	—

Data for the four English schemes are sourced from National Statistics Online: Neighbourhood Statistics http://www.statistics.gov.uk/ and is for Local Authority areas. In this context, it refers to the lower tier of local government, including non-metropolitan districts, metropolitan districts, unitary authorities and London boroughs in England.

Unless otherwise stated, data for EarthShare records are figures from Nairn, a Scottish Ward, and are sourced from The Highland Council: Ward Statistics, http://www.highland.gov.uk/

[1] 2005.

[2] Source: Scottish Executive: Health Statistics http://www.clearingtheairscotland.com/

[3] Rented from the Council, Scottish Homes & the Housing Association, 2001.

[4] Source: General Register Office for Scotland: 2001 census report to the Scottish Parliament, www.gro-scotland.gov.uk

[5] Average tariff score of all pupils on stage 4 roll, for Inverness, Nairn & Lochaber (Scottish Parliamentary Constituency level) 2005. Source: Scottish Neighbourhood Statistics: Quick Profile Report, http://www.sns.gov.uk/

[6] 1999–2002.

[7] 2005.

[8] Total deprivation calculated as a value out of 1, (which is the most deprived neighbourhood in England), based upon factors such as levels of crime, health deprivation and income deprivation.

Moorland is located, exhibits higher than average levels of long-term illness, lower than average educational scores and average household incomes which are considerably below those for East Cambridgeshire, Bath and north-east Somerset, and Nairn. While we do not have fully comparable data for the Abruzzo region, location for the Adopt a Sheep scheme, we can note that the population density was 1.169 people per hectare in 2001, compared with the Italian average of 1.891 people per hectare. The region has experienced significant rates of emigration, especially in the 1970s, and is characterized by an ageing population. Between 1991 and 2001, the share of population under 25 years of age decreased from 31.8 per cent to 26 per cent, whereas the share of population over 65 years of age increased from 16 per cent to 20 per cent. Per capita Gross Domestic Product is under the national average and represents about 84 per cent of the EU average (European Commission 2004).

SUMMARY AND OUTLINE OF THE BOOK

In this chapter we have set the scene for our research by illustrating the ways in which many of the current problems with food are intrinsically related to the 'disconnected' nature of relationships between food producers and consumers. 'Disconnection' is a concept which evokes the complex contradictions in contemporary food supply, whereby vast quantities of cheap foodstuffs of consistent quality and appearance, are made available through spatially extended supply chains, which obscure the 'hidden' costs of food production. These hidden costs include the environmental damage caused by productivist agriculture and current models of food distribution and retail; the economic and personal cost to farmers and growers both in the United Kingdom and abroad, whose profit margins have been eroded through aggressive retailer pricing strategies; and the burden of an unhealthy diet which threatens the most vulnerable sections of society. Not only are certain costs hidden, but 'disconnection' results in a situation where the origins, production methods and contents of many foodstuffs are obscured from consumers. These factors, we argue, are now driving producers and consumers to experiment with different forms of 'reconnection', which address some of the anxieties we have outlined. The rest of this book is concerned with how, why and with what impacts, 'reconnection' is occurring. To this end, Chapter 2 examines the discursive construction of the idea of 'reconnection', arguing that it is important to be aware of the ethical frameworks within which both discourses and practices of 'reconnection' are embedded. Given this, we find that the literature on the ethics of care offers a key set of ideas for understanding the reflexive construction of producer and consumer identities, motives and practices as they strive to build projects of 'reconnection'. We argue that these emergent 'alternative' food practices should not be seen as dualistically opposed to 'conventional' ones, but rather, should be understood in terms of the relationships and co-dependencies which operate *between* entities in different spheres of food production–consumption activity. Chapter 3 then presents a detailed description of the forms of 'reconnection' which we studied, within a framework of seven 'analytical fields'. Chapter 4 discusses the identities, motives and practices of the producers and managers involved in our six study schemes. Chapter 5 presents a detailed analysis of the identities and motives of consumers participating in the schemes and Chapter 6 considers the ways in which their practices help to construct and strengthen relations of care with others, as well as problematizing commonly accepted notions of choice and convenience. Finally, Chapter 7 presents conclusions and reflections as we assess some of the implications and possibilities of a more 'reconnected' food system.

CHAPTER 2

Conceptualizing 'Alternatives' within a Framework of Care

INTRODUCTION

Food is the one thing which is nice in our lives which we don't have to feel guilty about. So if something is marketed and as long as it's got a nice flavour then we'll be happy to eat it. And especially people who are rushed, you know, you've got your family, you've got your dog, you've got this that and the other, you've got to get down to sort out your mother because she's fallen down the stairs or whatever, and there should be a duty of care. And across society I think that is vanishing ... Right from the top. From the Managing Director of McDougals or Kerry Foods ... if they're marketing food they should market good food. And if the accountant comes along and says 'this is not a viable line anymore', then I think they should be honest and say 'we've got to put the price up' ... and there is a viable price going back to the producer so he can be comfortable ... and pay the heating bills in the winter. (Ann, a Farrington's customer; retired professional, interviewed in 2004)

Ann, a customer in Farrington's, a West Country farm shop, reflects on the way in which food often has to be fitted into busy lives, lives that are shaped in no small way by the daily act of caring for others: children, parents, pets and so on. Like many of the respondents in our research, Ann moves easily from discussing food to reflecting on the very nature of society itself. For her, the 'duty of care' which is so fundamental to society is 'vanishing', and by reference to the need for 'honest' pricing strategies which return a fair profit to the producer so that he can meet his own basic needs, she shows the breadth of her understanding of the notion of caring responsibilities across the whole food system. Ann's words provide us with a useful starting point: her identification of the significance of care as shaping our daily lives is central to our analysis. Our engagement with the academic and grey literatures, material produced by 'alternative' food providers, and with producers, consumers and others through empirical inquiry, has led us to an understanding that 'caring for food' is an important element underpinning the expressions of 'reconnection' which we have researched. We argue that a broad ethic of care for others (variously defined) acts as an important moral foundation upon which many decisions regarding food are taken. Moreover, this ethic of care can endow the discourses and practices of 'reconnection' with radical and transformatory potential. To develop this argument, we draw here on two main bodies of literature: first, research on 'alternative' food provisioning, and second, the literature on the 'ethics of care', which together provide ideas about power, relationality, and the reflexive co-evolution of producer and consumer identities, motives and practices. The chapter thus contributes to the continuing debate about emergent 'alternative' food practices by arguing that these should not be seen as dualistically opposed to 'conventional' ones, but rather, should be understood in terms of the relationships and codependencies which operate *between* entities in different spheres of food production–consumption activity. The chapter also examines the discursive construction of the idea of 'reconnection', arguing that three broad discourses can be identified. While some of these discourses appear to converge, they emanate from quite different political, economic and moral agendas and can be used to prop up current relations of inequality within the food system, just as they can be used to challenge them. It is important, therefore, to be aware of the ethical frameworks within which both discourses and practices of 'reconnection' are embedded. In other words, not all 'reconnection' promises radical change. In the rest of this chapter we lay out the conceptual foundations for our analysis, by dealing first, with the relational nature of the 'alternative', and second, with the notion of an ethic of care both in general terms, and in relation to food.

UNDERSTANDING 'ALTERNATIVE' FOOD PRACTICES: A RELATIONAL APPROACH

The Trouble with 'Alternative'

The concept of the 'alternative' in relation to food has generated considerable debate. Much of the initial research on 'alternative' agro-food networks began with the idea that their 'alternativeness' is attributable to the nature of the supply chains they use. 'Alternative' supply chains are generally considered to be 'shorter', in symbolic and material terms, than 'long, complex and rationally organised industrial chains' (Marsden et al. 2000a: 424; see also Murdoch et al. 2000). According to Renting et al. (2003) the critical difference between 'alternative' or short food supply chains (SFSC) and 'conventional' networks is that the former have fewer links in the chain which extends from producer to consumer, and that the food reaches the consumer embedded with information about its origins and production methods. In other words, information and quality cues attached to food and communicated by the people selling the produce, allow consumers to make value judgements about the relative desirability of specific food in accordance with their own knowledge or experience of, the place or type of production (Marsden et al. 2000a). However, more recent empirical work has begun to question this dualistic understanding of the 'alternative' versus 'conventional'. Ilbery and Maye (2005), for example, demonstrate that small-scale local food producers in Scotland have to 'dip in' to 'conventional' nodes in the food chain, such as abattoirs, processors and wholesalers, in order to get their products to the market.

One of the principal difficulties with the word 'alternative' is that it implies a choice between one thing or another different thing – between 'this thing' or 'that thing'. However, when applying it to the food system, we start to see that the differences between elements are often blurred. Once the structures and relationships involved in food chains are examined, it is often apparent that the 'alternatives' on offer are not actually very distinct from the choice that they are supposed to be 'alternative to'. So, for example, is 'organic' food truly 'alternative' if it is mass produced, or has travelled several thousand miles, perhaps by plane, in order to be retailed through a supermarket, or if its production relies on the exploitation of migrant workers (see Guthman 2004)?

Much of the early research and discourse about 'alternative' foods tended to use the term to stand for a collection of other terms such as 'local', 'organic,' 'speciality' or 'community', and latterly 'low food miles'. The immediate problem with this is that each of these terms is also highly contestable and potentially non-definable. How far can we go before food stops being 'local'? How are 'organic' standards defined and by whom? How are they regulated? What foods should be labelled as 'specialities'? Whose 'community' are we talking about? Are high food miles always bad? And so on. We have a situation where one contested and fuzzy concept ('alternative') is used to stand for other contested and fuzzy concepts. Moreover, the use of such terms is generally embedded within a binary mode of thinking, whereby the 'alternative' is dualistically opposed to the 'conventional'. So for example, in the North American school of thought identified by Goodman (2003), the 'alternative', with its emphasis on environmental and social justice, is presented as part of a critique of neo-liberal politico-economic relationships (Kloppenberg et al. 1996; Grey 2000; Hassanein 2003). European scholars on the other hand, suggests Goodman, have tended to see the 'alternative' in terms of the potential for small businesses in peripheral rural locations to carve out niche markets for their 'value-added' products on the margins of the agribusiness/large retailer complex (Marsden et al. 2000a; Marsden et al. 2001; Marsden et al. 2002; Marsden and Smith 2005). These are arguably quite distinct and non-reconcilable usages of the same term.

In practice we find this dualistic 'alternative/conventional' approach problematic. Maxey puts it most clearly when he states that perhaps the first and foremost limitation of 'alternativeness' is 'its ontological root within a binary opposition' (2007: 59). Other authors have also questioned this binary framework. Watts et al. (2005), for example, propose the idea of 'weaker' and 'stronger' 'alternatives', and Ilbery and Maye (2005) suggest that food enterprises could be considered as 'hybrids', which mix elements of 'alternative' and 'conventional' supply chains and rarely operate exclusively in either category (see also Slee and Kirwan 2007). As Maxey (2007) notes, one of the advantages of the concept of hybridity is that it can disrupt taken-for-granted boundaries around, for example, different forms of food provisioning. Yet, as he warns, binaries may remain latent even within hybridity and, as mooted by Holloway et al. (2007), such an approach can still leave 'alternative' and 'conventional' food notions intact, as distinct entities or 'pure' categories which can be 'dipped into' in when argument demands. Moreover, Maxey cautions that, '[I]n perpetuating analysis of "alternative" food, then, we may inadvertently naturalise, normalise and legitimise highly problematic practices and products labelled "conventional".' (2007: 60)

This argument is strengthened by reference to the recent debates concerning 'alternative' economic spaces. Leyshon and Lee (2003) build on the work of Gibson-Graham (1996) to argue that within what they present as a 'fragile and susceptible capitalism', there are possibilities for the proliferation of economic spaces and practices centred predominantly around social, ecological and ethical concerns rather than capital accumulation alone. Their profusion of examples of 'performing the economy otherwise' (Leyshon and Lee 2003: 16) suggests that global capitalism can be challenged and is not necessarily as hegemonic as is sometimes perceived. Massey (2000) has also argued that the notion of a coherent totality or structure which cannot be challenged by the weak is politically problematic, as it ascribes a constancy to power which fails to account for the 'fraught, unstable and contingent' (Massey 2000: 280) nature of power structures of capitalism. Having said this, she acknowledges the very pervasive story that is told of inescapable globalization and economic liberalism, which are often portrayed as necessarily overcoming ways of performing 'alternative' economics, with 'every attempt at radical otherness being so quickly commercialised and sold or used to sell ... With all of this, one might as well ask what are the, and where are the, possibilities for doing things otherwise?' (Massey 2000: 281). Indeed, we can see examples of this occurring within the food sector, whereby there has been a proliferation and expansion of practices which could be labelled as 'alternatives' but which may exhibit fundamental differences in aims, ethos and practices.

There is also a risk of romanticizing 'alternatives' so that they are not subject to the same degree of critical reflection as what might be termed more 'mainstream' food systems (Massey 2000). This romanticization of the 'alternative' often takes a spatial dimension in the association with an idealized notion of the 'local'. The 'local' has been celebrated as fostering closer, more authentic relations and providing a counter-hegemony to globalization. Yet important questions have been raised about the ways in which 'normative localism places a set of pure, conflict-free local values and local knowledges in resistance to anomic and contradictory capitalist forces' (DuPuis and Goodman 2005: 359). Such 'unreflexive localism' is characterized as romantic by DuPuis and Goodman, who argue it can deny the realities of the politics of the local 'with potentially problematic social justice consequences' (2005: 359). They also argue that many of the actors in US 'alternative' food movements and other local-based social movements are middle class and white; reforms are thus steered to serve particular interests, reflect particular visions of perfection and maintain traditional relations of power.

A romanticization of the 'alternative' can also lead to so-called 'defensive localism' (Winter 2003a), which is argued to be elitist, reactionary and appealing to nativist sentiments and xenophobia. It is important, therefore, to avoid essentializing 'place'. Instead, as Massey argues, it is necessary to retain an understanding of 'space' as open and interactional. This creates possibilities for a genuine politics which can 'make a difference' (Massey 2005: 11). For Massey, 'space' must be seen as the product of interrelations, and as a sphere in which distinct trajectories coexist. 'Space' must also be recognized as always under construction, never finished and never closed: 'a simultaneity of stories-so-far' (2005: 9). The restructuring of spatial relations is seen as central to moving towards more just social, economic and political relations, including a redistribution of control over how 'space' is produced. Although she argues that there are fundamental inequalities of power, the idea that power is relational and everywhere in social and economic relationships suggests that there are always possibilities available for re-imagining and restructuring those relationships towards different ways of doing things. We return to the intersection of social and spatial relations in the second part of this chapter, when we consider the utility of care ethics as a framework for interpreting producer–food–consumer relationships.

Our research engages with other issues beyond the challenge to binary constructions of 'alternative'. First (and discussed more fully in Chapters 4 and 7), the word 'alternative' is in fact rarely used by food producers, food project workers, business managers or consumers to describe themselves or their activities, even though they are so characterized by academics and others. Indeed, some argue the term is counter-productive, contributing to a marginalization of their activities (Seyfang 2006 arrives at a similar conclusion). Second, if we take the long view, practices described as 'alternative' have historically often been considered the norm. So, for example, delivery of food to households is not new – the milk float, fish van and others have long been a part of the food provisioning landscape. Organic farming is also not new – as its proponents remind us, all farming was effectively 'organic' before the industrialization of agriculture. Much food was also locally grown and consumed before industrialization and so local foods, too, are not new; indeed they trade on their historical associations with particular places. The tendency to associate 'alternative' with 'new' ways of doing things can therefore also be misleading. Trentmann (2007) makes a similar point in relation to 'ethical' consumption, which is often seen as part of a new 'moral' economy whereby consumers express care for distant others through the purchase of fairly traded goods. Yet as Trentmann observes, 'caring for distant others with one's purse is not the preserve of affluent postmodern shoppers, nor the novel outcome of the current age of globalisation' (2007: 1082). He argues that contemporary ethical consumerism traces its genealogy back to antislavery and co-operative movements, empire shopping and free trade campaigns.

Here and elsewhere (Holloway et al. 2007), we argue that, given the array of enterprises and schemes that proactively differentiate themselves by purposely, or necessarily, trading at the margins of industrialized food production, it is no longer sufficient, or accurate enough to simply merge them all under the heading of 'alternative'. Nevertheless, we recognize the term as a useful shorthand, and indeed so employ it in this book. But in so doing we insist that it is only by focusing on the identities, motives and practices of those involved that we can get to the heart of what is critically distinctive about 'alternative' food production—consumption. Moreover, the types of relationships which these 'alternatives' can engender, and the ethical frameworks within which they are embedded are, we suggest, at the heart of their radical and transformatory potential. Indeed, one of our main arguments is that the one feature which 'alternative' food practices share is the attempt to create 'closer' relationships between producers and consumers. This, in the expression of 'reconnection', we suggest, is the distinctive contemporary manifestation of the 'alternative', although we do acknowledge that there have been previous historical moments when reconnection has been sought, but for different socio-cultural reasons, notably the cause of building solidarity between home consumers and producers located in imperial outposts (Trentmann 2007).

'Reconnection' — Bringing Producers and Consumers Closer Together

The practices and relationships through which 'reconnection' may be achieved are diverse; we examine in detail those which emerged from our research in the empirical chapters of the book. As argued in Chapter I, the 'disconnection' in the food system is fundamentally linked to the growth of industrialized food production. The very word 'reconnection' implies a revival or re-establishment of a 'lost' or damaged connection, a return to previously existing and presumably now broken sets of relationships and practices. It resonates with a sense of nostalgia for a Golden Age when things were better, when consumers knew where their food came from, farmers earned a decent living, the environment was not degraded and human health was not threatened. Nostalgia is a powerful emotion, which can be tapped into successfully by marketers seeking to capitalize on our capacity for idealizing the past. As such, discourses of 'reconnection' are easily appropriated and used in advertising campaigns by powerful retailers whose procedures may bear little resemblance to the practices of 'reconnection' being performed by other actors in the food system. It is also worth noting that although the word 'reconnection' suggests a revival of something lost, the practices that are enrolled under the banner of 'reconnection' in fact share continuities with practices from earlier times and may never have entirely disappeared. Moreover, opposition to the disconnecting tendencies of industrialized agriculture is as old as industrialization itself, and has continued ever since – hence our emphasis on the co-evolution of 'disconnection/reconnection'. So for instance, the publication of Lady Eve Balfour's (1943) *The Living Soil*, in which she advocated a sustainable approach to agriculture, proved to be the catalyst for the formation of the Soil Association in 1946.

'Reconnection' is also not just a two-way relationship between the people constituted as producers and consumers (thought of here as 'purchasers'). Spouses, partners, children, friends, colleagues, soil, animals, plants, certification, institutions, technologies and artefacts all help to mediate 'reconnection'. The material and symbolic properties of food are especially important, and may change in response to organic, metabolic and climactic factors, as well as shifting fashions for different foods and ingredients. Through relationships of 'reconnection', consumers accept and even welcome the ways in which food's properties may change. So, for example, as Lamine (2005) argues, consumers involved in Community Supported Agriculture (CSA) and box schemes accept that the qualities of the products they receive may not be as consistent as those they might purchase in a supermarket, in that they may vary in size, shape, taste and even whether they have 'bugs' in them. However, in accepting such inconsistencies, consumers can reduce what Lamine describes as 'qualitative uncertainties' in relation to food safety, origin and tastiness. Producers, meanwhile, can reduce 'quantitative uncertainties' relating to sales and prices by embarking on 'local partnerships' with their 'subscribers'.

'Reconnection' is a *process* rather than an end-state, and it conveys a sense of 'doing and becoming.' It is also not always explicit or a central focus: participation in 'alternative' food practices is often only one aspect of people's lives, which may or may not resonate with other important ideologies and practices. As with the idea of 'alternative', those involved seldom conceptualize such practices in terms of 'reconnection'; these are largely the perceptions and labels of academics and others. We here tease out three major sets of relationships, which various actors are currently seeking to 'reconnect'. While this is not intended to be an exhaustive review of all discourses of 'reconnection' (for example, it is limited to the United Kingdom), it should illustrate the point that 'reconnection' is by no means a coherent concept and that it can be subject to appropriation for different commercial and political purposes. Many individuals have contributed towards the construction of the discourse of 'reconnection'. While the language, terminology and metaphors used may vary, their accounts are linked by a general belief in the need to 'reconnect' elements in the food system. The following brief discussion of the ideas of some of the most influential voices is provided to show the ways in which diversity is 'held together' through three discursive constructions of 'reconnection', which are summarised in Table 2.1. Discourses of 'reconnection' often combine all the elements suggested in the table (market, product–process–place and nature) and may also incorporate others (e.g. health, spirituality). Nevertheless,

Table 2.1 Discursive Constructions of 'Reconnection'

'Reconnect' What?	Examples of Proponents
Producers with their market	UK Government; European Commission; farming associations, e.g. FARMA
Consumers with product– process–place	Niche market producers and retailers, e.g. regional speciality foods and quality foods; large retailers, e.g. Marks & Spencer, Sainsbury's 'Taste the Difference' range, Tesco's 'Finest' range; campaigners, e.g. Slow Food
People with nature	Campaigning organizations, e.g. Soil Association, Sustain; academics/ campaigners

different actors prioritize different aspects, depending on political and commercial agendas, as shown in the following discussion.

Reconnecting Producers with Their Market   The need to 'reconnect' producers with their market is emphasized particularly strongly by policy-makers at national government level in the United Kingdom. The policy concentration on 'reconnection' was crystallized largely in response to the outbreak of foot and mouth disease (FMD) in England in 2001. While this was not a direct threat to public health through food consumption, the outbreak caused concerns about air and water pollution associated with the disposal of over 6 million culled animals and raised the public's sense of unease about some of the practices of contemporary farming and food distribution. Notably, this incident highlighted the increased separation of consumers and food producers and the degree to which food origins are obscured within the industrialized food system. As noted by Winter (2003b) improvements in road transport since the 1960s mean that livestock can be transported long distances to be slaughtered in large volumes in order to supply meat to central distribution depots. Between the two outbreaks of FMD in 1967 and 2001, the number of auction markets in England and Wales had declined from 380 to 180 and the number of abattoirs in Great Britain had fallen from 2,200 to 360. Within this context, 'a powerful cocktail of concerns arose encompassing animal welfare, the power of the supermarkets, the role of dealers and the weakness of farmers in the food chain' (Winter 2003b: 54).

The FMD outbreak also intensified a sense of public mistrust in key actors such as government, scientists and large retailers. One of the main policy outcomes of the crisis was critical scrutiny of the food system resulting in a number of policy initiatives to shorten and simplify food chains (Winter 2003b). As a result, the Government Policy Commission on the Future of Farming and Food (2002), which was launched in response to FMD, presented 'reconnection' as its central theme, arguing that 'the real reason why the present situation is so dysfunctional is that farming has become detached from the rest of the economy and the environment' (2002: 6). At that time, the Commission reported that taxpayers were paying £3 billion annually on agricultural support in the United Kingdom and yet farm incomes were at a historical low. The countryside had been degraded by intensive farming systems and relationships between farmers and consumers were often 'confrontational'. Indeed, several authors had already suggested that a new moral consensus had arisen, in which farming was associated not with rural stewardship and 'benign authority' in rural matters (Seymour et al. 1997), but with environmental damage, animal welfare issues and food and animal health scares (see e.g. Goodman 1999). Consumers were thus exhibiting 'unease' about food safety and wholesomeness and also about farming practices and the apparent 'mismanagement' of the countryside.

The Commission argued that the farming system was unsustainable and that '[T]he key objective of public policy should be to *reconnect* our food and farming industry: to reconnect farming with its market and the rest of the food chain; to reconnect the food chain and the countryside; and to reconnect consumers with what they eat and how it is produced' (2002: 6, our italics). The Commission thus presented a vision of 'a profitable and sustainable farming and food sector' that is internationally competitive, is 'a good steward of the environment and provides good food and healthy diets for people in England and around the world' (2002: 9). Under the umbrella of 'reconnection', the Commission advocated reform of the Common Agricultural Policy, encouraging local competitiveness (e.g. local foods), farm diversification and new land uses (e.g. energy crops) (Winter 2003b). On the strength of the Commission recommendations, 'reconnection' has been adopted as a key priority in the United Kingdom's Strategy for Sustainable Farming and Food (Defra 2002b). 'Reconnection' in this strategy,

implies a clear understanding, business by business, of the changing market, and then action to make the best use of the market opportunities identified. But there are vital common themes; the importance of both reducing unnecessary cost and adding value is likely to go hand-in-hand with the pursuit of higher quality and that quality will need to be recognized and verified to assured standards. (Defra 2002b: 15)

In other words, the emphasis is on 'reconnection' by producers, in terms of improving their understanding of the changing nature of their market opportunities, and developing fleetness of foot to respond. The strategy identified as initiatives to help this process:

- *adding value*, including the promotion of local and regional foods and farmers' markets;
- *assurance schemes*, to help re-establish consumer confidence;
- *organic action plan*, to help create a sustainable and competitive organic farming and food sector;
- *export promotion*, offering tailored assistance to smaller producers;
- *improving efficiency* along the food chain;
- *public procurement*, ensuring that British producers can be fairly considered, within procurement rules;
- *farm diversification*, helping farmers to exploit new markets and new sources of income while remaining in farming;
- *business advice* to assist producers in pursuit of these objectives.

Mirroring this policy discourse, the National Farmers Union also aimed for 'agriculture and horticulture to be a dynamic, market-focused, modern and profitable industry' which will 'offer solutions to society on the quality and security of its food supplies, the management of the countryside and the mitigation of climate change' (NFU Plan November 2006–2007). Indeed, there are now many examples of current attempts by the agricultural sector to 'reconnect' with consumers, not only in terms of developing direct selling relationships, but also in terms of trying to inform and educate people about farming activities. This information transmission has employed, for example, agricultural shows (for a critical examination of the idea of 're-imaging' agriculture, see Holloway 2004), and during 2007, *Farmers' Weekly* ran a 'Kids Connect' campaign, which was described as 'a major initiative aimed at teaching children the facts about food and encouraging farmers to host more school visits and go into the classroom' (*Farmers' Weekly*, 13 July 2007: 26). There is also a wider industry-led initiative to run a Year of Farming and Food from September 2007, first proposed by the charity Farming and Countryside Education (FACE) and endorsed by Defra, the former Department for Education and Skills, the Department of Health, the Royal Agricultural Society for England, and many other organizations within the food and farming industries. The aim of the initiative is to give young people direct experience of the food chain and the countryside.

Clearly, the underlying sense is of a need to inform a consumer public which is perceived as misunderstanding the nature of production. So, for example, 'there is an urgent need to target the public both as tax payers providing support to English agriculture and as consumers purchasing food.[1] It is essential that we have a better understanding of consumers' attitudes if we are to develop an effective communications strategy' (Institute of Grocery Distribution 2005b: i). In other words, the reasons for 'disconnection' are seen as being on the public's side; they are either ignorant of food as a biological and social entity, or they regard the industry as overbearing, wealthy and interested only in profit rather than the public good; either way, they need 'educating'. In practice, as our research and others' have found (e.g. Draper and Green 2003; Weatherall et al. 2003), people are not as ignorant as portrayed; many are quite well informed about contemporary practices and motivations of food system actors, and may well see the latter as implicated in generating and maintaining 'disconnection'. They are also aware of not being in touch with those who actually produce the primary products, many of whom they recognize as also having little decision-making capacity.

Some aspects of the policy discourses of 'reconnection' in fact potentially converge with radical anti-globalization discourses, despite their explicit location within drives towards the increased liberalization of trade, the discontinuation of price supports for agriculture and the continued growth of global capitalism. For example, among campaigners who have stressed the need for farmers to reconnect with consumers, Bové and Dufour (2005) use the language of the left-wing political tradition and advocate civil disobedience as a means to achieve their ends, writing within a context of resistance to 'rampant globalization'. They lay down principles for the creation of a new agriculture, which will create a renewal of trust between farmers and citizen-consumers and reintegrate farmers into society, and propose a World Charter for Farming to be based on 'Six Pillars of farming Wisdom' (2005: 167):

1. increasing the number of farmers and reducing the concentration of production in Europe and throughout the world;
2. protecting natural resources and respecting the environment;
3. rebuilding consumer confidence by ensuring the quality, safety and flavour of products;

4. reintegrating farming into rural society;
5. maintaining the diversity of the animal and the plant population;
6. working for sustainable development.

In their words, the Charter is a 'social contract bringing together farmers and citizens'. Another illustration can be found in the work of Hines (2000), who advocates 'localization' as a form of opposition to the 'new theology of globalization' (2000: vii). His manifesto is not anti-trade, but instead argues that the gap between producers and consumers must be shortened so that there is a 'better chance for the latter to control the former' (2000: x). His polemic calls for action to promote local self-sufficiency as a means to end international debt crises, environmental destruction and the continued impoverishment of the majority of the world's population. While there is not space here for a full critical analysis of these manifestos, what this discussion begins to show is the existence of distinct political nuances, and even potential contradictions within discourses of 'reconnection'.

Reconnecting Consumers with Product, Process and Place This discourse is based on informing consumers about the origins of products and also about the ways in which product qualities are derived from place of origin. As with the idea of reconnecting producers with the market, this dimension of 'reconnection' is prone to appropriation by actors with fundamentally different agendas. Two examples can be used to illustrate this point. The first is the case of 'quality' food products which are marketed on the grounds that they are specialities of particular places (Ilbery and Kneafsey 1998; Ilbery et al. 2005). The production of high quality regional speciality foods has been heralded by some as the basis for a new economic dynamic in areas excluded from the productivist logic of industrialized agriculture (Ilbery and Kneafsey 1998; Marsden et al. 2002). Such products rely on processes of certification and the circulation of symbols of quality and authenticity, in order to establish relations of trust between consumers and producers who may be physically distant. The appeal of such products lies in their ecological, aesthetic and moral qualities, which are in turn 'embedded within producer-consumer relationships in which notions of trust, regard … and "connectedness" are given prominence' (Holloway and Kneafsey 2004: 267). The success of such connection depends on products reaching consumers 'embedded' with information about product, process and place (Marsden et al. 2000a). This information can be communicated through the use of regional imagery to appeal to pre-existing aesthetics concerning rural identities and lifestyles (Kneafsey and Ilbery 2001), or through the use of labels of origin which, in the EU, can be carried by 'typical' products. Several authors have identified the French *appellation d'ôrigine controlée* and EU's Protected Designation of Origin (PDO) and Protected Geographical Indications (PGI) schemes as important expressions of 'local', 'quality' or 'endogenous' food systems, which potentially facilitate a 'reconnection' of people, products and place (Ilbery and Kneafsey 2000; Ilbery et al. 2000; Marsden et al. 2000a; Barham 2003). So for example, Barham writes that they 'hold the potential of re-linking production to the social, cultural or environmental aspects of particular places, further distinguishing them from anonymous mass produced goods' (2003: 129). This in turn offers small-scale producers an opportunity to carve out a niche for themselves in order to sustain their businesses, communities and traditions.

The Slow Food movement is also an example of an attempt reconnect consumers with product, process and place. Emphasizing everybody's right to pleasure, the movement aims to protect the heritage of food, tradition and culture that make this pleasure possible. The movement is founded upon the concept of 'eco-gastronomy', which is 'a recognition of the strong connections between plate and planet' (Slow Food 2007). According to their principles, 'Slow Food is good, clean and fair food. We believe that the food we eat should taste good; that it should be produced in a clean way that does not harm the environment, animal welfare or our health; and that food producers should receive fair compensation for their work.' Members of Slow Food consider themselves as co-producers, not consumers, because 'by being informed about how our food is produced and actively supporting those who produce it, we become a part of and a partner in the production process.'

The uptake of PDOs and PGIs in the United Kingdom is lower than in France, Spain and Italy, reflecting both the relatively weak tradition of producer co-operation in the United Kingdom and the long-term erosion of direct consumer knowledge and understanding of food origins and production processes. This vacuum has also left space for large retailers to move in and take advantage of growing consumer demands to know more about their food origins. This is illustrated by our second example of 'reconnection' with product, process and place: the British high-street retailer Marks & Spencer has developed and marketed a new brand of chicken, the 'Oakham White'. As Jackson and his colleagues (2007) argue, the company was able to command premium prices for a staple product by emphasizing quality, provenance and taste. The brand was developed as a direct response to consumer demands for 'chicken like it used to be' and consists of a standard breed of bird (the Ross 508), reared on non-GM, cereal-based feed, free from antibiotic growth promoters. The stocking densities are slightly lower than industry average and the growing cycle is on average 4–5 days longer than a standard broiler chicken. The product is marketed with the picture of a 'typical' Marks & Spencer farmer on the pack and the name of the farmer who raised the chicken (not necessarily the same individual). The name 'Oakham White' was carefully chosen to appeal to positive associations with the countryside and because it sounded 'British'. Interestingly, Jackson and his colleagues' work echoes Cook and colleagues' (1998) idea of the structural ambivalence inherent in contemporary consumer attitudes to food origins. Transparency, one of their industry respondents point out can be a 'double-edged sword' in that '[O]n the one hand it provides an opportunity to highlight differences in agricultural production. On the other hand, it risks alienating consumers who would rather not be reminded that they are eating an animal' (Jackson et al. 2007: 325).

Most retailers, Marks & Spencer included, express support for British agriculture and farmers; nevertheless, a continuing tension between producers and retailers is evident within the food system. Those whose role is to defend local food producers suspect the supermarkets of trying to appropriate the local food sector. Thus, for example, FARMA (the National Farmers' Retail and Markets Association) has launched a 'Friends of Local Food Campaign', encouraging consumers to buy direct from farmers in order to support local food producers and hence local communities and economies. They argue that supermarkets are seeking to profit from 'localness' at the producers' expense, and without bearing the costs and risks of small-scale local production (National Farmers' Retail and Markets Association 2007).

'Reconnecting' People with Nature   This strand of 'reconnection' is most clearly expressed by campaigning organizations and individuals who seek to emphasize the environmental, health, socio-cultural and economic benefits of re-engaging with nature. So for example, non-governmental organizations and campaigning organizations such as the Countryside Agency (2002), the Soil Association (undated), and the Council for the Protection of Rural England (2001) have argued for various forms of 'reconnection' through relationships between farmers and consumers, often located within the context of calls for greater 'sustainability.' Indeed, this idea of 'reconnection' extends beyond food, to include the commodification of the farmed environment through rural tourism and leisure services.

One of the most sustained engagements with this idea of 'reconnection' is provided by Pretty (2002) who links it to an environmentally sustainable agriculture which will nevertheless provide sufficient food for all the world's population. Within a general framework that argues for the fundamental importance of human connectedness with nature, Pretty draws on the concepts of bioregions and foodsheds to convey the integration of human activities within ecological limits. Bioregions are diverse areas with many ecological functions, which 'connect social and natural systems at a place people can call home' (Pretty 2002: 117). Foodsheds, following the work of Kloppenberg (1991), are conceived as 'self-reliant, locally or regionally based food systems comprised of diversified farms using sustainable practices to supply fresher, more nutritious food stuffs to small-scale processors and consumers to whom producers are linked by bonds of community as well as economy' (Pretty 2002: 117). Rejecting the dualistic separation of humans from nature which characterizes the industrial mode of food provisioning, Pretty argues that food should be regarded as a commons, rather than a commodity. A key feature of common pool resources is that they are interdependent systems in which individual actions affect the whole system: 'If these actions are co-ordinated, then individuals will enjoy higher benefits (or reduced harm), when compared with acting alone. But if this joint management breaks down, then some may benefit greatly in the short term by extracting all the benefit for themselves. In this case, the likely outcome is damage to the whole system' (2002: 157). Pretty cites many examples of participatory development, social learning and co-operative projects which, he argues can be part of an urgently needed 'revolution', not only in agriculture and food production–consumption, but in human–nature relationships and understanding.

Critically concerned with food policy and health, Lang and Heasman (2004) call for a 'radical' (in their sense meaning 'having the power to change peoples' thinking') and integrated perspective which links human and ecological health. They argue that an ecological paradigm which promotes a diet which is good for biodiversity and in turn good for human health should be supported by governments and citizens alike; in their words, 'the goal of food and health policy surely must be for humanity to be at one with nature' (2004: 307). Some of these ideas have been taken up recently, if not explicitly, by the Welsh Assembly Government, and the Scottish Parliament, in their consultation documents on the future of food for Wales and Scotland (respectively the *Wales Quality of Food Strategy*, and *Choosing the Right Ingredients: The Future for Food in Scotland*: Discussion Paper).

Having identified these three broad sets of 'reconnections', we now turn to theorising the radical potential of 'reconnection' with arguments based on feminist thinking on the 'ethics of care', a powerful framework within which to understand the evolution of identities and practices by those involved. A focus on 'care' also helps to distinguish between what we might describe as 'neo-liberal' and 'critical' discourses and practices of 'reconnection' because it enables us to consider what motivates the actions of those involved.

CONCEPTUALIZING 'RECONNECTION' WITHIN A FRAMEWORK OF 'CARE'

We here focus on the identities, motives and practices of those involved in 'doing reconnection', drawing on ideas from feminist literatures. Two key themes are identified and discussed: the first is a more general point, namely that 'caring' is a central and defining human activity which has radical political potential. The second examines more closely the relationships between 'care' and the production and consumption of *food*.

The Importance of Care: Personal and Political

Ideas about the 'ethic of care' developed within feminism and detailed debates have evolved surrounding the nature of such an ethic, its importance to feminist thought, its limitations and its links to an ethic of justice (Larrabee 1993; McDowell 2004). Our interest here is in the articulation of care and relations to others as a position from which decisions are taken and practices develop. This literature offers us a lens through which to see the actions of producers and consumers as based in, and belonging to, their *relationships* to others. In focusing on care we also open up a space where we can think about emotions such as happiness, love and guilt – all themes that were in fact priorities for our interviewees, but which are not always seen as appropriate in academic analysis. As Bondi (2005) argues, it is possible that a focus on emotions has radical potential, particularly when drawing on psychotherapy's theory of practice, whereby emotions are understood as intrinsically relational. She stresses that emotions arise and flow *between* people rather than belonging to one person or another; a focus on emotions can thus provide an insight on 'the betweenness that is constitutive of relationships' (2005: 442) and helps to unsettle claims to the position of the 'rational knower'.

The concept of an 'ethic of care' was developed by a psychological theorist, Carol Gilligan, in her 1982 work, *In a Different Voice*. She examined the moral reasoning employed by women facing difficult decisions relating to abortion, and asserted the existence of a care framework built around a sense of connection to and responsibility for others, empathy, and a sense of self profoundly interrelated to others rather than separate from them (Larrabee 1993). Prior to Gilligan's work, traditional studies of the development of ethical frameworks had been based largely on research with males, and the notion of a 'justice' framework which centred on ideas of duty, obligation, rights and a detached sense of self, had come to be regarded as the mature form of moral reasoning. In fact, Gilligan (1993) does not posit the 'ethic of care' and 'ethic of justice' as mutually exclusive, despite what critics may have argued, but rather insists that the 'ethic of care' must be recognized as a distinct and important aspect of moral reasoning. She also claims it is not limited to women, although it emerged through working with women in her study.

Joan Tronto's writing on care is of particular significance to our work because she proposes that 'care' can be used as a basis for rethinking the moral boundaries which preserve inequalities of power and privilege while 'degrading 'others' who currently do the caring work in our society' (1993: 101, see also Tronto 2006). Fisher and Tronto (1990: 4) define 'caring' as: '*a species activity that includes everything that we do to maintain, continue, and repair our "world" so that we can live in it as well as possible.* That world includes our bodies, our selves and our environment, all of which we seek to interweave in a complex, life-sustaining web' (cited in Tronto 1993: 103, emphasis in original). Tronto (1993: 103) draws attention to several features of this definition of caring, which can be summarised as follows. First, it is not restricted to human interaction with other humans – caring can also occur for objects and environment (to which we would add animals). Second, caring is not presumed to be dyadic or individualistic. Care is too often defined as a necessary relationship between individuals, notably mother and child, but this can lead to a romanticization of that relationship. Third, the activity of caring is largely defined culturally. Fourth, caring is ongoing. It can characterize a single activity, or can describe a process. Finally, and crucially, care implies reaching out to something other than self and implicitly suggests that it will lead to some kind of action – therein lies its political potential. More precisely, '[S]emantically, care derives from a notion of "burden"; to care implies more than simply a passing interest or fancy but instead the acceptance of some form of burden' (Tronto 1993: 103). By taking on this burden people can challenge inequalities and assert their relationships to others and the world more generally.

Tronto (1993) is careful to point out that, although the range of care is broad, not all human activity can be characterized as 'care'. For instance, to pursue pleasure, create art, fulfil desires or market new products are not 'care'. 'Care' involves making the concerns and needs of others (and not necessarily, or only, human others) a basis for action. As Lawson puts it '[C]are ethics begins with a social ontology of connection [...] Care ethics understands all social relations as contextual, partial, attentive, responsive and responsible' (2007: 3). Both Lawson (2007) and Tronto (2006) argue that 'care' must be understood as something that everyone is and can be involved in, and that everyone needs. By recognizing that we are all recipients of 'care', we expose our interdependence and reject notions of care that situate it in the private family or intimate relationships alone. Rather, care is a social responsibility and should be recognized as such.

Much of the work on 'care' focuses on the marginalization of care givers, showing how caring activities are devalued, underpaid and disproportionately occupied by the relatively powerless in society (Tronto 1993, 2006; McDowell 2004; Lawson 2007; Milligan et al. 2007). Our research is not concerned with this aspect, but the usefulness of the ideas is that the vocabulary of 'care' can act as a means of connecting broad political and social aspirations with the consequences and effects of actual practices (see McDowell 2004; Jarvis 2007; Lawson 2007). 'Care', then, is not merely disposition but must be understood as *practice* (Tronto 2006; Lawson 2007). As Smith (1998: 16) notes, there is a distinction between caring *for* others (beneficence) as well as caring *about* them (benevolence): the former implies 'doing' something – taking action. A focus on 'care' thus constructed then forces us to think about real needs and to consider how these needs should be met. That in turn, prompts questions about what/who is valued in society (see also Tronto 2006). In relation to the value of food, and as noted in Chapter 1, there is a need to consider to what extent, and how, care can be practised in terms of food production, trade, distribution and ultimately consumption.

Care and Food Production–Consumption: Identities, Motives and Practices

We turn now to a discussion of how the framework of 'care' can be used to locate the relationship between the identities, motives and practices of producers, consumers and others.

Producers' Identities, Motives and Practices within a Framework of Care   A growing body of literature is concerned with the idea of 'careful' consumers, which is also related to the ideas of 'concerned' (Weatherell et al. 2003) and 'ethical' consumers (Barnett et al. 2005a; Harrison et al. 2005). There has been less work and writing on the construction of producer subjectivities in relation to ethical frameworks of care, although some work is emerging, which is starting to trace the relationships between producers' identities, ethical frameworks and care practices. In their research with growers involved in Community Supported Agriculture in Iowa, for instance, Wells and Gradwell (2001) found that concern for land, water and other resources, non-human nature, people, community, place, the future and a need to make a living, were all motivational aspects. Moreover, the growers they interviewed revealed the 'primacy of relationships' as they spoke of 'closing the gap between grower and eater, and between people and nature; of land, plants and animals as community members, not commodities; and of moving from control of nature to partnership and respect' (2001: 117). Wells and Gradwell (2001) characterize Community Supported Agriculture as 'caring-practice', in contrast to industrial agriculture, which, they argue, fails the criterion of care-sensitivity. Rather than this being a dualistic care/non-care distinction between industrial farmers and CSA farmers, it is probably more appropriate to examine the ways in which different farmers care differently, to different degrees and for different things. Adopting a focus on producer reflexivity, Stock (2007) also draws attention to the notion of stewardship, in the sense of caring for the land and thus for the people affected by its health, as an important element of the construction of 'good farmers' amongst organic growers in the US Midwest. The farmers he worked with demonstrated an 'inherent understanding of their role as protecting and ensuring the health of human beings, including family members, community customers and, in a larger, global sense, the world, by trying to work towards the education of new farmers and customers' (Stock 2007: 95). Their work in caring for the soil can be seen as a moral act, in that their practices are attempts to remake what they see as a 'flawed system' based on instability and injustice. Drawing on Whatmore's (1997) notion of relational ethics, Stock suggests that the soil can thus be regarded as an intermediary through which farmers direct moral action towards individuals and the place in which they are rooted (Stock 2007: 96).

The producers discussed by Wells and Gradwell and Stock conceive of their own identities, at least partly, in terms of their roles as carers for various entities, including people, animals, soil, water, family, community and environment. This sense of identity as 'care-giver' thus shapes producer motives and in turn informs their practices. In our own research, we highlight a range of producer identities, motives and practices consistent with this sense of 'care-giver', including the desire to build direct relationships with consumers. We also explore the blurring of producer–consumer subjectivities through practices in which the eaters of food also become involved in its growing. These aspects are explored more thoroughly in Chapters 4, 5 and 6.

Consumer Identities, Motives and Practices within a Framework of Care   In relation to consumers and the act of consumption, associations between care and identities, motives and practices can perhaps be more readily drawn. To discuss the role of care in food consumption is in some ways to discuss the obvious: food is a marker of who we are, what and who we care about. It reflects – and also helps to constitute – our identity as individuals, members of a family or household, peer groups of various kinds, communities, and ethnicities or nationalities. How we obtain our food, what we do with it and the symbolic meanings constructed through its consumption are part of our relationships with the material, social and cultural world. Food is of course also a powerful source of emotions – of pleasure and disgust, as well as being quintessentially mundane and 'everyday'. Food is often symbolic of love and care – as in its offering to outsiders as a transferable gift or as a shared meal to which others may be invited as a demonstration of affection and care. Taking Fisher and Tronto's (1993) definition, it is clear that food is integral to the construction and maintenance of our bodies, selves and environments and is deeply implicated in ethics of care at individual and societal levels.

Consumption in general is an arena in which it has been suggested that people can care for others both close and distant. The act of carefully seeking out and selecting goods – including food – for other people has been portrayed as an act of love. As Miller (2001) argues, people appropriate goods in order to enhance their devotion to other people – notably children, partners and friends. Research on 'ethical' consumption – notably fair trade – has also explored the abilities of consumers to think about the lives of people from whom they are emotionally and physically removed but to whom they are related through goods which are produced and consumed. Geographers in particular have been concerned with the critical problem of how an ethics of care can instil a sense of responsibility towards different and distant others (e.g. Smith 1998; Silk 2000; Friedberg 2004; Popke 2006). As Barnett et al. (2005b: 24) clearly express, there is 'a widespread and taken-for-granted assumption that spatial distance can be thought of in terms of a barrier, beyond which the reach of responsibility becomes problematic in a way that is assumed not to function in relations of proximity'. In an effort to 'fix' the problem of the spatial barrier, many geographers have argued for a need to 'reconnect' the separated moments of production, distribution and consumption in order to 'restore to view a previously hidden chain of commitments and responsibilities' (2005b: 24) (e.g. Hartwick 1998; Castree 2001). Within this model, knowledge is seen as the key factor motivating responsible conduct. Barnett et al. (2005b) are critical of this approach because first, it focuses on the responsibilities of individuals (rather than collective actors) and second by privileging knowledge, it downplays other features which may influence peoples' dispositions towards the world around them (2005b: 25).

As such, Barnett and his colleagues seek to introduce a different approach to conceptualizing ways of being ethical: '[R]ather than assuming that ethical consumption is a self-reflexively conscious practice set off against non-ethical consumption, we start by assuming that everyday consumption practices are always already shaped by, and help shape, certain sorts of ethical dispositions. We propose that everyday consumption routines are *ordinarily ethical*' (2005b: 28; emphasis in original). They thus take 'ethical' to refer to the everyday activity of constructing a life by negotiating practical choices about personal conduct. From this critical perspective, they go on to develop an interpretation of ethical consumption as a process whereby consumers' ordinary, practical moral dispositions are re-articulated by campaigning organizations and businesses. While their concern is explicitly with ethical consumption (e.g. Traidcraft) conceptualized as a form of 'action-at-a-distance', what is particularly useful for our purposes is the idea of everyday consumption routines as 'ordinarily ethical'. Moreover, as Popke makes clear, to suggest that ordinary dispositions to care are mobilized via deliberate representational strategies (on the part of corporate retailers, for example) is 'not to suggest that the acts thus engendered are necessarily devoid of moral or ethical purchase' (2006: 510). In other words, it does not dilute their significance, nor their potential as drivers of change.

We do not argue here that, of those characterized as producers or consumers in our research, all are engaged deliberately in 'ethical consumption/production' – although some of them do self-consciously try to 'be ethical'. Rather, they all undertake daily practices and decisions within ethical frameworks of their own making. These frameworks are in many cases inseparable from the cares they shoulder for other people and entities, which are discussed more fully in Chapter 5. Moreover, as noted by Barnett et al. (2005b), ethical consumption does not only bring to light existing ethical dispositions but might also provoke new ones. In the chapters that follow we provide evidence to suggest that this can often be the case; we observe a 'graduation effect' (Chapter 5), whereby consumers refine and develop their ethical frameworks through their consumption practices. While we agree with Barnett and his colleagues (2005b: 30) that consumption can be thought of as a key site of 'ethical self-formation', we caution that it is not necessarily an 'arena' in which 'people are made up as selves who can exercise freedom and responsibility by exercising their capacities to choose, where these are understood to be a realization of the innate, private right of individual autonomy'.[2] Rather, our conceptualization – supported by the analysis in the following chapters – suggests that choice is in practice often constrained by many factors, including time, money, family circumstances, and also constrained by frameworks of care which include elements of responsibility and commitment towards particular producers or providers of food. Interestingly, the choice to accept responsibility towards others, can in itself limit future choices by the setting of personal boundaries around particular forms of consumption behaviour.

Choice involves decision-making on the basis of knowledge. It suggests an element of power and duty. Thus, fair trade initiatives are built on the idea that consumption choices are actions which can make a difference. As Sassatelli notes, within this context 'choice' is regarded as 'a public, other-related, and therefore, moral action, rather than a self-interested, private and therefore a-moral affair' (2004: 373). Indeed, government and retailers alike claim that the real drivers of change within the food system are consumers themselves, who potentially wield power through the collectivity of their individual demands. People are said to 'vote with their feet'; companies only produce the food commodities and processed products that customers want, and that this is known by what they buy (see also consumer power as 'voting' discussed by Gabriel and Lang, 2006; Clarke et al. 2007). Electronic point of sale (EPOS) facilities and 'Just in Time' distribution systems are said to enable the decisions of millions of people engaged in everyday practices of shopping for food to trigger effective market response (Marsden et al. 2000b). In practice, 'choice' is seldom as 'free' or as simple as it seems, and many people express a sense of unease over the economic and social power which the major food companies have both over retail siting and size, and over what food is produced and distributed. People still largely use the mainstream sources for food shopping – for consumption – not least because most have few other options. 'Consumer choice' is the mantra, but as Galbraith (1974) argued some thirty years ago: the ideology of 'choice', however illusory it may be in reality, is critical to the success of those with power, who co-opt and employ it to deflect challenges over where power really lies. The food system in contemporary societies exemplifies this apparent ambiguity: that 'more choice' (or more apparent choice) masks a lack of effective decision-making. The 'consumer', when it comes to food, may in fact struggle to be the key driver of change, and to demonstrate their 'ethic of care': hence the increasing discontent and desire for 'something different', which underpins the research presented here. The concept of consumer choice – so often held up as the reason for supermarket success – is itself challenged by the voices of consumers we heard. They raised critical dilemmas concerning the nature of 'choice': what are choices between? Must I make this choice? Who decides what options I can choose from? The complex interactions between care, choice and convenience are examined in more detail in Chapter 6 (see also Soper 2007a; 2007b).

Of course, we do not regard an 'ethic of care' as unproblematic. As many authors have pointed out, care has potential to be exclusionary, partial and irrational (Smith 1998; Popke 2006). It can demand resources for those who are known and loved while overlooking the needs of more deserving others (Tronto 2006). So, for instance, much work on care stresses its embodied character, and that it is often associated with locally embedded relationships. The same can be said of work on 'alternative' food provision. So, for example, the 'spaces of reconnection' described by Hendrickson and Heffernan (2002) in their account of the Kansas City Food Circle are physically proximate and the relationships of trust they describe are embedded in a particular locale: 'Producers feel a responsibility to produce healthy, wholesome food that will be eaten by people whom they know. Eaters feel a responsibility to producers who are members of their community' (2002: 303). Similarly, Sage emphasizes the significance of face-to-face transactions in his study of 'good food' networks in south-west Ireland, where 'good food is strongly associated with spaces that are sites of transaction, where food changes from the hands of the person who produced it to the person likely to be party to its consumption' (2003: 51). The embodied co-presence of producers and consumers is crucial to many expressions of relocalization, such as Farmers Markets, Community Supported Agriculture and delivery schemes (Hinrichs 2000, 2003; Holloway and Kneafsey 2000). 'Reconnection', then, is often thought of in physical terms. It can be argued that an 'ethic of care' arising out of this would tend to be restricted to those with whom we have some immediate contact and familiarity. As DuPuis and Goodman note, the 'local' is a concept that 'intrinsically implies the inclusion and exclusion of particular people, places and ways of life' (2005: 361). However, even critical approaches to the 'local' can back-handedly reinforce its idealization: as noted by Smith (1998), 'nearness is no guarantee of beneficence'. Moreover, contemporary technologies can enable the construction of direct relationships between spatially distant producers and consumers. In work on Internet-mediated food schemes Holloway (2002) shows that consumers can obtain an element of 'remote control' over how their food is produced. This 'electronically mediated folding-in of space produces effects of scale that make the conventionally distant close and within an ambit of care' (2002: 78). In other words, the Internet-mediated schemes which Holloway writes of have potential to disrupt usual assumptions about the relationship between proximity and care:

> While relations of care have often been assumed to be most significant where the carer and the object of care are in close geographical proximity (Smith 2000), in the case of these schemes, ethical relations based on electronically mediated encounters during which customers invest in the production of food are played out over greater distances, and between urban and rural, and potentially over international, spaces. (Holloway 2002: 78)

While Holloway suggests that relations of care may be established across space, he is careful to stress that more research is needed to fully explore this. In our own project we have further explored the extent to which caring practices can be said to occur through the Internet-mediated 'Adopt a sheep' scheme (see Chapter 4 in particular). By examining relationships that are established over large distances as well as within local areas we are able to explore the potential for care to relate to people and places beyond the immediate locality or close community.

SUMMARIZING REMARKS

In this chapter we have developed two broad conceptual themes, which provide the framework for the empirical analysis presented later in the book. First, we have tried to trouble the concept of the 'alternative' in relation to food. Throughout the book, we try to be sparing and careful in our use of the word, and a central concern of the research has been to explore just exactly what is understood by the term by different actors engaged in different food production–consumption relationships. Throughout, then, 'alternative' is taken to be an unstable concept and as such is treated with caution. Moreover, and drawing on our theoretical predisposition towards relational approaches, our focus is consistently on the relationships which are formed by, and through which, 'alternatives' are practised. Within this context, discourses and practices of 'reconnection' are, we suggest, a defining feature of the 'alternatives' we examine in this book. These discourses and practices in turn, are distinguished by the ethical frameworks within which they are embedded, and we propose that a broad ethic of care, understood as a consideration of, and preparedness to take action about the needs of others (not only human others) is central to the identities, motives and practices of those we have engaged with during our research. During our conversations with producers and consumers we were often engaged in discussions of care: care for people, places, plants, animals, soil, water and for relationships and ways of life. Notions of care permeated our participants' discussions of their involvement in 'alternative' food practices. Yet the notions of care that were drawn on were diverse and the things being cared for were various. Consumers each constructed their own 'careful geographies' of consumption focused on different scales, objects and actors. In the empirical chapters which follow we chart some of these geographies as we examine the identities, motives and practices of the producers and consumers involved in six different attempts to forge 'reconnections' through food.

CHAPTER 3

Analytical Description of Six 'Alternative' Food Schemes

INTRODUCTION

Having laid out the principal elements of our conceptual framework in the previous chapter, we now turn to a detailed analytical description of our six examples of food 'reconnection' (please note, a full discussion of our research methods is presented in Appendix I). The material presented here is important for contextualizing the interview-based data which follows in the next three chapters. In effect, this chapter acts as a bridge between our theoretical and methodological discussions, and the empirical findings. We continue using the word 'alternative' as a shorthand, and to acknowledge its contemporary resonance, despite the shortcomings of the concept discussed in Chapter 2. We begin with a brief account of how we dealt with the literature and discourses around the term and its practices, and the selection of six different schemes or activities, to enable us to engage with 'producers' and 'consumers' practising/participating in ways of obtaining food 'outside the mainstream'.

Before schemes could be chosen for detailed research, it was necessary to construct a database from which potential cases could be selected. In devising the criteria for inclusion in the database (which are reproduced in Appendix I; see also Venn et al. 2006), we began to engage seriously with the question: what is an 'alternative' food network/scheme/initiative? When we began our research, market trend analysis (Mintel 2003) and non-governmental reports (Sustain 2002; Foundation for Local Food Initiatives 2003; Working Group on Local Food 2003) suggested an exponential growth in the organic, speciality and local food and drinks sectors, but there was a lack of agreement on what actually constituted an 'alternative' food scheme (for example, is 'speciality' food necessarily 'alternative'?) and subsequently the breadth and size of the target population. A key theme bridging the diversity of the 'alternative' food schemes reported in the literature began to emerge around the notion of distinctive ethical frameworks. So, for example, producer co-operatives could be built around shared desires to farm 'responsibly' and provide quality, artisanal products in an attempt to circumvent the homogenizing legacy of conventional food production (see Collet and Mormont 2003; Stassart and Whatmore 2003; Wiskerke 2003). Thus, 'alternative' ethical frameworks were 'different' to those found in 'conventional' food production–consumption relationships usually in the sense that they were an attempt to 'counter' or 'resist' prevalent modes of industrial scale production. How exactly this 'difference' was constituted and performed from the perspective of consumers remained under-examined.

In addition to reviewing the literature, we also invited a specially convened panel of experts to review our selection process and so by combining insights from the panel with concepts from the literature review we developed a framework for sourcing examples of 'alternative' food schemes (see Appendix I). One of the first critical insights from the panel was their recommendation that the word 'alternative' be used with caution. For several of the panel members the word was unhelpful because of its connotations of 'radical' and 'fringe'. For those working to make local, organic or ethical foods 'mainstream', the label of 'alternative' was seen as potentially restrictive and damaging to the cause. For the purposes of the research project, however, it was necessary to keep working with the 'alternative' label until its conceptualization could be improved. The aim was to develop a comprehensive and inclusive working understanding of 'alternative' food practices, while simultaneously contributing to the development of more specific concepts and tools that would reveal the variability of 'alternative' food schemes as called for by Renting et al. (2003).

Having collected in excess of 140 entries in the database (the actual figure for schemes is much higher given that a number of the entries relate to umbrella bodies representing a number of individual schemes), we conducted a content analysis of the promotional materials produced by schemes in order to better understand the ways in which they represented themselves and their aims. This analysis illustrated the various descriptors utilized by schemes to differentiate themselves from their competitors and demonstrated that 'alternative' food projects are not necessarily always driven by profit maximization and market penetration. In numerous instances, consumer and community groups utilize food procurement as a mechanism for tackling social injustices and inequalities, and consequently issues of food access and affordability are seen as legitimate attributes. Given our focus on the nature of producer–consumer relationships, we created a typology of relationships into which our database entries could be fitted; this has already been reproduced in Chapter I.

ANALYTICAL FIELDS FOR DESCRIBING FOOD SCHEMES

While the typology of producer–consumer relationships was a useful starting point which enabled us to select six examples for detailed investigation, during the course of the research, we developed a methodological tool that assists us in moving beyond the prevalent 'alternative–conventional' dualism discussed in Chapter 2 in order to describe the constitution of food production–consumption in more complex and relational ways. We have set out a series of interrelated analytical fields, or areas of engagement or significance, which enable us to examine the symbolic, material and embodied aspects of production–consumption and understandings of power and agency as relational effects.[1] This is a shift away from a process of categorization of food relationships as *either* 'alternative' *or* 'conventional'. Instead, the fields allow a mapping of particular food initiatives in relation to a set of interrelated arenas and processes. Importantly, this allows us to demonstrate how these arrangements have particular effects, such as the ability of a food scheme to endure through time, to counter prevailing power relations and/or to restructure producer–consumer relationships. At the same time, it has to be understood that the mapping is a process, rather than a definitive and static representation of a scheme. We emphasize here that the idea of these analytical fields emerged *from* and *during* our research and we have applied the fields to our case studies as a means of making sense of their particular and general characteristics.

Table 3.1 sets out the categories or fields we used to characterize the matrix of relationships across which the particularities of individual schemes are distributed. The table gives examples of what can be included in each field in the cases of the schemes represented in our database. The fields described here are particularly relevant to cases in which food moves directly from producer to consumer, reflecting our pragmatic decisions over criteria for selecting the case studies, and further fields might be necessary in relation to other sorts of producer–consumer relationship. The fields used here nevertheless indicate the methodological value of this strategy for describing and starting to analyse food schemes. The fields are described as follows:

- *Site of food production*: the place where food is grown and/or processed. It includes a wide range of contrasting sites, including some which have a degree of permanence and are established within traditions of food production in the UK (e.g. farms) and others which are more ephemeral and makeshift, occupying 'new' or temporary sites like ex-industrial

Table 3.1 Analytical Fields for Describing Food Schemes

Heuristic 'Analytical Field'	Examples from Database of Food Schemes
Site of food production	Community garden, school grounds, urban 'brownfield' sites, farm, rented field, allotments...
Food production methods	Organic, biodynamic, consumer participation, horse ploughing...
Supply chain	Local selling/procurement, Internet marketing...
Arena of exchange	Farm shops, farmers markets, home delivery, mobile shops, PYO...
Producer–consumer interaction	Direct selling, email, newsletters, cooking demonstrations, food growing work (e.g. weeding parties), farm walks, share/ subscription membership schemes...
Motivations for participation	Business success, making food accessible, social/environmental concerns, anxiety avoidance, sensory pleasure...
Constitution of individual and group identities	Customers, participants, stakeholders, supporters groups, children's groups, disability groups, care-givers, women's groups...

'brownfield' sites, spaces within school grounds or small areas of rented farm land. In some cases, for example where commercial farmland becomes part of a community-supported agriculture scheme, the nature and meaning of the space involved changes as particular modes of food production are engaged with and different types of producer–consumer relationship are established. Spatial scale and location is also important here. For our schemes their relatively small size, in terms of food production area, and their position in relation to, for example, particular groups of consumers, other producers, or institutions which support their operations, is important to how they operate.

- *Food production methods*: many schemes emphasize the ways food is grown and prepared, in particular where these are thought to challenge the prevalence of industrial interests in agriculture. The emphasis placed on these methods, such as 'organic' production, may also be interpreted as demonstrating producers' assessments of consumers' motivations to consume food produced in these ways. These might include consumers' anxieties over the use of pesticides or artificial fertilizers etc. Food growing is thus seen in this field as the result of producer–consumer relationships, and in some cases (especially the co-operative or community-supported schemes) negotiations, rather than simply a product of growers' decision-making.
- *Supply chain*: although we are wary of the term 'food chain', as it can imply a one-way relationship between food production and food consumption, we use this field to indicate a sense in which food literally moves between different arenas, via different technologies and organizations of movement. Our schemes thus use supply chain mechanisms ranging from 'low-tech' methods of local supply to use of the Internet and airfreight to supply an international consumer base. Again, producer–consumer relationships are key to understandings of these food chains, as they are involved in the construction of particular supply chains and are also mediated by the supply chains.
- *Arena of exchange*: the concrete and meaningful spaces in which food is exchanged. At one level the field refers to the site in which exchange occurs, such as a shop or market stall. But at another level it also refers to what the exchange is actually *of*, both materially and non-materially. In the schemes included in our research, food itself is both material, with particular sensory and physical qualities, and is embedded with significance for both producers and consumers, symbolizing, for example, a particular locality, a particular way of growing food, or means of earning a living, and/or particular producer–consumer relationships. Food is usually exchanged for money, but in other cases for, for example, work, communal activity, LETS, longer term financial commitments (such as in share or subscription schemes), and also, at least in part, a sense of 'regard' (Sage 2003) and other intersubjective aspects of producer–consumer relationship (see below).
- *Producer–consumer interaction*: the material and symbolic, formal and informal 'meeting points' of consumers and producers in food networks are emphasized in this field. Interaction might thus be face-to-face, or

involve communications at a distance through various technologies (e.g. one-way communication through advertising, or inter-communication via email or telephone). The importance of this interaction is in the establishment of particular sorts of intersubjective and spatio-temporal relationship which influence the ways food schemes emerge and change over time. These interactions are thus important processes of effecting change, contributing to the changing spatial relationships involved in our particular examples, and in the ways they are explicitly or implicitly engaged in challenges to dominant food systems. This field is in some ways similar to the preceding one in its emphasis on connection, but emphasizes the social aspects of that connection in contrast to the material dimension noted in the arena of exchange.

- *Motivations for participation*: describes the reasons people have for participating in particular food schemes as consumers or producers, and relates these reasons to both the ways in which people think about food (including imagining how things can be done in a different way to the mainstream) and forms of behaviour. Motivations clearly are subject to change and there are likely to be shifts within and between producers' and consumers' motivations, and processes of negotiation between differently motivated actors. Motivations and behaviours are thus seen as 'becoming', rather than as a fixed part of stable identities. Motivation is important here as it allows us to examine how participants describe and explain their own participation. It also points to the importance of producer–consumer relationships in the ways that each has an understanding of the motivations of the other that in turn influences their own behaviours. Thus, for example, a producer's understanding of consumer anxieties about pesticides in food or the environmental costs of globalized food networks might influence his/her use of, respectively, 'organic' production or localized marketing methods. Similarly a consumer's perception of a producer's ethical commitment to growing food in particular ways might encourage them to source food from that producer.

- *Constitution of individual and group identities*: this final field is closely related to the previous one, but attempts to account for the ways in which particular food networks, first, depend on or assume particular subject positions or identities, and second, actually produce or reproduce particular subjectivities. For example, ideas of the 'ethical consumer' are important in some food networks, alongside others which produce particular group identities, such as food schemes centring round women, ethnic minority groups, or people with disabilities. More widely, this is part of an argument that a food network or scheme is never simply external to the producers and consumers, but both produces and is produced by the people involved. This field, then, allows a sense of subjective 'becoming' in relation to food production–consumption. We use this field to account for the co-constitutive relationships between human identity and the field of shifting spatial and social formations making up the heterogeneous food networks people participate in, and which is played out in their diverse food provisioning practices.

The descriptions illustrate first, how particular arrangements allow schemes to work, and second, how in the cases we are interested in, these arrangements allow them in different ways to offer possibilities for resistance to locations of power in food systems (whether or not this is an explicit objective of a scheme) and engagement in active remaking of food production–consumption relationships in accordance with their particular ways of imagining 'better' food networks. The descriptions thus attempt to illustrate how effects of agency and power in relation to food are produced by social, economic and spatial relationships between and within fields. In the next section, we provide a more detailed description of each case in relation to these fields.

SALOP DRIVE MARKET GARDEN

Salop Drive Market Garden is described as 'a three-acre site which provides a working market garden for people to learn at first hand about food production, undertake healthy exercise and learn about healthy eating and lifestyles' (http://www.idealforall.co.uk). Salop Drive is located in Sandwell, an economically depressed urban borough in the West Midlands (see Table 1.2). This local context is important for understanding the principal aims and ethos of the scheme, which are discussed in more detail below. Table 3.2 outlines some of the key aspects of the project in relation to our analytical fields. The site of food production was formerly an allotment site which had fallen almost derelict over a period of about fifteen years. Much work was needed to reclaim the overgrown site and then improve the soil, which was severely compacted once the clearance had finished. Green waste from Herefordshire council was used to improve fertility. Access roads have been installed and purpose-built wooden offices erected which serve as meeting and resting places for people working on the site. Six commercial sized poly-tunnels are now in place and the produce is grown 'sustainably'. The site of

Table 3.2 Salop Drive Market garden, West Midlands, United Kingdom

Heuristic 'Analytical Field'	Brief Description
Site of food production	1.1 ha in the heart of a deprived inner city housing estate.
Food production methods	Organic
Supply chain	Fruit and vegetable bag deliveries
Arena of exchange	Consumers pay a fixed amount per bag, depending on size of bag required. Consumers can also volunteer to work on the site and will often receive free produce in return.
Producer–consumer interaction	Consumers are frequently consulted by scheme workers. Use of leaflets, newsletters, questionnaires, workshops and organized social/educational events.
Motivations for participation	The scheme was established to encourage healthy living and healthy eating, with a specific focus on involving disabled people. Consumer participation driven by desire for fresh, accessible, good quality and cheap vegetables.
Constitution of individual and group identities	Consumers are local residents, community members, users and participants; scheme workers (growers) try to work in consultation with the users of the scheme.

food production – unlike many sites of industrial food production – is thus highly visible because it is surrounded by houses and flats and is also quite accessible (see Figure 3.1), although this was an aspect project workers were trying to improve still further at the time of research. In 2003 seventy-four bags of fruit and vegetables were delivered each week to three drop off points at local residents' homes and at an Independent Living Centre in the

Figure 3.1 Volunteers plant out seedlings at Salop Drive Market Garden. Photo courtesy of Ideal for All, Salop Drive Market Garden.

borough. If necessary, the bags are bulked up with produce bought from a local supplier. The scheme also offers leisure, social and learning activities, which include basic and intermediate skills training, community events and celebrations.

At the time of research, the scheme was staffed by a horticultural site worker, a development worker and a support worker. However, volunteers are central to its survival and from its very beginnings, one of the key aims of the scheme has been enable people with disabilities to participate in the work. In terms of producer–consumer interaction, therefore, the Salop Drive market garden is represented – and organized – as a 'user-led' scheme, with participatory processes at its heart. The scheme was originally driven by local and regional food policy initiatives dating back to 1995 and is now managed by Ideal for All, an organization set up in 1996 to offer services for disabled people living in Sandwell and beyond. Local residents and users of the scheme have regularly been consulted and the garden is portrayed as an outcome of the vision and hard work of many people. Questionnaires, workshops and social events such as community lunches and visits to other gardens have all been used to encourage community interaction with the scheme. Leaflets, recipes and newsletters are included in the vegetable bags, and the garden has also supplied vegetables to Healthy Living Network Community Cafes and regular cook, grow and eat workshops (Ideal for All, 2004). A small number of mini-allotments are also available on site and these are tended by local residents and people referred from the Independent Living Centre. A wildlife garden has been created and there are plans to build more seating and create herb gardens and raised beds to further increase accessibility for those with disabilities.

Regarding the motives for participation, the scheme is first and foremost concerned with encouraging healthy eating and healthy living, with a specific focus on involving disabled people. The scheme aims to contribute to the government's national agenda for encouraging people to eat five pieces of fruit and vegetable a day. The scheme is not, therefore, driven by a profit-making motive, although it does seek to become self-supporting and decrease its reliance on public funding. From the perspective of the residents and consumers involved, our research indicates that the key motives for participation are the freshness and quality of the produce, along with the convenience of the delivery system. Consumers also reported that they have tried new vegetables and learned new cooking skills as a result of being in the scheme. They also appreciated the positive contribution that the garden makes to the community in terms of providing a social contact point for people who would otherwise be isolated and generally encouraging people to 'get involved'. For those involved in volunteering at the garden, there are many benefits including the enjoyment of getting out of the house, meeting new people, getting some physical exercise, relaxation, stress-reduction and gaining a sense of pride and satisfaction from seeing the results of their work. In relation to the final analytical field in our table, Salop Drive presents a clear case of the co-constitution of individual and group identities in the sense that the scheme workers are highly attuned to the needs of the local community and the disabled volunteers in particular. As such, growing decisions are made in response to these needs rather than in response to commercial pressures. The scheme is very much a partnership between different actors and consumers tended to identify with the scheme itself rather than any individual growers or staff members. They recognize that the scheme is about much more than simply the production of food; it has community and environmental dimensions which were greatly appreciated by the consumers involved. Many of the consumers have also been able to develop new food-related skills and knowledge.

This scheme then reveals much about the diversity of activities and agendas which can be pursued within differently structured producer–

consumer relationships. Importantly, this case is about so much more than 'reconnection' in the sense of supplying local food for local people. It has a broader agenda of widening participation, promoting wildlife conservation, environmental sustainability and crucially, improving public health not only by increasing access to fresh fruit and vegetables but also by enabling people to enjoy the physical and mental health benefits associated with growing their own food. While resistance to the dominant food system is by no means an overt aim, this scheme can be thought of as a form of resistance for those marginalized by such systems – those who cannot easily access supermarkets because of physical disability, lack of private transport, low income and so on. Examining the case in terms of our analytical fields allows us to identify just how this particular scheme can empower groups and individuals to participate more fully in the production of their food and also exert more control over their own health and well-being.

EARTHSHARE

Established in 1994, EarthShare is the longest running Community Supported Agriculture scheme in Britain. Subscribers fund the growers' salaries, plus the rent of land from a local farmer, and in return receive their share of produce as an organic fruit and vegetable box each week. Subscribers are also expected to do three workshifts a year; however, there is an option to increase the fees in order to avoid this contribution of labour. The scheme operates in the same area as the Findhorn Foundation – a spiritual community – but although the Foundation is a major subscriber to the scheme there is no other formal control and subscribers need not necessarily have any association with the Foundation. When EarthShare was established the goal was to make organic produce available to local people without increasing food miles.

EarthShare produces organic vegetables and soft fruit in a field rented from an organic farm. An immediate difference is evident between this small, seemingly ephemeral site (there are no farm buildings beyond a couple of wooden sheds) and the established large-scale modes of crop and livestock agriculture which surround it. Growers at the nearby Cullerne Gardens are contracted to supply EarthShare with salad vegetables grown in poly-tunnels. Consumers pay either an annual subscription or a monthly direct debit, and receive a weekly box of produce. Table 3.3 provides some details of the scheme in relation to the analytical fields. We focus here on the way in which the particular arrangement of this CSA produces a sense of power and agency in relation to food, which makes it different in important ways from the other options for food provisioning that are available to consumers in this locality, which would tend to centre around the use of supermarket retailers. This sense of a different way of imagining food provisioning is emphasized by EarthShare, which contrasts its produce with that available from supermarkets in terms of its physical qualities (e.g. taste, seasonality and freshness) and its ethical associations (in terms of the differential social, economic and environmental effects of the different modes of production–consumption). As the EarthShare website says (2005), 'EarthShare does a lot more than provide organic vegetables'. The vision of food production and consumption that EarthShare promotes is one in which agency within the local area is produced by producers, consumers and the production–consumption relationship. People's food practices then, as producers or/and consumers in EarthShare, are represented as being able to achieve social, economic and environmental benefits which contrast explicitly with the very different effects of supermarket food provisioning. This achievement is effected in a number of different ways. Here we present just two, relating particularly to the fields of arena of exchange, producer–consumer interaction, individual and group identities and the motivations associated with producers' and consumers' involvement.

First, the relationship between producers and consumers in EarthShare is very different to those effected by supermarkets, and is presented as one emphasizing closeness and connectedness. Beyond 'mutual knowing' between producers and consumers, however, EarthShare involves other production–consumption practices associated with a production of agency and identity within food production–consumption. Consumers subscribe to EarthShare and are identified as scheme members, giving them a sense of commitment to the scheme and generating a sense of participative ownership in the scheme. This is developed further by the expectation that members participate in working groups ('weeding parties'), thus contributing to food production and producing corporeal engagement with the materiality of food and the 'nature' involved in growing food. In terms of identity, then, the differentiation between producers and consumers evident in mainstream food provisioning is blurred, with consumers having social agency (through their position as subscribing members of a scheme) and material agency (through participating in growing and consuming food). At the same time, a particular arena of exchange is produced, involving the exchange of food in return for a combination of money and work (this novel arena of exchange can be further supplemented by exchanging food for services via the local LETS scheme – subscribers can pay up to 20 per cent of their fees in

Table 3.3 EarthShare Community Supported Agriculture, Near Forres, Scotland

Heuristic 'Analytical Field'	Brief Description
Site of food production	c.9 ha rented land; close to Findhorn Foundation
Food production methods	Organic; mechanical and horse power; consumer involvement in growing
Supply chain	Box delivery
Arena of exchange	Money, work and LETS exchange; food embedded with ethical value
Producer–consumer interaction	Website, notes in boxes, working parties, social events; emphasis on 'closeness', connection and commitment
Motivations for participation	Social, economic and environmental concerns; desire for fresh, seasonal produce
Constitution of individual and group identities	Consumers are participants, sharers, subscribers to values; group growing work

LETS[2]). Part of what EarthShare represents then is the possibility of a challenge to the purely money exchanges which are prevalent within capitalist food production–consumption, and their conjoining with different forms of exchange associated with different types of social relationship.

Second, and in a related way, participation in EarthShare is represented as associated with wider economic, social and environmental effects, and with subscription to particular value systems related to this mode of food production–consumption. Here, participants' (as producers, consumers and both) motivations are important, and relate to the particular way of imagining food production–consumption which is, in practice, achieved by the ways in which this scheme functions as described by its arrangement across the fields. EarthShare thus contrasts the food it produces with supermarket produce, partly in terms of its lower money cost, but also, significantly, in terms of a particular ethical vision of what the effects of food production–consumption in a locality should be. For example, it is suggested that participation in a CSA encourages the circulation of money within local economies, provides employment opportunities, and creates a sense of community and mutual support. Importantly, discussion with EarthShare participants indicated that, although there was a range of personal reasons for an initial engagement with the scheme, over the duration of their involvement they had become increasingly enrolled into, and motivated by, the wider value system in which the CSA is situated. As such, consumers' motivations and identities are as much produced through their participation as leading to participation to begin with.

EarthShare is clearly open to being categorized as an 'alternative' mode of food production–consumption. However, what we are able to illustrate is that it is the particular arrangement of the CSA in relation to our analytical fields which produces particular forms of agency and identity associated with food production–consumption, and which allows the practical expression of a particular vision of food production–consumption which is associated with a particular set of social, economic and environmental values. As such, although something like EarthShare alone does little to rebalance the power relations within food networks more widely, it represents an example of a proliferation of different ways of thinking and doing things within a wider capitalist economy, and establishes, at a small scale and through a particular spatial arrangement of production–consumption, a locus of power which is expressed through its ability to persist in time and space and to at least raise an explicitly oppositional voice against the majority of food provisioning practices in its locality.

WATERLAND ORGANICS

Waterland Organics is based on a mixed organic farm in Cambridgeshire and sells organic fruit and vegetables direct to the public through a box scheme. Set up in 1995, on an initial plot of five acres (at the time this made it the second largest organic operation in Cambridgeshire), it started with just thirteen deliveries. The scheme has since expanded to over 100 customers and now runs throughout the year, having originally shut down over the winter months. It has also joined the Eostre Organics co-operative in East Anglia, which is a producer co-operative which buys produce from them and also supplies produce that they cannot grow. The producers' overriding

Table 3.4 Waterland Organic Box Scheme, Cambridgeshire

Heuristic 'Analytical Field'	Brief Description
Site of food production	Mixed 49 ha organic farm in Cambridgeshire
Food production methods	Organic; 8 ha sugar beet, 8 ha mixed vegetables, 33 ha under grass and grazed by sheep
Supply chain	Direct from farmer to consumer
Arena of exchange	Box scheme
Producer–consumer interaction	On the doorstep, newsletter, recipes, website
Motivations for participation	Producer: business viability in competitive retail sector, desire to sell locally and have direct contact with consumers. Consumers: organic food foods, desire to buy direct
Constitution of individual and group identities	Consumers are customers; producers are farmers and retailers

motivation for setting up the box scheme was to grow food that was sold locally and to have direct contact with the people that ate the produce. Table 3.4 describes Waterland Organics in relation to the analytic fields.

In terms of the analytical fields, Waterland occupies a relatively permanent site in the farmscape and material provided on the Eostre Organics website emphasizes the longevity of the Robinsons' connections to the area, whereby both sides of the family 'have farmed in and around the Cambridgeshire fens since at least the 1600s'. Records also show that 'some of the family members were involved in wild fowling until the mass drainage of the Fens took their livelihoods away, and in the late 1800s one of his [Paul Robinson's] ancestors was hanged at the end of the Littleport Bread Riots' (www.eostreorganics. co.uk). There is thus a definite attempt to establish connection, to evoke a sense of history and perhaps also to suggest an element of resistance or rebellion to more powerful forces – note the references to livelihoods 'taken away' and an ancestor hanged. Such information does not strictly bear any relation to the quality of the food produced by the Robinsons, but it is used here to establish trust by suggesting the existence of deeply embedded knowledge and practices and perhaps also, to create a sense of the Robinsons as being of resilient 'underdog' character; people able and willing to stand up to injustice. Later on the web page, reference is made to Paul's completion of a three-year horticulture course, again reinforcing the sense of his inherited knowledge of farming practices combined with up-to-date knowledge gained at college. Reference is also made to the problems encountered by the farm when supermarkets moved into organic retailing and custom was lost, and also to the 'troublesome' and 'unreliable' relationships with supermarkets. What is presented here is thus a complex mix of messages whereby a sense of continuity with the past is emphasized at the same time as a sense of the radical and oppositional. The fact that the production methods are organic is a feature which means that this business can be folded into the 'alternative' umbrella but at the same time, aspects of continuity with the past are emphasized. Moreover, once the motives for participation of producers and consumers are examined, it again becomes clear that these are far more complex than a desire to create an 'alternative' food system and indeed, consumer and producer motives and expectations do not always align neatly with each other. So, for example, the Waterland website suggests that you may want to try a vegetable box 'If you are in the Cambridge area and value the environment and your food' (www. waterland.org). This suggests that a Waterland consumer is someone whose ethical framework prioritizes the environment and food, rather than other aspects such as price. Indeed during interviews it did become clear that some Waterland consumers were lost when supermarkets such as Waitrose started selling organic ranges and it became clear that they were not buying food for the same reasons as Paul was producing it – in his words, because it was 'local, it's fresh and cutting down on food miles'. The motives for participation and constitution of consumer identities are examined in more detail in Chapters 5 and 6. For the moment, our aim is to illustrate how structuring of our discussion around these analytical fields enables us to problematize and 'complexify' the notion of 'alternativeness' and the nature of producer–consumer relationships within our case studies.

FARRINGTON'S FARM SHOP

Farrington's Farm shop is located on a tenanted, traditional mixed-farm just outside Bristol. The farm comprises a herd of 230 dairy cows, large-scale potato growing and an award winning farm shop (National Farm Retailer of the Year, 2004). The shop sells over 4,000 product lines, including home-produced crops and locally sourced produce to a customer base of 8,000. Set up in June 2001, the farm shop now includes a coffee shop, new kitchens for the production of breads and cakes and meals for the coffee shop, customer toilets and new farm attractions for visitors. The working farm is at the heart of their business and represents their ethos of selling direct from farm to consumer. Table 3.5 describes Farrington's farm shop in relation to the analytical fields. The shop retails products from the farm as well as a wide range of other products that are sourced 'locally' as far as possible. Geographically, then, the site of the shop and its relationships with a network of food suppliers identified as local to it, are important to its function and to the way it represents something different for the consumers who purchase food from it. For example, consumers value the opportunity to see the cows and to watch milking at the same time as purchasing food, something which clearly contrasts with the experience of supermarket shopping. Yet Farrington's resembles 'mainstream' supermarket retailers in some key ways. For example, it has a loyalty card scheme which involves about 4,000 consumers, and retails processed foods and ready meals (both made on site) as well as fresh produce (see Figure 3.2). Where produce is unavailable locally, national and international sources are used but the business explicitly tries to source food in ways which do not compete 'unfairly' with local and United Kingdom suppliers. In contrast to EarthShare and Salop Drive, but in common with Waterland, consumers are represented here as customers, and the shop's owners as farmers and retailers: the identities of producer and consumer remain distinct and there is no formal sense of consumers' participation in production–consumption except as customers engaging in the exchange of money for food. Nevertheless, the particular arrangement of food production–consumption across the analytical fields draws attention to some of the ways in which some things about what makes it work implicitly counter prevailing power relations in food networks. We identify two here.

First, although not everything is grown or processed on site, the scale of the business is small enough to allow consumers to feel that they know the operators and employed staff, and that this is a reciprocal knowledge. This sort of knowledge is associated with consumers' feelings of trust and commitment to the shop which, for them, differentiates their relationships with Farrington's from their relationships with local branches of national supermarket chains. Although superficially, then, the arena of exchange in this case is characterized by money payment, the exchange is simultaneously

Table 3.5 Farrington's Farm Shop, Somerset, England

Heuristic 'Analytical Field'	Brief Description
Site of food production	Processing and some growing on working tenanted farm; products sourced from wide range of local (preferentially), national and international suppliers
Food production methods	Variable; no commitment to specific production methods. Food processing on site
Supply chain	Retailing of home-grown and bought in foods; leasing of part of shop for a butcher's counter
Arena of exchange	Farm shop and café; visibility of working farm; money exchanged for food
Producer–consumer interaction	Retailer–customer or employee–customer in the shop; loyalty card; website
Motivations for participation	Producer: business viability in competitive retail sector. Consumers: quality foods, dislike of supermarkets
Constitution of individual and group identities	Consumers are customers; producers are farmers and retailers

reliant on relationships of regard (following Sage 2003) which are necessarily associated with consumers' understandings of the identities of the shop's owners as directly 'present' in the food they retail (implying both a relationship of proximity and a closeness to *how* food was produced). Second, although for its operators the main motivation is to sustain a viable business, for consumers the farm shop presents an opportunity for them to circumvent, or counter, prevailing supermarket modes of retailing

Figure 3.2 Farrington's Farm shop – a range of frozen and processed meals is available. Photo by E. Dowler.

food. They claimed, for example, a dislike of supermarkets, and valued the opportunity to buy 'local', 'quality' food. The production of a particular mode of consumer agency is thus emphasized in analysis of this food network although the empowerment of consumers was not a reason behind its establishment. Similarly, the shop owners' decision to retail home-grown and locally sourced products as far as possible, has the effect of countering established power relations in food supply in a similar way to that seen in relation to EarthShare and Waterland.

MOORLAND FARM

Moorland Farm is a traditional 280-hectare family farm selling 'natural beef' from their closed herd of grass-fed Aberdeen Angus cattle (Table 3.6). At the time of initial interview the Scotts were selling a third of their produce direct to the public through their farm shop and the rest through a circuit of

Table 3.6 Moorland Farm, Somerset, England

Heuristic 'Analytical Field'	Brief Description
Site of food production	280 ha family farm set in an environmentally sensitive area of the Somerset Levels, rising to a height of over 150 m on top of the Mendip Hills
Food production methods	Aberdeen Angus cattle are raised on grass, according to traditional methods used 100 years ago. Growth promoting hormones and routine antibiotics are not used. The animals are slaughtered at local abattoir and returned to the farm's cold store, where they are hung for 2–3 weeks to bring out full flavour and texture. Meat is butchered at the farm
Supply chain	Meat is retailed direct to the public via farm shop and stalls at farmers' markets
Arena of exchange	Farm shop and farmers' market stalls; money exchanged for food
Producer–consumer interaction	Retailer–customer in the shop/stall
Motivations for participation	Producer: business viability; Consumers: quality beef
Constitution of individual and group identities	Consumers are customers; producers are farmers and retailers

regular farmers' markets in Somerset. When they started selling their produce in 1996, their initial goal was to sell everything they produced direct to the public and to withdraw from conventional food chains. They achieved this and demand for their meat now regularly outstrips supply. Moorland farm is an interesting case because on reading about the characteristics of the farm and its produce, it fits easily into the 'alternative' category. The supply chain is short and direct, the product is of high quality and distinct provenance and the contact between producers and consumers is direct. Their leaflet makes use of language and imagery which can be understood within the context of a nostalgic discourse of 'reconnection'; the front cover features a black and white engraving of an Aberdeen Angus and is accompanied by a quote: 'It tastes wonderful, just like beef used to. I know exactly where is comes from every time I buy'. Inside the leaflet, the beef is described as 'old fashioned' and raised using a method used by the farmer's great grandfather 'a hundred years ago'. There is thus reference to times gone by and also to the traceability of the product. The beef is also marketed under the trade name of 'Natural Beef' and there are frequent references to the cattle's 'natural lifestyle' and the 'natural environment' in which it is raised. Each animal can be 'traced back for generations' and they 'are treated as individuals with great dignity and respect'.

Yet on delving into the motivations for participation and the constitution of identities (the last of our two analytical fields) this initial perception is problematized. The Scotts turned to direct retail because they felt that their business would not survive if they stayed in conventional relationships. They are extremely committed to raising Aberdeen Angus in a 'traditional' and 'respectful' way, but they have no desire to change the world or promote 'alternative' food systems. They believe in the quality of their product and attribute their success to this. They assume that consumers like knowing who has produced the meat, where it has come from and that it has been grown to traditional methods. Recognizing the importance that consumers attach to direct contact with the producers, they have not gone down the route of box deliveries. They do not undertake any marketing beyond having produced 5,000 leaflets in 2003. They do not maintain a website and while they may be listed in some local food directories, this was not a marketing strategy of theirs. It could be argued that the Scotts, in maintaining their personal presence at their shop and farmers markets contribute towards practices of 'reconnection', but their own sense-making of this made no reference to discourses of 'reconnection'. Instead, they emphasized the quality of their product and put faith in the ability of consumers to recognize this and recommend it to others. Our research with the consumers who buy from Moorland showed that the presence of the farmer at the stall was very important in that it enabled consumers to reinforce feelings of trust and respect for the producers and their produce. While recognizing the importance of their regular customers, it was only rarely that the farmers treated such customers differently to non-regular customers (e.g. occasionally a small discount might be given to a regular customer making a large purchase).

'ADOPT A SHEEP'

This sixth and final case concerns a scheme in Italy which allows people located anywhere in the world to 'adopt' a milking sheep on an Italian mountain farm and receive the products of the farm (cheese, salami and wool) by post (see Figure 3.3). There are currently around 1,100 adopters. For 190 euros an adopter receives a certificate of adoption, an identity card and photo of 'their' sheep, two kilograms of pecorino cheese of any seasoning and size, two kilograms of juniper-smoked ricotta, one pair of trekking socks, one kilogram of *salamelle di tratturo* (sheep-salami) (alternative for vegetarians one kilogramme of *Caciocavallo*) and five litres of olive oil. Freight costs by priority mail are included. Cheaper packages are available at 140 and 80 euros, each offering a reduced range of products.[3] Table 3.7

Figure 3.3 Entrance to the Abruzzo National Park in Italy, home to the 'Adopt a sheep' scheme. Photo by L. Venn.

Table 3.7 'Adopt a Sheep' Scheme, Anversa, Abruzzo National Park, Italy

Heuristic 'Analytical Field'	Brief Description
Site of food production	1,100 ha of high mountain pasture and farmstead located in a depopulating village in the Abruzzo national park; farmstead also has processing plant, shop, accommodation and restaurant
Food production methods	'Biological' (organic); emphasis on 'traditional' breeds, farming and processing methods; use of local 'wild' herbs. Produce is high money value speciality cheese, wool and meat
Supply chain	Regional: speciality food shops. Global: air freight
Arena of exchange	Adoption relationship; money transaction; food highly embedded with (1) qualities derived from locality and (2) ethical value
Producer–consumer interaction	Internet technologies – 'closeness at a distance'; farm visits and holidays
Motivations for participation	Producer: develop a sustainable business associated with concern for local economy, community and environment and for 'traditional' farming and processing. Consumers: similar concerns and/or 'conspicuous consumption'
Constitution of individual and group identities	Consumers represented as concerned individuals and connoisseurs. Producers as upholders of 'traditional' practices and values

illustrates schematically some of the important features of the scheme in relation to our analytical fields.

The scheme was started by Manuela Cozzi, who was inspired to take steps to preserve what she saw as traditional ways of life and rural landscapes by establishing a mode of enrolling consumers into a food production and consumption network. This particular scheme can be understood at different scales. On the farm itself, the 'Adopt a sheep' scheme is part of a series of linked enterprises aiming to add value to the farm produce, including a farm shop (Figure 3.4), accommodation for visitors and a restaurant. Second, within the locality, it is part of a wider co-operative network of 140 farms supplying high value sheep's cheese and meat to specialist retailers and restaurants, together with agri-tourism projects. The co-operative, which began in 1977, has received funding from the EU LEADER programme, and is thus linked into EU rural development ideology. It also hosts about ten 'WWOOF-ers' every year (volunteer workers participating in the 'World Wide Opportunities on Organic Farms' programme) and these individuals bring ideas and knowledge as well as labour power to the farm. Finally, this set of on-farm, local and European relationships allows the 'Adopt a sheep' scheme specifically to be part of an international supply chain network of communications and transportation technologies allowing farm produce to be mailed anywhere globally. Adopters are located, for example, in Japan, the USA, Australia and the UK. These sets of local and international relations reproduce an arena of exchange which deploys the trope of 'adoption' to establish and attempt to sustain relations of close connection and care between the farm and consumers of cheese and meat. The food itself is represented and experienced as meaningful in different ways in this arena. For example, as the product of 'your sheep' it carries the significance of the 'adoption' trope. It is also strongly identified by the producer with the physical and ecological characteristics of the locality, ideas of tradition, and the importance of sustaining local communities and economies. In this sense we can identify the motivations of Manuela as the producer and founder of the scheme as a key analytical field for this scheme. Her motivations, as she stated to us and as evidenced on the scheme website, are to preserve a particular type of rural economy, community and environment, characterized by what are represented as traditional lifestyles, foods, relations of production and human–livestock–natural relationships. These are, for her, contrasted favourably against urban lifestyles and industrialized foods, and people's loss of a connection with rurality and food production. Her scheme thus attributes special values to the food itself, but in association with attempts to challenge what she sees as the relationships of power within society and its food supply system which threaten her ideal types of rural existence.

A central mechanism for these attempts to attribute value to food and challenge dominant power relations is the website through which the scheme's relationships with adopters and potential adopters are mediated,

Figure 3.4 The shop selling cheeses, meats and wool products from the 'Adopt a sheep' scheme. Photo by L. Venn.

so that the analytical field of producer–consumer relationships is also key to our understanding of this particular scheme. The website uses photographs and text to do three things. First, it draws attention to the sensual qualities of the local environment and the farming experience, evoking in viewers a vicarious experience of tastes, sights, smells, sounds and textures. In doing this, attempts are made to 'virtually' establish sensual connections between viewers and place, thus enrolling viewers into a representation of the place as special, but vulnerable and worthy of protection. Second, it makes an argument about the special value of 'traditional' rural lifestyles, communities, economies and environments, and urges that these are worthy of viewers' concern and support. Included within that are representations of farm workers and local people as having the authentic knowledges and practices needed to reproduce this specific rural environment and 'traditional' community. Third, it constructs a picture of the viewer as both a connoisseur of particular foods and sensual experiences, and as an ethically concerned consumer. In this way a particular identity is constructed for consumers to align themselves with. This perhaps contrasts with a sense we get from consumers that their participation in the scheme is more to do with its novelty, as something to be conspicuously consumed *in itself* alongside the consumption of cheese and the vicarious consumption of distant lifestyles and environments. This has meant that, despite the attempt to enrol consumers into lasting relationships with the scheme, 60 per cent fail to renew their adoption subscriptions after the first year. Having said this, some adopters do visit the scheme and Manuela was able to tell stories of individuals and families who return year after year. Indeed, Manuela does not believe that people can be reconnected through the Internet but rather, the Internet offers a point of first contact through which people can be encouraged to visit the farm and rediscover rural life for themselves.

What seems more important in making this scheme possible is the motivation of the producer, and her agency in developing a representation of consumer subjectivity and the pleasures of consumption that, for whatever reasons, people will actually buy into. This outline description of the arrangement of this particular scheme across our analytical fields again points to the particular aspects of the scheme which make its operation possible, and allow it in some ways to challenge established power relations in the food supply system by the way specialist cheeses are produced. We emphasize in this case the importance of the producer's motivations, the representation of potential consumers as connoisseurs and ethically motivated individuals, the deployment of the 'adoption' trope in attempts to enrol consumers into relations of care, the spacing of the scheme's local and global connectivities, and the way those connectivities are effected through the use of communications and transport technologies.

SUMMARIZING REMARKS

This chapter has provided an analytical description of the selected food schemes, which is important for contextualizing the empirical data presented in later chapters. Tables 3.8 and 3.9 provide an overview of all of the schemes, split into two broad themes: food production and exchange, and constitution of identities, motives and practices. The tables clearly illustrate the range of relationships and activities that can be encompassed within 'alternative' food initiatives. In the next chapter, we examine in more depth the identities, motives and practices of the producers and growers who founded the schemes.

Table 3.8 Overview of Food Production and Exchange in the Schemes

Analytical Fields: Food Production and Exchange	Site of Food Production	Food Production Methods	Supply Chain	Arena of Exchange
Salop Drive	1.1 ha in the heart of a deprived inner city housing estate	Organic (but not certified)	Fruit and vegetable bag deliveries	Consumers pay a fixed amount per bag, and can also volunteer to work on the site, often receiving free produce in return
EarthShare	About 9 ha of rented land; close to Findhorn Foundation	Organic; mechanical and horse power; consumer involvement in growing	Vegetable boxes delivered to pick-up points	Money, work and LETS exchange; food embedded with ethical value
Waterland	Mixed 49 ha organic farm in Cambridgeshire	Organic; 8 ha sugar beet, 8 ha mixed vegetables, 33 ha under grass and grazed by sheep	Vegetable boxes delivered direct from farmer to consumer	Box scheme
Farrington's	Processing and some growing on working tenanted farm; products sourced locally (preferentially), nationally and internationally	Variable; no commitment to specific production methods Food processing on site	Retailing of home-grown and bought in foods at farm shop; butcher's counter leased	Farm shop and café; visibility of working farm; money exchanged for food

Table 3.8 (*continued*)

Analytical Fields: Food Production and Exchange	Site of Food Production	Food Production Methods	Supply Chain	Arena of Exchange
Moorland	280 ha family farm set in an environmentally sensitive area of the Somerset Levels, rising on top of the Mendip Hills	Cattle raised traditionally, on grass. No growth-promoting hormones or routine antibiotics used. Animals slaughtered at the local abattoir, then returned to the farm where hung and butchered	Direct retail to the public via farm shop and stalls at farmers' markets	Farm shop and farmers' market stalls; money exchanged for food
Adopt a Sheep	High mountain pasture and farmstead (with processing plant, shop, accommodation and restaurant) located in a village in Abruzzo national park	'Biological' (organic); emphasis on 'traditional' breeds, farming and processing methods; use of local 'wild' herbs. Produce is high money value speciality cheese, wool and meat	Regional: speciality food shops and restaurants. Global: air freight	Adoption relationship; money transaction; food highly embedded with (1) qualities derived from locality and (2) ethical value

Table 3.9 Overview of Identities, Motives and Practices in the Schemes

Analytical Field: Identities, Motives and Practices	Constitution of Individual and Group Identities	Motivations for Participation	Producer–Consumer Interaction
Salop Drive	Consumers are local residents, community members, users and participants; scheme workers (growers) try to work in consultation with scheme users	Established to encourage healthy living and eating, with a specific focus on involving disabled people. Consumer participation driven by desire for fresh, accessible, good quality and cheap vegetables	Consumers frequently consulted by scheme workers. Use of leaflets, newsletters, questionnaires, workshops and social/educational events
EarthShare	Consumers are participants, sharers, subscribers to values; group growing work	Social, economic and environmental concerns; desire for fresh, seasonal produce	Website, notes in boxes, working parties, social events; emphasis on 'closeness', connection and commitment
Waterland	Consumers are customers; producers are farmers and retailers	Producer: business viability in competitive retail sector, desire to sell locally and have direct contact with consumers. Consumers: organic foods, desire to buy direct	On the doorstep, newsletter, recipes, website
Farrington's	Consumers are customers; producers are farmers and retailers	Producer: business viability in competitive retail sector. Consumers: quality foods, dislike of supermarkets	Retailer–customer or employee–customer in the shop; loyalty card; website
Moorland	Consumers are customers; producers are farmers and retailers	Producer: business viability; Consumers: quality beef	Retailer–customer in the shop/stall

Table 3.9 (continued)

Analytical Field: Identities, Motives and Practices	Constitution of Individual and Group Identities	Motivations for Participation	Producer–Consumer Interaction
Adopt a sheep	Consumers represented as concerned individuals and connoisseurs. Producers as upholders of 'traditional' practices and values	Producer: develop a sustainable business concerned for local economy, community and environment; 'traditional' farming and processing. Consumers: similar concerns and/or 'conspicuous consumption'	Internet technologies – 'closeness at a distance'; farm visits and holidays

CHAPTER 4

Growing and Selling Food: Producers and Production

INTRODUCTION

> When you are on your own a lot, and working with the boxes you don't actually get to see anyone that you don't already see everyday like family, so you end up grovelling around in the mud and you think 'well why am I doing this?' And it's not until you go off the farm and speak to people, and they say 'thanks' that you get real meaning, it gives you a sense of satisfaction. Positive feedback gives you the strength to go on. (Paul Robinson, Waterland, 2004)

In this chapter, we examine our six case studies from the perspectives of food producers. We recognize that referring simply to 'producers' is problematic because in some schemes individuals act simultaneously as producers and consumers, so that the boundaries around these categories are uncertain and blurred. We return to this in later chapters as we consider the various ways in which those who engage with schemes as consumers also come to participate in production. Here, however, the focus is on those who are the primary producers, or managers, of their respective schemes, as identified in Chapter 3. As such it draws on material collected during the two rounds of producer interviews. The chapter consists of two main sections. The first focuses on the constitution of producer identities in relation to their schemes, and on the motivations behind producers' engagement with particular sorts of food production practices. We explore how producers discuss their own identities and how they describe their own relationships with their schemes. In the second section, we look in more detail at the practices that enable producers to develop their own particular forms of interaction with consumers. First we examine the 'enabling' relationships which have been formed with institutions and individuals (touching also on the 'disabling' encounters producers have experienced in establishing and running their schemes), and second we explore producer attitudes towards and relationships with consumers. Throughout, we emphasize the ways in which producer identities and motives are located within frameworks of care for particular places (particularly sites of production), or are bound up with wider social and/or environmental concerns. The analysis tries to convey something of the diversity of ethical frameworks which are developed by producers involved in these 'alternative' food schemes, and also emphasizes the idea that these frameworks can be thought of as always 'becoming', being reconsidered and sometimes reworked in relation to changing circumstances and encounters with different people, entities and ideas.

PRODUCER IDENTITIES AND MOTIVES

This first section of the chapter looks at the identities of scheme producers, their backgrounds and motivations. Inevitably, material discussed in this section overlaps with some of the discussion in the following section, emphasizing the relationships between the organizational functioning of particular schemes and the issues of subjectivity, identity and interpersonal relationships raised in this section. In turn, then, we here look at, first, the producers' backgrounds and the way in which this relates to the construction of their identities; second, their discussion of their motivations in participating in 'alternative' food projects, in particular how their involvement allows the expression of care for people, place and environment; and finally, their ethical positions.

Producers' Backgrounds, Identities and Motivations

In all of our cases, producers had a strong association with food and farming either through family ties, a history of farming in the family and area, work experience or academic training. This association is strongly bound up with the ways in which producers cared about sites of food production, food production practices and food itself. For example, at Waterland, Paul Robinson's parents were both from farming families, and he trained at agricultural college. Similarly, at Farrington's, Andy Jeffery was from a farming family and returned from a non-farming career to run the family farm, and at Moorland, Peter Scott came from a farming and veterinary background. In other cases farming experience had been gained through employment. Thus, at Salop Drive, staff working on the site had employment experience in market gardening and city farming. At 'Adopt a sheep', Manuela Cozzi had worked in agricultural science at an Italian university while keeping sheep on a very small scale, before turning to commercial farming as a way of attempting to realize her social and environmental objectives. As such, then, we might suggest that an association with farming and, in most cases, the rural, is central to producers' identities – their sense of themselves and their place in the world. This can be referred to as disposition, in the sense that such individuals are disposed in some way towards involvement with farming and food. This is, perhaps, expressed in two further ways. First, we argue that their backgrounds in producing food provided all producers with a 'sense of belonging' and care about, first of all, the practices of food production, and second, to the geographical area in which they were engaging in these practices, even if they were not originally from those places. This sense that incomers to an area can develop deep attachments to place was illustrated, for example, by the case of 'Adopt a sheep'. Despite originating from Tuscany, Manuela Cozzi expressed a passionate attachment to the Abruzzo region, and a sense of care for its environment and culture, which had become articulated through her establishment and management of her farm and the 'Adopt a sheep' project. The second expression of identity related to food production was evident in particular for those producers who have a family tradition of farming in particular places, and this is the feeling of intergenerational care and responsibility towards both the farm and the practices that sustain it as both a site and an enterprise. Paul Robinson (Waterland) and Peter Scott (Moorland), for instance, expressed their desire to maintain family traditions, and in several cases, protecting the existence of the small family farm was reported as the driving force behind a continued association with agriculture.

However, involvement in 'alternative' food projects has meant that in addition to identifications with the role and place of 'farmer' or 'food producer', even those from 'traditional' farming backgrounds have had to become something other than simply food producers; producers in all schemes have had to be adaptable, flexible and willing to be much more than a farmer or grower in the conventional sense. To an extent, this reflects the calls for all farmers to attempt to 'reconnect' with customers and consumers which we identified in Chapter 1 and have explored more fully in Chapter 2, and which has been expressed in the increasing market-orientation, which, it is argued, farming must have. For producers in our case studies, however, their relationships with consumers, and the many different roles that they must perform as a result means that their identities have become flexible, and perhaps reflect a disposition on their part towards 'alternative' ways of being a food producer. For example, Paul Robinson (Waterland) described how part of his role was now to educate consumers – for example about the implications of the late spring 'hungry gap' (that period when winter crops were coming to an end and summer crops were not yet ready for harvest) – and to stimulate their continued interest in the box scheme by providing novelty and difference:

> People do seem to enjoy it and by bringing that little something extra like Italian broccoli or mushrooms it just gets people interested. So we chop and change it just to keep people interested.

So, although business-orientation is important, it is inevitably shot through with, and related to other objectives and desires, such as care for the soil or a wish to deploy particular farming techniques. Exploring producers' motivations, then, becomes important, although in all cases it is problematic to try and simply identify a straightforward reason for their initiation of, or involvement with, a particular project.

In some cases, the motivation behind a scheme could be associated with a moment of 'crisis' in an existing food production business. Andy Jeffery (Farrington's), for example, described how the incidence of BSE in the late 1990s reduced the farm income at the same time as investment was being made in extra cattle and milk quota, leading to a progressive state of indebtedness. Considering giving up altogether, Mr Jeffery attended a Farm Retail Association conference as part of a consideration of alternative pathways for developing the farm business. Here, he listened to an Australian expert on farm shops who listed a number of things that any farm shop should have. Mr Jeffery realized that their existing small farm retail scheme did not meet these requirements, but was inspired to persist with on-farm retail and to develop and expand the farm shop. A similar crisis point was experienced by both the Robinsons (Waterland) and the Scotts (Moorland), both of whom had relied on marketing, respectively, vegetable crops and beef, to supermarkets. When prices they received through such channels were greatly reduced, direct marketing through box schemes (Waterland) and a farm shop and farmers' markets (Moorland) presented themselves as opportunities to sell produce in such a way as to retain a greater proportion of what consumers paid for the product.

Ethics, Pleasure and Food Production

Yet even for these producers, and also for those producers whose projects did not arise from moments of crisis, the motivations associated with their projects went beyond a response to difficulties experienced with conventional food production businesses, and were related to ethical positions on how food production should be practised. In some instances, producers talked in visionary terms about the objectives that underpinned their involvement. Evident for example in the case of EarthShare, this related to its nature as an enterprise that emphasizes care for particular social and ecological concerns alongside the need to be financially sustainable. In a rather different manner, the unusual siting of Salop Drive on an urban 'brownfield' site is closely related to the social objectives underpinning its functioning as a project – for example, the inclusion of people with disabilities, the enhancement of community life and the provision of nutritious food for people with limited access to fresh produce. 'Adopt a sheep' had been founded with a specific, perhaps quite radical aim in mind. As such, it is associated with one of the most clearly articulated ethical frameworks of all the initiatives we have examined. Manuela Cozzi wants to use an 'alternative' food production–consumption project to preserve what are regarded as 'traditional' rural ways of life, rural communities and a particular mountain ecology in a particular place she cares about. As Ms Cozzi said, 'sheep are important to the whole environment of the mountains', and on the scheme website, the phrase 'adopt a sheep – defend nature' emphasizes a perceived interconnectedness between 'wild' nature and agricultural practice. Going further, particular 'traditional' practices and even breeds of livestock are part of this sense of interconnectedness between 'natural' and 'cultural' elements of a particular place. Thus, transhumance practices are seen as particularly significant, as is the local Sopravissana breed of sheep. Referred to by Ms Cozzi as the '4×4 sheep' for its ability to access remote upland pastures, it is regarded as particularly well adapted to local conditions, but due to its relatively low milk yields, it has been displaced on many farms by higher-yielding breeds imported from Sicily and Sardinia. Ms Cozzi's aims are clearly articulated within a framework of sustainable rural development, underpinned by the project's association with the EU's LEADER rural development programme. 'Adopt a sheep' and its related enterprises are driven by the energy and passion demonstrated by the producer who has no immediate connection to the area, yet who is motivated by a sense of care for the local community and environment which appears to be as important as maintaining a viable business. However, the ethical ideals and aims associated with 'Adopt a sheep' nevertheless demand that economic viability is also sustained, and the rationale for the 'Adopt a sheep' scheme (as part of a wider set of activities such as cheese making and *agriturismo*) was an economic demand to add value to sheep's milk and wool, both low value products.

Ecological, economic and social concerns underlie other initiatives, but have become expressed in the rather more mundane contexts of more-or-less conventional business practices. At Waterland, for example, Paul Robinson had been driven by a personal questioning of agribusiness and agrichemicals, derived from his experience of employment in a major agrichemical company. He cared too about the decline of the family farm, which seemed to be being precipitated by the very organization he was working for, and expressed a sense of intergenerational responsibility in terms of a need to care for the soil of the farm and to develop farming practices which mirrored the 'natural' processes occurring in the farm's woods and hedgerows. Returning to the family farm, his response was to investigate organic production methods and join the Organic Growers Association and British Organic Farmers (formerly the producer arm of the Soil Association), in a stated desire to remodel the farm's food production strategy in an attempt to mimic the 'natural' cycles seen in the farm's uncultivated areas. In this case, as in others, such motivations have become tangled up with desires for 'reconnection' with food consumers. Paul Robinson expressed the satisfaction he obtained from growing and selling food to the consumer, instead of hiding behind the corporate structures of supermarkets:

> *Interviewer*: Was a motivating factor for the box scheme that you could have direct contact with the people that are eating your food?
>
> *Paul Robinson*: Definitely, that was a lot of it, I wanted to know that it was being sold locally and have that direct contact and actually one of the good reasons for me of having that direct contact was that not only did it build up a relationship while all the BSE stuff was going on but that they knew, you know I had to look them in the eye and say this was my veg, you can't hide behind a corporate structure, like a lot of the supermarkets do, you know it's there, that's mine and if it's not mine I know exactly where it has come from.

Again emphasizing the pleasure to be gained from particular modes of food production, Peter Scott (Moorland) discussed the family's wish to maintain 'traditional' or 'natural' forms of beef production based on breeding cattle using pure-bred Aberdeen Angus bulls. This mode of farming was a source of great satisfaction, and allowed them to develop a specialist market for relatively expensive meat products, thus contributing to a profitable business.

During interviews with producers, it was clear that they did draw a great deal of pleasure from what they do, and this pleasure was in all cases tied to an ability to relate their project to an ethos of 'care' – although perhaps for many such a formal term – ethos – is inappropriate for what was discussed in general terms. Yet, ethos (like ethics) relates to notions of 'spirit', 'attitude' or 'disposition', and as such word permits a representation of how motivation becomes expressed in terms of something which guides the direction of individual projects. In other terms, the ethos of a project relates to those things the relevant producer cares about. The comments below represent such statements of 'ethos' from two different producers; in both cases they suggest principles which can be associated with how their business functions:

> We pride ourselves on supplying many of our own lines and reducing food miles wherever possible. (Andy Jeffery, Farrington's)

> Sustainable tourism has not been done much in Abruzzo but it holds things together. People can see where their produce comes from and feel a connection … The scheme is driven by the desire to re-introduce people to the local environment. (Manuela Cozzi, 'Adopt a sheep')

This sense that individual projects are underpinned by a particular ethos, or ethical framework, emerged in several ways from the six case studies. In part, the projects' ethical outlooks were expressed in terms of their stated relationships with *other* projects in their localities. Producers at Waterland, Salop Drive and EarthShare, for instance, all claimed to exist within relationships of mutual respect, rather than competition, with other producers. This was felt to allow their coexistence and mutual benefit. At Waterland and EarthShare, producers acknowledged the existence of informal 'gentleman's agreements' with other producers. Thus, for example, Pam Bochel (EarthShare) stated, 'I mean I would never advertise EarthShare in Inverness for example, because that's [*competitor's*] patch and he would never advertise his box scheme in Forres …' At Salop Drive, the notion of competing with existing suppliers was particularly problematic because of the public funding the project had drawn on, and because of the overall objectives of the project. The organizers were clear that they did not want to interfere with the businesses of local greengrocers, especially as they had given produce away in the first year in order to raise the project's profile and create an initial group of customers; their aim is to get people eating more vegetables rather than swapping allegiances from one source to another.

Alongside these inter-business issues, ethical concerns were also articulated with regard to producer–consumer relations. The implications of these are explored more fully below, but here we mention two illustrative examples. First, at Moorland, Peter Scott described their direct marketing of beef in terms suggestive of his recognition of an ethical relationship between the business and its consumers. He cared, for instance, about the 'authenticity', 'integrity' and 'quality' of the produce, and about 'honesty' towards consumers. The way in which the farm business operates, that is, with all animals being bred and reared on the farm rather than bought in, allows the functioning of this relationship since consumers are able to *know* about the production process, by visiting the farm shop and seeing the farm, by questioning the producers, and by reading the publicity material.

Such ethical concerns also have particular implications, however. In the case of Moorland, Peter Scott explained a *business* dilemma in terms which showed how this produced a simultaneous *ethical* problem: at the time of research the farm could not produce enough beef to meet consumer demand, but buying in animals or meat would, he felt, compromise the essential and ethical 'integrity' the current operation both produces and is dependent on. He would no longer be able to honestly describe the product as 'farm reared'. The issue of how to expand, then, is not simply a business issue but needs to account for the nature of the ethical relationships between producers and consumers that are foundational to the success of the business.

A further example can be drawn from 'Adopt a sheep', where a very different sense of an ethical relationship between producers and consumers was articulated by Manuela Cozzi, in terms of an attempt to engender social change, based on caring for a particular environment in an active and quite ingenious way. For her, the project offered opportunities to reconnect consumers, particularly urban consumers, with the rural areas, 'nature', farming and food production she cared about. This was contrasted in particular to the food many urban people consume, which tells consumers only what manufacturers want them to know and hides the 'real' origins of what is consumed. More than this, however, such a 'reconnection' is associated with an ethic of care which suggests that it is only through contact with, and knowledge of, the countryside and food production, that people can reach moral maturity: a radical sense of a need for 'reconnection' with agriculture and rural nature was therefore essential to this scheme. Ms Cozzi argued that many social and environmental problems are rooted in a society where adults no longer know how to take care of, and responsibility for, others. In her terms, this meant that they never grow up. There is thus apparently a powerful moral geography associated with this scheme. As she put it, 'to be an adult means to be able to care for things ... only the rural community can teach people how to care for the environment'. As such, she hosts school visits during which she aims to teach children about food, farming and rural life, and to take responsibility for what they do, as well as hoping that the adoption and tourism projects which are part of the farm business will perform the 'reconnections' she argues are needed. This particular ethical perspective is thus reliant on a set of distinctions between concepts of rural and urban, in which rurality is positively associated with care, tradition, a particular view of adulthood, and sustainable community, economy and environment, and the urban is associated with a problematic alienation of people from first, their food and how it is produced and second, the possibility of human ethical 'maturity'.

Other producers too expressed their identity in part as an 'educator' of consumers, and what producers said about this role provided insights into the reflexive and sometimes ambiguous nature of producer identities. Manuela Cozzi, as discussed above, clearly saw her role as educational; she had attended courses on teaching children, and has a 'school farm' on site where children do practical activities such as cheesemaking. Similarly, staff at Salop Drive host school trips for local, inner-city children. In other cases, producers were rather more uncertain as to what extent an educational role should be part of their work. At EarthShare, for instance, Pam Bochel commented that:

> my role's not to educate people and to try and influence the way they think, but maybe it is, maybe part of EarthShare's role is education in that, you know, we're trying to educate people into seasonal eating again. Well no actually that's interesting because we're not trying to educate people. People have to become educated about seasonal eating in order to enjoy EarthShare ...

Similarly, Andy Jeffery (Farrington's) narrated how, within his scheme, there had been discussion about the extent to which education of consumers could occur. The following comment is in the context of a decision about whether to use butter or margarine in their home-made cake recipes (the former is popularly seen as unhealthy, and is more expensive and harder to work with, but the latter is seen by the producer as 'bad' for you as a more 'artificial' product). Following the decision to use butter, and as a result to increase the shop prices for the cakes, the interviewer asked whether consumers had actually noticed.

> We've had this debate. I'm not sure they have. No, I'm not sure they've noticed. We've had this debate about if we're going to be ethical then you know; the trouble is what are we trying to do? Are we trying to educate the whole of the

world? It's a bloody difficult job to do. How can we … and if you start trying to preach to people … it turns them off.

In these reflexive comments, there is clearly an uncertainty about the producers' own role, the roles of the projects, and consumers' roles. We do not suggest here that a clearly defined role as 'educator' is one that producers might or might not 'adopt', but argue that such comments are an important indicator of producers' perceptions of and relationships with their scheme's consumers, a point which we return to later in the chapter.

In part, the role of 'educator' is a response to producers' awareness that at least some of the consumers they supply with food do not share their ethos, or ethic, of food production–consumption – they do not necessarily care about the same things, or care in the same ways. This seemed to matter most for EarthShare, in that consumers who perhaps did not fully understand the ethos were more likely to complain:

> … if people join EarthShare thinking it's an organic box scheme and there's carrot fly [an insect whose grubs might decimate the carrot crop], they're going to phone up and complain and they're going to say, 'this isn't good, I want to leave', and of course they can't leave because they've signed up for a year.

Producers for others schemes were more sanguine about motivational 'gaps'. The next exchange, with Paul Robinson (Waterland), shows first, that the producer is aware that consumers' motivations are likely to be multifarious, but that second, for him a key motivation is simply to be able farm organically, and that as such, the reasons for consumers' custom are at this level of no great concern.

Paul Robinson: My whole reason for doing it is to make the farm, so I can keep the farm, you know, and I want to farm it organically and, you know, people are … I don't know, getting it because it's local or because it's … I don't know, whatever, I can't think of what other reasons there could be, but … or fresher, then that's ok by me as well 'cos I still get to farm it the way I want to farm it, you know.

Interviewer: So there's no right or wrong reasons why people might join?

Paul Robinson: No, not as far as I'm concerned. No.

Interviewer: What about if they're doing it because it's a status thing and they like having you deliver …?

Paul Robinson: That's ok [laughs] … I mean I don't mind anything, yeah, as long as I get the money.

The comments indicate that there is a sense in which producers' attempts to understand their consumers can run into problems of comprehension, of being able to make sense of the perspectives and motivations of others. We return to a discussion of producers' perceptions of consumers and producer–consumer relations in the next section of the chapter, foreshadowing the discussion of consumers' perspectives on these relationships in subsequent chapters. First, however, we explore the wider range of relationships with organizations and individuals which have both 'enabled' and sometimes caused problems for producers and their schemes.

RELATIONSHIPS WITH 'ENABLERS' AND CONSUMERS: PRODUCERS' PERSPECTIVES AND PRACTICES

'Enabling' and 'Disabling' Relationships and Food Production

Although we have focused above on the identities and motivations of individual producers associated with the different schemes, the functioning of all of them was clearly dependent on relationships with a range of individuals and institutions. As producers explained, many of these relationships were initiated during the earliest stages of attempting to establish businesses or projects, and were related to deficits of both finance and knowledge or skills. Establishing such relationships thus enabled the initiation of a project. Examples include those associated with rural development policies at national and international scales. Moorland, for instance, was assisted under the United Kingdom Rural Enterprise Scheme in establishing a cold room for meat storage, while Farrington's received grants from the United Kingdom Rural Development Agency and Community Action Fund, and 'Adopt a sheep' is part of a co-operative enterprise supported by LEADER. In addition to these relationships, some schemes had authenticating relationships with certifying organizations (e.g. Waterland requires certification to sell produce labelled as 'organic'), and all producers mentioned the professional advice they had received from experts in particular sorts of farming or food marketing. Others, such as EarthShare, had benefited from their proximity to organizations sharing an interest in 'alternative' lifestyles. In EarthShare's case this is the Findhorn Foundation, which is a major subscriber (taking seventy-five subscriptions for its kitchens and ten to sell on in its shop). A noticeable finding was that, in accordance with the arguments of, for example, Ilbery et al. (2004), much of the 'alternative' activity which formed the focus of the research was underpinned by, indeed often inseparable from, 'conventional' modes of production–consumption. Thus, for example, at Waterland, the Robinsons discussed their history of relationships with supermarket buyers at the same time as operating their vegetable box scheme, and the Jefferys at Farrington's ran a conventional dairy and potato farm alongside the farm shop. As discussed in Chapter 2, this interconnectedness of the 'alternative' and 'conventional' continues to make these categories problematic. Alongside these relationships with institutions, particular individuals were often cited as having had an important effect on project establishment. Farrington's, for example, had benefited from an association with a highly regarded local butcher, who moved from supplying the farm shop with produce to actually opening and operating a butcher's counter in the shop itself. In this case, the butcher's experience of dealing with bureaucracy (e.g. health and safety regulations) was clearly a valuable input into the business. Informal discussions with friends and contacts doing similar things were also cited as important, for example by Paul Robinson (Waterland), in stimulating a shift into 'alternative' food production projects.

The relationships outlined above are those which supported schemes as they were initiated and which contribute to their ongoing viability. Other relationships were nevertheless experienced as obstacles to the success of particular schemes. In some cases, these were related to legal and planning constraints on what a particular scheme was able to actually *do*. At Moorland, for example, attempts to gain planning permission to develop a farm shop in the neighbouring village failed, preventing the establishment of a new site of exchange and the creation of new producer–consumer relations, and forcing the scheme to continue relying on a less suitable shop location and their presence at farmers' markets. In the case of EarthShare, it has been the legal constitution of the scheme which has led to a chain of problems limiting what the scheme has been able to achieve. Set up as a 'company limited by shares', this constitution has prevented EarthShare applying for funding from external sources. In turn, this has affected the economic valency of the scheme, which, in particular, has made it unable to purchase land, so that it is reliant on relatively short-term leases of land. As a tenant, EarthShare is unable to erect any permanent structures on the leased land, placing restrictions on what the scheme can achieve; for example they are unable to accommodate WWOOFers (volunteer workers participating in the 'World Wide Opportunities on Organic Farms' programme). As a final example, Salop Drive, because of its particular nature as an urban scheme with social objectives, has experienced a second type of temporal fragility, relating to the three-year project funding cycle which predominates in the

United Kingdom's public sector. One of the main constraints on the project was the amount of time that staff spent on looking for funding sources.

This series of quite mundane obstacles and problems points to the sense in which the establishment of particular sets of 'alternative' producer–consumer relationships is a process of dealing with very ordinary, everyday issues – negotiating planning rules and funding patterns, dealing with seasonality in crop production, or negotiating legal bureaucracy and complexity. It is also a process, however, of dealing with the consumers themselves. The remainder of this chapter, then, is devoted to an extended discussion of the practices associated with producer–consumer relationships in the schemes, and of the way that such practices are related to producers' sense of their own identities and to their perceptions of the consumers of their food.

Producer–Consumer Relationships: Producers' Perspectives and Practices

Fundamentally, these producer–consumer relationships are associated with the exchange of food, money and labour within a scheme. Each of our case studies was thus associated with a very specific set of relations of exchange between producers and consumers, tied to particular geographical sites and to a specific temporality or rhythm. At Moorland, for example, the sites of the farm shop and regular farmers' markets the producers attend are associated with a relatively straightforward exchange between producers and consumers of money for food, although of course the exchange might at the same time be overlain with other meanings and associated with relations of trust, sociability, and so on, as is explored in Chapters 5 and 6. At Waterland, EarthShare and Salop Drive there is a reliance on a network of sites and individuals through which vegetable boxes are delivered. At Waterland, for example, some customers, known as neighbourhood representatives, are given a price reduction for their own box in exchange for taking delivery of other boxes for their neighbours, and at Salop Drive 'local agents' receive a free box for organizing box delivery to their neighbours. However, while at Waterland the exchange is, like Moorland, of money for food, at EarthShare the exchange is complicated by the expectation that consumers also contribute labour during 'workshifts' or 'weeding parties' in part payment for their food and by the possibility of using LETS (Local Exchange Trading Scheme currency units) in exchange for food. At Salop Drive the money–food exchange is made more complex by the non-business community objectives of the project. Finally, 'Adopt a sheep' works through a combination of information and communications technologies and transport technologies, and the exchange of money for food is played out through the 'adoption' conceit in which consumers seem to receive 'free' food in exchange for the annual payment which cements the apparent relationship of care between the consumer, the sheep, the rural community and the farmed environment.

Although the exchange of food for money is clearly fundamental, first, the way in which such exchanges happen and are part of the fabric of different projects is important, and second, relatedly, exchange simultaneously involves a series of other things bound up with the material exchange. Clearly, very different exchange mechanisms are deployed by the different projects. Some deliver to consumers, using door-to-door delivery systems (Waterland) or 'pick-up point' delivery systems (EarthShare). In both instances, the concept of having food delivered in such a way is key to the identification of the project as 'other' to conventional modes of food provisioning. Other businesses, such as Moorland and Farrington's, rely on consumers to attend shops or farmers' markets, functioning thus in a way similar to 'conventional' retail outlets. The sense that, for some producers, there is more to the process than the exchange of food for money is highlighted in comments like the following from Paul Robinson (Waterland), which ends by presenting an imaginary exchange between a delivery driver and a consumer. It illustrates the importance placed on the direct encounter between producer and consumer at the point of delivery, in contrast to other schemes where delivery drivers are employed who are not directly involved in, or knowledgeable about, the food they deliver:

> Yeah, I mean [some competitor schemes have] got van drivers and I'm convinced that … well, a lot of them don't see the produce other than in the box. They don't really know anything about it, and that's just one thing that we would say about … you know, I think I've said this before but I mean of all the people I've had deliver vegetables for me over the years, I mean, sometimes we do it mostly ourselves, but if it's someone else who's fitting in for us or when we're really busy doing other things, they're people that have worked on the farm, and I think that really does need to be done rather than have, you know, a delivery driver coming and you load him up, because, you know, on the doorstep, you know, 'Oh, beetroot, oh, what do I do with that?' 'I don't know. I haven't got a clue, love.' 'Did you harvest it this morning?' 'Don't know mate.'

Here then, the possibilities for exchanges of knowledge and practical skills are bound into the exchange of food for money, and are integral to processes of the production of trust and 'reconnection'.

Examination of the networks of relationships which surround, or constitute, individual schemes illustrates first, that such relationships are usually established in order to deal with relatively mundane issues to do with the material exchange of food between producers and consumers, but that second, the relationships in some cases at least can be quite fragile, as noted by Paul Robinson (Waterland) who commented that, in advance of the annual inspection, 'the Soil Association inspector would ring up and his first question would be, "Are you still in business? Do you still need an inspection?"'. This fragility can be encountered in different ways, but can be understood as part of what actually makes such schemes seem 'alternative' to mainstream food production–consumption.

Much of this fragility is related to a temporality that differs in some way from that which consumers expect from their 'conventional' food suppliers. Several producers, for example, pointed out that the seasonality of their production, particularly in relation to vegetables, meant that they had at times, particularly when they had only recently been established, been unable to supply customers for at least part of the year – the so-called 'hungry gap'. At Waterland, for instance, Paul Robinson reported that during the hungry gap, particularly during the early years of the box delivery scheme, customers would find other sources of produce and that it was necessary to almost have to start the delivery round up again each year. Similarly, at Farrington's, supplies of potatoes grown on the farm were intermittent during the producers' initial forays into direct marketing – it was necessary to close down the scheme for two months during the summer to await the maturity of the next potato crop. At Salop Drive, which does not supply year-round, there have also been concerns about intermittency of supply, both in terms of the need to re-enrol people into the scheme after a break, and in terms of worrying about how the sometimes quite vulnerable consumers of Salop Drive's produce would continue to access healthy food during periods when no produce was available, thus showing how care for consumers interplays with practical challenges. These problems of continuity of supply cause clear difficulties for producers related to the 'natural' constraints on their production systems, yet are also directly related to what is meant to be 'alternative' about their schemes – for example their seasonality, localness or 'closeness' to natural cycles. As such, the 'hungry gap' can be seen as a 'bio-social' phenomenon, a term emphasizing the relationality of the ecological and the human in such situations.

The differences in expectation between producers and consumers connect to the ways in which producers attempted to establish and maintain communication with consumers. Central to notions of 'reconnection', communication between producers and consumers can be linked to exchanges of information, a process of education, but also to the fostering of relations of care within particular projects. The investment which went into communication differed according to the nature and extent of the 'connectedness' different producers desired. For example, Paul Robinson (Waterland), Andy Jeffrey (Farrington's) and Manuela Cozzi ('Adopt a sheep') were clear that 'reconnection' with consumers was an explicit aim of their projects. For others, such as Peter Scott (Moorland), this was not the case, although communication still mattered in terms of marketing produce and informing consumers – certainly a style of 'reconnection' but differing from the more profound relationships sought by the aforementioned producers. For many producers, however, communication and 'reconnection' were experienced as a problematic process, however desirable they were. We summarise producers' comments on the obstacles faced by schemes in their attempts to establish 'reconnections' with their consumers in the following list.

1. Recruitment of consumers
    • Marketing and publicity
    • Differences between producers' and consumers' motivation for involvement with a scheme
2. Frailty of consumer loyalty
    • Failure to fully enrol consumers into a project's ethos, leading to lack of consumer commitment
3. Intermittent produce supply
    • Periods of disconnection
    • Difficulty of re-establishing connection
4. Delivery systems
    • Lack of time for personal interaction
    • Delivery structures that make interaction unlikely
5. Labour resources
    • Tension between work demands and interaction.

Projects approach producer–consumer communication in different ways. What we argue here is that such communication is not simply an effect of the way in which a project is constituted, but is instead fundamental to how the project is envisioned and how, in practice, it functions. 'Adopt a sheep' is the clearest instance of this, as the project's publicity and marketing is almost wholly reliant on Internet-based modes of communication. Although Manuela Cozzi stated that her aim was to encourage consumers actually to visit the site of production, in practice producer–consumer communication takes place largely by email, while the wider, global, presence of the project is achieved via its website, which when initially launched achieved 200,000 'hits' in 48 hours, and produced around 500 emails per day. In this instance, then, 'reconnection' is to an extent virtual, although at the same time it is mediated by the materiality of the food which is exchanged as a result of the 'adoption' mechanism.

In contrast with the 'virtual', and effectively quite distanced process of 'reconnection' achieved by 'Adopt a sheep', projects like Moorland have deliberately maintained the significance of face-to-face contact between producers and consumers by selling only through their small on-farm shop and through farmers' markets. Indeed, Peter Scott said that they had rejected the idea of a box marketing scheme because it would jeopardize the one-to-one producer–consumer interaction they valued, where consumers were able to ask questions about the provenance of meat and obtain advice about how to use different cuts of meat. Although they did produce a leaflet explaining their production process, Peter Scott claims that they don't advertise since they believe that 'word of mouth' publicity is best – in other words, that the best advertisers they have are current customers recommending their products to other potential buyers. Pam Bochel (EarthShare) made similar comments, arguing that they preferred word of mouth advertisement:

> the scheme just grew by word of mouth, this is the best way to grow as there is a lot of potential for dissatisfaction, especially if people don't understand the seasons and risks associated with food growing and harvesting.

This is largely to do with the fact that those consumers who hear about EarthShare from friends or acquaintances will be more likely to understand the aims and ethos of the scheme and will be able to make contact on the basis of having had time to consider the proposal:

> … most new members come though by word of mouth. Plus, we've found that advertising locally in papers and shops has meant that the people who join after seeing our notices don't always appreciate the ethos of the scheme. (Pam Bochel, EarthShare)

In other cases, processes of communication have evolved as projects have developed, and have particularly become more formalized as projects have grown and become established. At Farrington's, for instance, Andy Jeffery argued that at the outset, communication about the farm shop proceeded by word of mouth, a mode of communication which was found to be powerful in increasing consumer numbers, and which is still highly significant for them in recruiting consumers:

Each week we get nearly 20 new customers who have never been before, and they've usually heard about us through word of mouth.

Yet more recently, as the shop has grown, 4,000 regular Farrington's consumers have become shop loyalty card holders, giving the producers access to their personal details, which have then been used to communicate with them via a regular newsletter. At the same time, however, attempts have been made to create two-way processes of communication, with consumers given the opportunity to provide feedback to the producers via questionnaires and surveys. This more participatory mode of communication has been developed furthest by project workers at Salop Drive, who, instead of simply surveying consumers as a form of market research, spend a lot of time attempting to find out exactly what consumers want by integrating them into project decision-making through various participatory exercises (Salop Drive was, too, the only scheme which consulted its members before agreeing to participate in our research). Table 4.1 summarizes the main modes of producer–consumer communication used.

Table 4.1 demonstrates that the majority of communication is producer led, where producers set up leaflets, newsletters and websites to communicate their business ideas and offerings to consumers. In many instances, these are one-way channels and even where feedback is invited, producers argued that these calls for information, advice or help are rarely reciprocated. As such, all producer-led schemes expressed difficulties and concerns about recruiting participants and creating mutually knowledgeable relationships. This could be explained by the fact that many of these schemes were set up by producers 'for' consumers, or as solutions to producers' problems of business viability,

Table 4.1 Main Forms of Communication Used by the Food Initiatives

Scheme	Face to Face	Newsletter/Box Notes/Leaflet	Website	User Questionnaires	Participatory Development
Waterland	Deliveries	Box notes	Y	Y	N
Farrington's	Shop	Newsletters	Y	Y	N
Moorland	Market/Shop	Leaflet	N	N	N
Salop Drive	Only if visit site	Box notes, leaflets	N	Y	Y
EarthShare	Only if visit site	Box notes, leaflet	Y	Yearly & when leaving	Y
'Adopt a sheep'	Only if visit site	N	Y	N	N

with little negotiation about the structure, organization or facilities required by consumers. In contrast, as highlighted above, from the outset Salop Drive has developed a process of consultation and participatory development, associated with the fact that the scheme was publicly funded and specifically set up in order to contribute to local health strategies and designed to be a 'community-led' project. Salop Drive producers thus did not assume that they knew what consumers wanted:

> The other thing we are doing, as well as the site works consultation, is a participatory appraisal day here we want people to come onto the site to feed into producing the vegetable leaflet, and gain an understanding of what people need along with receiving a bag and this could be to do with storage of veg, preparation or identification of unusual veg etc. (Veronica Barry)

Similarly, EarthShare does hold meetings where consumers have inputs into the production planning process – for example of what crops to grow. For other schemes, organizational structure was usually in place before consumers were invited to participate and in these cases, communication has been more concerned with explaining the remit, structure and purpose of the scheme to consumers. Here, for example, communication can be used to explain to people how the project is run, how farming/growing is practised, the different benefits the project has (for example, by reporting on wildlife seen on the site of production), and even on the difficulties faced by producers so that, for example, adverse weather conditions might be used to explain the lack of availability of particular items. Yet, for some, there was a wariness associated with communication, in the sense that there was a perceived risk of, according to Andy Jeffery (Farrington's), 'turning people off by preaching'. Yet, Farrington's is perhaps the most sophisticated and consistent of the initiatives in terms of communication with consumers. For example, loyalty card holders receive the 'Farrington Flyer' newsletter, which features articles about shop staff, the food and the environment. Farrington's also makes its food policy public in a written statement (see Box 4.1), and invests considerable time and effort in trying to communicate to consumers what it is that is 'different' about the farm shop, and to create some sense of 'community': for example, through newsletters, the farm shop becomes staffed by known characters, rather than anonymous checkout operatives. Farrington's policy also shows that for some projects, communication is part of negotiation with consumers. For example, there is a tension in the policy between a desire to draw on local suppliers and the stocking of lamb from New Zealand. The emphasis is thus placed on the *fairness* of the competitive

---

Box 4.1 FARRINGTON'S FOOD POLICY

[EMPHASIS IN ORIGINAL]

Our food policy is to source as much local produce as possible. To give you a wider choice, though, imported produce may be available. In these instances, the produce will not compete **unfairly** with British produce.

For example, New Zealand lamb is available as some customers prefer it. Most importantly, New Zealand farmers get no unfair subsidies and do not use hormones banned in Britain. Their production system is similar to ours, and so they are competing on a 'level playing field'.

We **do not** stock Danish bacon (they still use pig tethers), American or Far East chicken (they still use tiny battery cages) or Argentinian beef (Argentina has Foot and Mouth disease yet is still allowed to export – we aren't!). Our organic produce is British where possible, as the British rules are more stringent than elsewhere.

By shopping here you can be sure that you are **not** contributing to dubious farming practices, and also that the British farmer is being treated fairly.

---

environment in relation to lamb, and on consumer demand for New Zealand lamb, as a way of justifying stocking that product in contravention of the stated desire to source products locally.

In noting this, it is clear that producers' understandings of their consumers are highly important in making sense of the practices of 'reconnection' and the producer–consumer relationships which are associated with each scheme. It was possible on the basis of interviews with producers to compile a set of factors which they felt motivated consumers' involvement in their projects. The following quotes illustrate some of the most significant points which were made. These comments (which result from a question asking producers to comment on their consumers' motivations) reflect producers' perceptions of their consumers. In some instances (such as Waterland) producers had conducted their own market research, which influenced those perceptions.

> I think actually when they put it down on paper, what they tell me is it's because it's local, whenever possible it's ours and it's fresh, so it cuts down on food miles, yeah and it's the localness and I suppose yeah, the fact they're helping someone local. So it's food miles and local really. (Paul Robinson, Waterland)

> Well it's always organic, they always phone up wanting to enquire about the organic, they want an organic box … And then when I talk to them more, seasonal eating is important to them as well. (Pam Bochel, EarthShare)

I think it's because, well, I don't think organic is right up there, but I think it's because it's fresh and locally produced and contributing to, you know, a community project. (Tim Botfield, Salop Drive)

However, people like coming to a place that is 'on the farm' and getting meat direct from the producer who is very local. (Peter Scott, Moorland)

From such comments, a list of positive motivational factors ascribed to consumers can be drawn up, representing a collection of producers' perceptions of what consumers cared about. These included: a desire for organic produce, a desire for local produce, the seasonality of the produce, regard for animal welfare, the freshness, quality and healthiness of the food, the sustainability and traditional nature of the food production process, the ability to have an input into how food was produced, and a range of factors to do with the producer–consumer relationship, including care, 'reconnection', trust, fairness and morality. Producers also hinted at anxieties about conventional sources of food, which they suspected were influencing consumers' turn to their projects. For example, at EarthShare, Pam Bochel commented:

And I think there's been television programmes recently about supermarkets … And I think that maybe … sent a few folks scurrying to EarthShare.

From the producers' perspective, however, simply identifying a list of motivational influences is insufficient. Particular types of consumer, and particular types of relationship between themselves and consumers, were desired. Much of the discussion with producers revolved around the negotiation of these relationships, and the problems raised when consumers didn't behave in the 'right' ways. The actual type of relationship depended very much on the specific project, with some (such as EarthShare) assuming that consumers would have a direct, physical engagement with the work of producing food, and others (such as Moorland and Farrington's) regarding consumers more conventionally as 'customers'. Producers' comments indicated how they attempted to think about their particular projects in terms of what sort of relationships with consumers would result. At EarthShare, for instance, Pam Bochel showed concern for the scale of the project and the effects of that on producer–consumer relationships:

[the project founder] had always planned or aimed for two hundred [subscribers], but never to go above. I think his way of thinking was if there were more than two hundred then it's time to set up a second CSA.

There was a feeling here that at too large a scale, the desired relationships with consumers would be jeopardized. At the same time as considering the scale and structure of a particular project, and the producer–consumer relationships which would be produced, producers described the different types of consumer they had experienced. There was a clear sense in some instances that some consumers were 'right' for a particular project, while others were for various reasons problematic: the former were more likely to enter into the relationships of connection which project producers found desirable. Paul Robinson (Waterland), for example, commented that

> there is no typical box scheme customer, they're all different, so you can't please everybody and we do roughly what we think is right and that seems to keep people interested. Obviously some join for a week, decide it's not for them and leave, others join, don't eat all the veg and think well we'll buy it so that we do try and eat more veg.

He added that, 'I always try to be very honest when they phone up and try and tell them exactly how it is', for example in letting potential customers know that some produce is bought in from other members of the Eostre co-operative rather than produced on the one farm. There is a sense here of a need to 'filter' potential customers, in order to identify those who are 'right' for a particular scheme. Similar comments about the diversity of potential consumers were made by Pam Bochel (EarthShare):

> We have a core of supporters who have been with us since the beginning and these people are very dedicated and do understand the principles behind CSA and accept that sometimes boxes will be less full than other times because they appreciate that it depends on the season and the harvest. These people are also joined though by people who don't understand or appreciate these issues ... Some almost consider themselves to be customers much the same as [supermarket] customers and don't truly appreciate the difference, whereas others fully take on board the fact that they are subscribers of a CSA.

Comments such as these are particularly interesting in the way that they differentiate between 'core' and 'peripheral' consumers. The former are represented as a more committed group who appreciate and 'buy into' the values espoused by the project. The latter are represented as less knowledgeable, and as having a very different attitude to their engagement with the project. This is particularly likely to be the case where, from the producers' perspective, engagement beyond that associated with more conventional modes of retailing food is expected – so, for example, it is more likely that consumers at EarthShare or Waterland would be seen as not engaging with a project in an 'appropriate' way, in comparison with consumers at Farrington's farm shop, which is rather more akin to a 'conventional' retail outlet. This latter group is also represented as the group most likely to cause problems for such producers, for example by complaining about the quality of produce or not understanding why, for instance, produce might be unavailable at particular times. At EarthShare, again, then, Pam Bochel commented that:

> they have joined perhaps just to get organic produce and these are the ones who most likely complain because they expect the supply to be constant. It's then a case of trying to educate [them].

The idea that part of a producer's role is to 'educate' people has occurred previously in this chapter, and, as discussed above, emerged as an important dimension to producers' identities and roles. It is allied to a particular view of consumers as lacking knowledge and skills in relation to food – there was an understanding that consumers had become significantly 'disconnected' from food and its production, for example in terms of not being able to identify food items or appreciate the seasonality of crop production. Several producers, for instance, commented that consumers were sometimes anxious about dealing with unfamiliar items. For some, this leads to experimentation with new food items, while for others it can lead to an eventual withdrawal from involvement with the project. In this way, the process of 'reconnection' is seen to depend on education (although as noted above, producers do not necessarily explicitly identify with an 'educator' role). In other words, it is necessary to, in a sense, 'produce' newly knowledgeable consumers, so that they become the 'right' type of consumer to participate appropriately in a given project. The key point here is that forging 'reconnections' requires the presence of particular sorts of consumer, and particular relationships. Rather than necessarily pre-existing, such consumers may need to be 'made' through their interaction with the producer and the scheme. As such, what our producers are producing is not simply food, but subjectivities, connections and relationships.

However, from the producers' perspective, and as already indicated above, some consumers 'resist' their casting as particular sorts of consumer, by not engaging with a project in the expected fashion, or not at all. EarthShare, again, is a good example, since it in particular requires consumers to perform an active role in food production. Yet as Pam Bochel described, the enrolment of consumers into this mode of sharing the work of production is not fully successful.

Well about three quarters of them join ... planning to do their work shifts ...
Now probably out of those three quarters ... at the end of the subscription year
there's probably a third of those who don't do their work shift, because if at
the end of their year they haven't done them, I then invoice them on the work
shifts they have done.

And then if the crops don't do so well and people are getting less in their
boxes, they'll think, 'Oh, this isn't value for money. We'll leave.' So it's very
difficult to gauge it ... People have to really understand the principle of CSA
and some of our subscribers do join just because they want a box of organic veg,
some join because they really understand what it's about and they understand
that they're actually sharing in the risks of farming.

In these cases, then, those consumers who do not engage with the practice
of exchanging their own labour for food revert to a rather more conventional
exchange of money for food, with implications for the type and 'depth'
of 'reconnection' achievable through such a project. EarthShare is not the
only project which recognizes the fragility of some of the 'reconnection'
which is aimed for. At Farrington's, for example, Andy Jeffery was aware
of the potential ephemerality of some of his consumers' motivations, here
suggesting that issues of food ethics and the potential ecological effects
of food production and transport are possibly only temporary consumer
concerns:

Well, of the ethic ... this ethical ... food miles, that sort of thing, they
[consumers] might change their minds in a couple of years' time and say, 'Oh
sod it. Can't be bothered with that any more'

As such, then, producers were in general concerned with the levels of
commitment either displayed, or not displayed, by their consumers. For
them, this was indicative of the establishment of 'reconnection' – properly
connected consumers would demonstrate that they cared about the project
through their commitment and understanding, even (or especially) when
problems arose. The following comments, for example, were made by Paul
Robinson (Waterland) and Pam Bochel (EarthShare) respectively:

As soon as, sort of, [leading supermarkets] started selling organic produce,
those types of customers went actually. Because one year we lost ... I think we
were up to about 70 [boxes] and then the supermarkets started, you know, 'Oh
we haven't got any organic produce, we can't sell anything', and were all going
mad, you know, we were selling it everywhere and then they started stocking it,
and then yeah, those sort of customers just disappeared and we lost ... And

that was quite hard hit then, I think we lost about 14 customers when we went to start the box scheme again in the autumn, or in the summer, because ... yeah, they wanted ... I think they just started going to the supermarkets.

I suppose another possible threat to EarthShare is the growth in organic food, it's much more readily available, but that again goes back to what we were saying earlier about why do people join EarthShare, if they're really committed to the CSA then [a leading supermarket's] huge range of organic veg wouldn't affect them, but it's just the folk who join purely for an organic box which could be led astray.

In both cases here, reference is made to the competition for consumers with large retail chains, and this is used to differentiate between types of consumer: there are consumers who commit to the 'alternative' ethos of the project and share the same ethic of care as the producer, and those whose interest is more simply in obtaining 'organic' produce from the most convenient source (although this does not mean that this latter group does not 'care', but that what they care about and how that is expressed may be different).

In both the above quotations, some consumers are represented as easily 'led astray', as 'duped' by the convenience and choice of supermarket shopping, in contradistinction to those more 'committed' consumers who accept the ethical underpinnings of the 'alternative' projects even at a cost to themselves in terms of time, money, convenience, choice, and so on. This latter group are described by the same two producers in the following comments:

There's no doubt about it. The majority have been ... we've had some for ten years ... Yeah, we've had some for ten years, definitely. And then some maybe for nine or eight years ... There's been some for a long period, and there's some stick with you that you think they're slightly fussy and then they're still with you. (Paul Robinson, Waterland)

Well I mean the core group have stayed with EarthShare through thick and thin, right, when we had the bad winter they were still there. There was no question of them leaving, because they really understood what it's all about. (Pam Bochel, EarthShare)

What are represented here, then, is a group of knowledgeable, committed, 'connected' consumers, regarded as a fundamental and stable component of a project's food network.

The final point we wish to make here is about the difference between the rhetorics of 'reconnection', which pervade the concept of 'alternative' food networks, and a lived experience, which in many ways is quite different. Producers discussed how there was frequently a tension between their need or desire to interact with consumers in particular ways, and the demands of food production. Expressed another way, this is a tension between producers' motivations and the practices of food production and exchange. The following comment from Pam Bochel (EarthShare) illustrates that even in a scheme where in theory consumers spend some time working alongside the growers, it is possible to establish only relatively insubstantial relationships with the majority of consumers.

> I suppose I don't know them that well, it's just some have been in for years I'll know because I've seen them at events and … you maybe get to know them around Findhorn and Forres, but there's a lot … particularly now when there's been so many new people joining EarthShare that I just don't know them, and quite often I'll speak to them when they join, I'll speak to them on the phone and I'll think, 'Oh yes, I'll remember her because …', you know, there's something in particular, but after a few weeks, a month, I don't remember who they are and I feel quite guilty about that, but then I can't remember a hundred and ninety-five people, where they live and their phone numbers.

Other producers felt the same way, discussing how, for example, during the delivery of boxes of produce, it was difficult at times to reconcile wanting to talk to consumers with needing to stick to the delivery schedule. As Paul Robinson (Waterland) put it, 'you can spend a lot of time talking to people, but when you start, you can't stop, so you have to ration yourself and make a decision about who to speak to'. He also commented that although there were opportunities to further develop producer–consumer relationships, these take further time and commitment from both producers and consumers.

> … people actually see us face to face, you know, there's personal contact and there's all that and … and we've just got to build on that, you know, we've got … we've said before when we've been talking around the table is that we need to actually have farm visits…

In common with the other projects, there is clearly a desire among producers for a process of connecting with consumers, yet this needs to be articulated within the constraints and possibilities afforded by the specific constitution of an individual food production–consumption arrangement.

SUMMARIZING REMARKS: PRODUCERS' VIEWS ON PRODUCTION AND CONSUMPTION

This chapter has explored the six 'alternative' food endeavours from the perspectives of food producers. It has considered first, producers' identities, motivations, and the relations of care and ethical frameworks within which particular schemes are constituted, and second, it has examined the relationships which are essential to the functioning of particular projects: those with 'enabling' institutions and individuals and those with consumers.

The chapter has shown that producers care about food production, in terms of the food itself (the ways it is produced and marketed), the environmental and social conditions in which it is produced, the possibilities that certain modes of food production might contribute to ethically 'better' ecological and social relationships, and the relationships that they as producers have with consumers. Practices of food production have been shown to be related to ethical frameworks, which in different ways, to different extents and for different reasons emphasize care and an impulse to reconnect with consumers.

Producers' different perceptions of consumers, and their negotiation of different relationships with consumers, have been shown to be fundamental to how different schemes function in different ways, and are bound up with the ethical positions and expressions of care evident in relation to the 'alternative' food projects. We have argued that in some ways projects attempt to construct consumers who are appropriate for their purposes – consumers who, for instance, sympathize with the objectives or ethics of a project, who will commit to supporting a project in a desirable way, or who will be tolerant and understanding when problems arise.

The chapter has also emphasized that in many ways, achieving producer–consumer 'reconnection' is a relatively mundane process, from the management of growing, rearing and processing food, to the logistics of arranging marketing and delivery, to the negotiation of producer–consumer relationships through forms of communication. However, we have tried to demonstrate that these quotidian processes are in fact co-constituted with the more intangible dimensions of 'alternative' food schemes – producers' identities, the projects' construction of particular types of consumer, the nature and extent of 'reconnection' which can occur, and the ethical frameworks or particular relations of care embodied by different projects, for example.

So far, then, we have presented the perspectives of producers on this complex range of issues. We move in the next two chapters to consider the identities, motives and practices of consumers.

CHAPTER 5

Buying and Eating Food: Consumers and Consumption

INTRODUCTION

> If you think about where your food's come from and who's work has gone into getting that, the growing of it, the planting of it and getting it to you, and now when I'm doing the vegetables, I think, well somebody's been out in that field and you do feel better having those kinds of thoughts and it's not just an anonymous carrot [laughs] ... a lot of people have gone to a lot of effort. (Julie, EarthShare subscriber; office worker, interviewed in 2004)

This chapter examines our empirical research findings from the perspective of consumers who buy some of their food from the six schemes described in preceding chapters. This chapter is paired with the next in order to mirror the approach adopted in Chapter 4, where we examined the constitution of producer identities, motivations and practices. So, in this chapter we focus on consumer identities and motivations, and in the next we examine consumer practices. Both chapters draw on material collected during interviews, workshops and household research.[1] The overall aim of the chapter is to explore the utility of the framework of care as a lens through which to make sense of the complicated consumption behaviours of our respondents.

In writing this chapter, we wrestled with the problem of how to 'separate out' identities and motivations, when in practice, and particularly in relation to food consumption, they are fused together. Moreover, what is clear from our fieldwork is that the identities and motivations constructed by respondents are to some degree malleable and in a state of constantly 'becoming'; they can change over time in relation to life events. They are also both contingent on and the result of deliberative decisions (such as where to live or shop, what to buy). Furthermore, identities and motivations are constructed through relationships with friends, family, other consumers, producers, food, and have to be understood as relational. We also recognize that food selection, whether day by day or over a lifetime, is influenced by a range of biological, economic, social and cultural factors, which work at the level of the individual, family, household, or wider social group. Indeed, the complexity of behaviours labelled 'food choice' makes the process and outcomes difficult to study, and as Murcott (1998b) points out, even the notion of 'choice' is ambiguous. Definitions include: the act of choosing, the power of choosing, that which is chosen, and an abundance of items from which to select. It can refer to the selection of one commodity rather than another, to the selection of the wherewithal to construct a meal, or to the selection of a pattern of menus (see Beardsworth and Keil 1997). Moreover, the ability to choose, like the ability to care (understood in Tronto's terms as the ability to act on one's concerns), is constrained by factors such as income, time, location and availability of food supplies, as well as expectations and immediate life demands.

When consumers spoke to us about food consumption, the two concepts of identity and motivations were linked in complex ways and indeed, consumers generally found it easier to begin by thinking about what motivated them to participate in their particular food scheme, and from then to reflect on more abstract questions concerning their sense of identity. Whereas the producers' disposition and ethical frameworks were clearly bound up in, identifiable, and expressed through, their food production, or business, the relationship between consumer identities, motivations and practices appears far more complex. For this reason, we approach the empirical material slightly differently to the way it is approached in Chapter 4, by first of all discussing the factors that motivated consumers to engage with their 'alternative' food provider. Much of the data presented here cast light on the ways in which consumers perceived their own identities, particularly in terms of whether they were disposed to empathize with, take responsibility for, think about, and ultimately, care, for known and unknown others, communities and environments. After discussing consumers' initial motivations for participation we go on to examine the development of identities and motivations through processes of connection, 'reconnection' and entanglement between producers and consumers. Next, we explore the extent to which, for some consumers at least, there is evidence of a 'graduation effect' whereby the scope of care expands to encompass the consumption of other commodities besides food, or indeed, whether changes in food consumption practices 'followed' changes in practice relating to other products. Finally, we reflect on the extent to which an ethic of care can account for the identities and motivations of the consumers in our research.

CONSUMER MOTIVATIONS: CARES, ANXIETIES AND HEDONISM

At first glance, our data suggest that many consumers participated in these schemes for a range of reasons which are typical of the general consumer anxieties outlined in Chapter I. When specifically asked about why they had used the scheme, people mentioned issues which had concerned them *before* they joined the scheme (i.e. were motivating factors to join or shop in particular ways), or were things they had realized *since* joining the scheme/ using the shop or market (i.e. were part of a learning and engagement process). Some consumers saw schemes as risk management tools (which perhaps results in low eventual engagement), others, as differentiated lifestyle choices (which perhaps meant a greater involvement and commitment to the underlying ethos).

There were quite clearly complex and overlapping sets of motivations and desires, combining with circumstances which might have been coincidental (such as a new job, or new route to work, or house move, or meeting someone who used the scheme) or triggering (such as birth of a baby or retirement), which enabled changes in practice. Some had specifically sought out a scheme but had had to grapple with practical and logistical aspects before getting involved (Is there a scheme where I live or work? Are they taking on new customers? How do I receive/obtain produce? Can I carry/store/cook it? etc.), whereas others had just 'happened upon it'. Some simply said they wanted whatever the particular product was and/or what it represented, such as being 'good quality', 'local' and/or 'organic'. For many respondents, taste and freshness were paramount, and for some, there was no desire for 'knowing the producer's name or face.' When asked how much she knew about the scheme, Rebecca, a Waterland consumer replied:

> I don't know much and to be honest, it's not that I'm not interested, because I'm a snob or anything, but what is important to me is that it meets my needs as a consumer, and I also think it's because ... that's the only way he [i.e. the producer] can grow.

As the above quote clearly illustrates, consumer motivations are rarely simple, and data presented in the rest of the chapter will continue to reinforce this point. So, even when prioritizing her needs as a consumer, Rebecca still recognizes the needs of the producer and implies that she wants to support the producer in growing his business. Others were clear that they had sought out certain schemes because they were an extension of the way in which they wished to live their lives, such as avoiding using supermarkets, or being closer to production (again, these aspects are discussed in more detail, below). One Farrington's customer asserted,

> Yes ... I think it's something that I have thought about a lot at some time before [finding] the farm shop and then after, yes, this is a really good idea, I really should continue with this.

EarthShare participants at one of our consumer workshops were particularly clear that the scheme simply fitted their values and lifestyle:

> Opportune, I've been eating organic food for many years so it wasn't a big thing for me.

> Respondent: ... for us its very simple, myself and my wife, because we had been growing and eating organic food for years, and also for about eight years we had our own smallholding ...
> Interviewer: So it's sort of been a stable part of your ...
> Respondent: Absolute, inside and outside my life, our lives really, for years and years and years, eating organic food.

Other consumers would use whichever sources provided the best produce, including supermarkets. For instance, in Salop Drive Market Garden, members demonstrated an in-depth knowledge of the quality, freshness and price of fruit and vegetables at all local outlets and made their choices according to factors which best satisfied their personal circumstances.

Whatever the starting points, these did not map exactly on to the different schemes; in other words, it is not the case that we found more 'engaged' consumers in one scheme and less committed ones in another. People across the range had an underlying interest in some, at least, of the principles and practice of such schemes, and an openness and willingness to consider incorporating them into their daily lives, even though this meant changing shopping, budgeting, cooking or eating practices as a result, whether or not that had been their original intention. Thus, they adopted an identity as those who are prepared to act on beliefs and desires which may be quite widely held by the population at large but which are not necessarily put into practice, even though in so doing they might have had to seek out, or work at finding, schemes and opportunities which fitted into their schedules and lives.

Despite the complexity of motivations and desires, combined with circumstances, a number of common themes emerged as being important in encouraging people either to start a scheme in the first place, or continue using it, perhaps after starting it through happenstance or out of curiosity. These motivations can be thought of as interlocking 'cares' operating across different scales, from the home through to the local community, and the wider community of humankind, and encompassing concerns for people, food, animals, soil and ecosystems. We identify three key sets of motives: first, care for local economies, environments and future generations; second, care for health and wholeness; and finally, care *about*, rather than *for* transparency and integrity in food systems, including issues relating to science and governance. The distinction between 'care for' and 'care about' is important in this last set of motivations, for it distinguishes between actions which can be, and are, taken in order to benefit others in some way, and concerns, worries or anxieties about a particular situation or set of circumstances.

Care for Local Economies, Environments and Future Generations

Several generalized concerns were expressed about the nature of the food system. However, one, extremely common, particular concern, usually mentioned early in interviews or workshops, was about the loss of shops in the local area, and the potential future loss of amenities. For example, these EarthShare subscribers commented:

> you know I think it is very sad how the little local shops are being squeezed out ... you know, they opened a new [supermarket] in Forres [nearest town] about, I don't know it must have been about three or four years ago, and within something like about two months the local fishmonger had closed. And he just put a big sign saying 'Closed because of [supermarket]'.

> ...something like [supermarket] gets way too much power ... there's [supermarket] in every town and you can't get away from it, there's nothing else can almost exist, which sucks.

People spoke with passion and understanding about the viability of the local economy, both in terms of jobs and in terms of its food production ecology. They wanted to support both their local community and smaller, sometimes local, food producers, even in some cases recognizing this was at extra cost or inconvenience to themselves. For example, this Moorland consumer explained:

> I think unfortunately these [supermarkets] will displace the local shops eventually, but we try and support numerous places including the local 10 o'clock shop as they are useful occasionally, to make them feel wanted. Plus, my milkman is struggling so I want to support him even though it's not the best milk.

Respondents also recognized the impact of their actions on local economies elsewhere; thus, concern was not limited to the immediate locale but to places further afield, and this is perhaps most clearly illustrated in the case of the 'Adopt a sheep' 'parents'. When asked to describe the most positive aspects of the scheme, the most frequent responses concerned respect for the environment and support for 'traditional' farming methods. Linked to the 'natural' aspects of the scheme, members enjoyed the sense of 'belonging' to a unique form of food production, which operated on a small scale and protected the physical environment and a rare, or 'antique' breed of animals. They recognized that the scheme supported a 'traditional' way of life and liked the idea of 'helping others'.

The awareness of economies and livelihoods elsewhere was also expressed in comments relating to fair trade. So for instance, this Farrington's consumer said:

> I always buy Fairtrade stuff again and I try in the vegetables to try and keep up with um current affairs so that I'm not promoting something that I disapprove of, so in [supermarket] I'm quite careful. Um, what else, er, I don't buy milk because I don't think they do a fair job for the um producers ...

Interestingly, she didn't know whether her choice of milk was actually any better for the producers, and there was often a sense of consumers trying to make the best decision on the basis of incomplete knowledge. Furthermore, as the comment below suggests, schemes such as Fairtrade are possibly undermined when they are supplied through conventional retail channels as peoples' fears about some supermarkets mean they may question the independence and/or integrity of the schemes:

> ... I wouldn't want fruit from Botswana unless the people that are doing it ... producing it, are getting a fair wage ... but you don't know with [supermarket]. (Farrington's consumer)

Furthermore, Fairtrade produce comes with its own ethical and moral contradictions. For example, consumers voiced their support for giving farmers a fair price both here and abroad but also identified that supporting this form of network meant having to swallow the 'food miles' associated with importing produce. Conversely, buying local food from farmers' markets, rather than foods grown overseas, raised moral dilemmas about the livelihoods of those unknown farmers versus the livelihoods of local or national producers:

> ... mostly I have to admit we shop in [supermarket], um, but I try not to buy green beans that have come from – although – I mean, it's a really difficult decision because you're supporting farmers in Kenya or Egypt or wherever, on the other hand, we can perfectly well produce green beans, so we should be, and then buying something else from them. (Moorland consumer)

Another key concern was damage to the local and wider (global) environment, the issue of 'food miles', the pollution associated with global food distribution and transportation, and the impact that this has on local communities through increased numbers of lorries on roads. People both criticized the practice of large retailers and commended their own scheme, over distances that food travels. However, some recognized the potential contradictions in their own practices in trying to source ethically, for instance, buying from direct-sell initiatives, which could involve driving longer distances or requiring others to do so. Although these ways of sourcing may not contribute as much to climate change as importing air freighted produce, nevertheless they were sometimes seen as problematic:

> [My husband will] sometimes comment about how ... you know, it's all very well saying that there's low food miles but he sometimes will say 'yes, but you've got these people that are all driving ten miles to Findhorn on their own in their cars' and I know that's not the case but do you know what I mean? So you just must be wrecking the ozone layer as much, as you know, one plane from Argentina full of masses of stuff ... (EarthShare subscriber)

> ... the only thing that slightly worried me about box schemes was, I mean I think the principle of box scheme is great, but they are driving around all over the place to get to you, and I kind of ... there's something not quite right about that as well. I almost ... I don't know how you'd get around that (Waterland member)

In some discussions there were people who spoke with almost idealistic concern about ecological sustainability: that people have an individual and personal responsibility to live in such a way that future generations' well-being is protected, even enhanced. A notable proponent of this way of thinking was Ian, an EarthShare subscriber, who when interviewed, expressed a clear sense of responsibility for, and care about, future generations:

> Of course for a lot of people, and certainly for ourselves, my wife and myself, it isn't the food so much, that's partly it, but it's really because you can't say that the present generation owns the soil, one can't say that a person from whom EarthShare rents the 22 acres owns that for you, he doesn't, he's the tenant for the ... you know, in a sense for the generations to come, and so ... I mean, we feel this very deeply indeed, you cannot hand over to your incoming people, your incoming generations, soil that is so desperately polluted and inert ...
>
> ... the land does not belong to the person who we think it does belong to, the laird, the farmer or whoever, the landowner, it belongs to the people who are going to come, and you could also say there's a very strong feeling up here, a very strong feeling indeed, that it belongs to the community of people who are inhabiting that area at the time and that community ... the community, not so much the individual, but the community, which is a different kind of feeling really, that community of people are responsible for handing over their birthright to the next wave of community that comes ...

For some, this had led them to move from particular jobs or places, to new ways of living (e.g. to be near Findhorn community, or to live in Somerset); for others, this awareness had been there, perhaps in nascent form, but had been activated or strengthened by the experience of involvement in the scheme as a different way of living and obtaining food. This was particularly true for EarthShare participants, but also in Somerset and Sandwell. Thus the experience of being in the scheme, with all that meant in terms of knowledge, trust, pleasure and relationships (with producers and with other consumers), had in turn affected both new roles as consumers, and reinforced or developed the beliefs and practices which had informed joining.

In several consumer workshops this connection to the integrity of the local economy was taken further, in an expressed desire to resist what were seen as global powers homogenizing, alienating and almost 'dumbing down' the consumer in the food system. For some, there was an intense desire for closeness (to production and producer, to processes and outcomes), and recognition of the need to preserve the connectedness of networks established by what were sometimes implied to be brave or challenging schemes, so that future generations could benefit from them and not be beholden to one type of food source.

Thus these expressions of care for localities and the people in them, and the meanings which could be ascribed to them as locations of production and employment, thriving economies and communities of interlinked peoples, households and practices, which need to be preserved not as museums but as living and sustainable systems, provided powerful examples in practice of 'caring' as Tronto defined it. In other words, care as action, as 'doing something' about a situation, however distant (in locality or relational terms) it may appear, rather than just expressing a regret about that which is less desirable, or a hope that things might change. Here were people prepared to try and effect change, who engaged and, however incompletely, sought to make things better – not just for themselves and their own households, but for their neighbours (defined as those within a wide locality), for distant others, and future generations.

Care for Health and Wholeness

Our respondents articulated a sense of caring about 'health' and 'wholeness', for self, other people and planet. Consuming a 'healthy diet' is a widely promoted essential towards living a healthy life, and, unsurprisingly, participation in schemes such as those we are discussing was for many a means of making conscious decisions about health. These encompassed a wide range of expressed benefits, including the obvious ones related to improvement in dietary quality through eating more fresh produce, particularly vegetables and fruit, which tends to follow from being in a box scheme or going to a farmers' market, and consuming milk and dairy produce, meat or fish which have been produced using traditional methods, and which are, therefore, more likely to provide more recommended nutrients (such as claims that grass-fed cattle and sheep give products which have different fatty acid profiles from intensively reared or cereal fed animals; see, for example, Harvey 2006). People also spoke of a desire to avoid 'processed' products, because of the unfamiliar chemicals perceived as being used in conventional, industrial food production. They often mistrusted food that had been, as they saw it, 'adulterated', which they associated with techniques to alter appearance or prolong shelf life artificially; and many disliked techniques such as the use of genetically modified organisms. Very often, these concerns were most sharply brought into focus in relation to the provision of food for dependent relatives, especially children. Indeed, a common catalyst for buying 'organic' and joining schemes was the desire to feed young children a healthy and less adulterated diet. Rebecca, a Waterland consumer specified that starting her son on solids was the main reason for joining the box scheme; she 'wanted nothing else but "organic"' and didn't want to 'pollute' him. David, a Moorland consumer, explained the lengths he went to, in order to get acceptable food for his son:

> ... when your time is that limited it's really hard and ... and sometimes I think well, you know, I dedicate a whole morning to kind of going and buying nice sausages and nice bread and all that and I really want ... I do it cos I want my son to have really nice food. I don't want him to have white plastic bread from [supermarket] and even their nice bread isn't that nice ...

The birth of a child was clearly a major life event which marked an opportunity for some consumers to change their practices and made them reconsider their priorities. As Mary, an EarthShare subscriber explained:

> You know, you grow and you become aware of your own body and health too of course, and it fits together. And if you have a child that's also a big responsibility, to think about how you're feeding them and ... what sort of home you are providing and so on ... I mean, I didn't give a damn when I was in my twenties, you know ... you change.

On the other hand, other parents told of how the pressure on their time, as a result of combining work and family commitments, reduced their ability to source food exactly as they wished, and led to more reliance on supermarkets for a one-stop shop.

Although not all the schemes were selling food labelled as 'organic', many people used the label as shorthand for a more desired type of food and food system. There were many reasons given about why 'organic' food was preferable, which again related both to anxiety about the appropriateness of the many artificial chemicals used in food production, including any 'cocktail' effects, an anxiety which extended to mistrust in official and private sector systems for assuring safety, and to a positive desire for better health both for oneself and the ecosystem. Two EarthShare workshop participants here discuss why organic food is important to them, and in so doing clearly illustrate the interrelatedness of health of self and environment, as well as the sensual pleasure of eating 'clean' food:

> I prefer to eat organically grown food. I think it's much healthier and I don't think we should be poisoning the ground, and it tastes much better, it's really simple, it's fresher ... I mean I have very clear priorities for where my money goes and one of the things is to eat clean and good food.

Two things really, it's a concern about health and, and also the sustainability of high input chemical farming, I think ultimately you know you've got to know what the organic produce could taste like then you realize exactly what you miss when you go into a high intensively grown set up. I mean the carrots actually taste of carrot.

The desire for/care for biological wholeness and integrity included respect for the soil, for other creatures and for natural systems for production and promotion of growth and well-being. Some consumers felt that there is a need for the use of some artificial chemicals to enable sufficient crop growth or protection for animals, but all expressed a great desire for transparency and to have confidence and trust in the system, in the producer and all involved in the food chain, especially supermarkets:

> I just think that my feeling about the supermarkets is they skim in at the bottom level that they can to get away with something. So they'll come in at the lowest possible level to get something as … as certified organic. (David, Moorland customer)

Thus, knowing exactly where your food has come from, how it has been produced, and sometimes even knowing the person who has produced it (including those who have grown, or slaughtered, or prepared or cooked it) is for some an essential component of making conscious decisions about health, and for expressing themselves as a 'conscientious' consumer:

> It [the food system] is one of life's mysteries, isn't it, because you can't see what you're buying, whereas when you go to Farrington's you know what you're getting. (Farrington's customer)

In fact, for some consumers, it was this knowledge and trust which mattered rather than the 'organic' label, which was simply used as a guide when there was no other means of gaining the relevant information about production.

This discussion illustrates that many people's thinking about, and caring for, health stretched beyond their own, personal, state to include the well-being of their household, community and wider environment. 'Well-being' could encompass ecological, economic and social dimensions, at the immediate local and wider national levels. The concept of health applied was not confined to a reductionist set of anxieties – 'absence of poisoning' or 'absence of disease' – but to a more holistic and integrated sense of a balanced, thriving and sustainable ecosystem. Furthermore, being healthy was not just desired for oneself, it was for the whole family and for one's friends and neighbours, indeed the wider community where possible. Expression of ideas about healthiness rapidly segued into the value of the social aspects of growing, preparing, cooking and eating food (for more on this, see Chapter 6) and of the pleasures to be had from variety (both of commodity and between commodities) and in recognizing seasonality (and being reminded about it through participation in a scheme). The quotes in Box 5.1 are illustrative of the sense of enjoyment and satisfaction experienced and expressed by virtually all our respondents in relation to food from their scheme. Notably, the food's symbolic and material qualities were often contrasted favourably with supermarket food.

Box 5.1 THE SENSUAL PLEASURES OF FOOD

I'd just made this lovely veg stew and, oh, I mean the taste of the carrots was just, you know, what carrots are supposed to taste like. Whereas if you buy it from a supermarket it actually doesn't taste of anything. (Ruth, EarthShare)

I mean the carrots, are just … when you're peeling them, you actually smell carrot … I mean, I don't think organic carrots from the supermarket … they don't taste any different. (Michelle, EarthShare)

… the tomatoes you get in the organic boxes are lovely and I mean, it doesn't matter how much vine branches you put onto … the supermarket ones, most of them are just tasteless … I mean, cauliflowers you can buy, you know you can buy cauliflowers that look so lovely and they just have no taste at all … (Michelle, EarthShare)

… you can just taste that some food is better produced, you know … you don't have to know what's gone on with the food, and be able to see that it's better produced, and you can look at their beef and tell that it's … it's not that horrible bright pink stuff that you get in supermarkets … you can tell it's nicer, and it tastes nicer. (David, Moorland)

Food was seen as part of a biological system and not something manufactured as part of a technocratic system, and this was regarded as a healthy understanding as well as a source of pleasure. There was acknowledgement that growing, rearing or producing food, and storing or preparing it, could entail hard work, but this too was seen as potentially healthy and also enjoyable. Mary (EarthShare) described how she 'loved' doing the workshifts:

I do sit behind a computer a lot and it's wonderful to go off on your bike you know and pick strawberries for an afternoon. Can you imagine? With this heavenly world around you up here and the views and, just lovely, I love doing it. Not for any idealistic reason, I just enjoy it. I enjoy pulling weeds up in the rain too.

There was also much expression of the healthiness of local and regional taste and culture; people could only be healthy who valued and enjoyed their food in all its aspects:

And its bound up with my feelings about food, I love cooking and I ... I love shopping ... um ... for that sort of food you know, looking to see the quality of the meat and talking to the butcher and things like that um, because, I invest an awful lot of quality of life in food. I don't see it as something that you get ... you know fast food for me um is really um ... it has no conceptual meaning at all 'cos I don't see food as fast I see it as a lingering pleasure. (Lilian, Farrington's customer)

Care about Transparency and Integrity in the Food System / Rejection of 'New Technology'

Almost the converse, or corollary, of embracing an ethic of care for environmental and personal health and well-being was the suspicion of, and sometimes rejection of, a good deal of the modern, highly technologized food system. Although sometimes presented in non-technical language, these views were not 'knee-jerk' Luddism or nostalgia for (imaginary) days when food was pure and unadulterated, but a clear-headed irritation or even anger at a perceived deliberate lack of transparency, not only in ingredients used, but also the people, processes and places where food is processed and manufactured. These comments from Farrington's consumers illustrate the point:

I just don't like processed food because you don't, you honestly do not know what goes on. The bagged lettuce and things — when I heard that there were more germs inside one of those bags because of the fact that they're not washed in clean water and you don't know who's actually putting them into the bags and whether the people putting them into the bags who were being paid to do it had washed their hands. So that made me think ...

I think they spray them ... the carrots never go off that you buy from the supermarket. They go all wobbly, the ones that you buy from the fresh [farm shop] ... and those iceberg lettuce last forever. I think they'll still be going at Christmas what we've bought now [from the supermarket]!

The necessity and appropriateness of such technological management of food was also often rejected. This was particularly expressed (unsolicited) in terms of production of widely available cheap chicken, which was seen as the epitome of foods which may have been subject to means of maintaining 'freshness' which disguise potentially negative signs of travel, storage or processing:

> I mean, like the chickens, I mean the thought of buying one of those slippery slimy chickens in the supermarket is just ... I just look at them when I'm going past and they're so cheap. They're amazingly cheap. They really are. But then I just think ... they're just grown, aren't they in a ... fattened and ... just sat in a thing and they just wash them off, fill them with water and things and throw them into a plastic bag and then you buy them. Well I don't want a chicken like that. I'd rather have a chicken once a month and pay, what, £8 to £10, £12 for a free range one. (Fiona, Farrington's customer)

> And you know it's like the chickens and the fact that you can buy two chickens for a fiver or something, they are, they are beyond belief the way these chickens are brought in from Indonesia, they all cost 10p, they're cryogenically frozen in some kind of suspension, so that when they get here they're unfrozen by a chemical process and then they say they're fresh. Because the fact they haven't been technically frozen as we would understand it; they've got a big Union Jack on them which, in minute writing, probably in a foreign language, says, packaged in the UK, and they sell them for £2.99 as 'fresh, and can be frozen', which they technically can. They're pumped full of antibiotics so they reckon in 20 years we will have no immunity anymore to antibiotics, it just freaks you out. (Joan, Moorland customer)

Where choices were available, people were adamant they preferred low-tech options, such as were on offer through the schemes they took part in. Of course, some of these also offer 'processed' foods, in that farm shops and market stalls sell all sorts of food products (jams, chutneys, sauces, pies, etc.) and 'Adopt a sheep' supplies cheeses and salami, but customers distinguished these from products produced on a large, industrial scale. For example, many of Farrington's customers, although they would not buy 'ready meals' from a supermarket, were happy to purchase Farrington's 'ready meals' because they knew they had been processed on site – and the cook was often seen in the shop and known to customers. They also trusted Farrington's to source other processed foods appropriately.

Customers and box scheme members alike did buy food from conventional supermarkets, as discussed in Chapter 6, but many expressed an increasing mistrust of mainstream retailer sourcing and tactics, as shown above. The use of technology by supermarkets and retailers was in fact directly acknowledged as a factor that contributed to dissatisfaction with these outlets and was often a reason why people wanted to stop using them as much as possible, especially for foods they considered susceptible to possible technical manipulation or which they perceived to be prepared in ways that suits the manufacturer/retailer rather than necessarily the consumer. People mentioned a range of technological processes used in production (technologically derived seeds, feeds, hormones, antibiotics, chemical applications), to manipulate foods (mass production, food factories) and methods to deliver, store and present products to customers on shelves in an apparently fresh state (radiation, chill freezing were often mentioned) but devoid of visible signs of these processes, which they often felt to be nontransparent and requiring too much technical competency and/or time, to be trusted implicitly. Conversely, part of the attraction of the schemes we were studying seemed to be that they allow consumers to avoid technologically driven food production and mass-produced commodities.

These findings demonstrate quite clearly the issues of trust and mistrust. People were not on the whole rejecting 'technology' per se, as far as we could tell; with one or two exceptions, they embraced the use of freezers, automatic machinery, cars where essential and other paraphernalia of contemporary life. What they disliked was the use of technology to industrialize food, to make it uniform, appealing and predictable, to manufacture flavour and taste, and to disguise realities of production, storage and transport. People wanted 'authenticity' in food, and mistrusted its absence and the lack of transparency; they also mistrusted those they saw as complicit in maintaining such opacity – which for many was epitomized by the large retailers/supermarkets.

What has emerged from this discussion of the main cares, anxieties and pleasures which motivated consumers in our research is that the means of addressing these issues lie within the construction of more direct relationships with the producers and growers of food. In the next section, we examine the ways in which these relationships are experienced by consumers in terms of a range of emotions from pleasure to guilt. We examine evidence of the ways in which participation in these relationships enables the reflexive and continuing development of care-oriented identities.

RELATIONSHIPS WITH PRODUCERS: CONNECTING, RECONNECTING, ENTANGLING

Our analysis of consumers' relationships with producers and schemes suggests that distinctions can be drawn between three overlapping forms of direct engagement: connection, 'reconnection' and entanglement. These can be defined as follows:

- *Connection* – a mutual exchange of values, sharing of common causes, feelings, opinions.
- *'Reconnection'* – an ability to invoke values, pursue modes of engagement which link to memories or constructions of older types of relationships in 'bygone times', perhaps also a desire to withdraw from contemporary consumption patterns and the food system.
- *Entanglement* – an increasing emotional, financial and practical engagement with a particular scheme which can contribute to and reinforce changes in behaviour, not only in shopping for/procuring food but also in using it and experiencing its effects on oneself and the household.

While connection and 'reconnection' can be partially established through printed and virtual media, which can convey information and values, for the majority of our respondents discussing things with the farmer or a contact person (the delivery van driver or employee in the farm shop) was the most important and enjoyable way of learning more about their food and its origins. While many found it hard to articulate exactly how they knew what they did, and the contribution the scheme they belonged to made, they were able to refer to the trust they had in the 'producer' (whether the grower, rearer, farm shop manager, etc.), and the fact that they knew them and could ask questions, or could hear them explaining to others the ethos of the scheme, which reinforced their own understanding. This is in a context of a tendency among many respondents to mistrust the validity of labels and certification on food. So for example, this EarthShare subscriber said:

> ... there's a lot of questions about certification, of organic things, so it's very important to know that the people who produce the food are genuinely committed and wouldn't let you down. That's much more important than to have the stamp of approval from the Soil Association ...

Unlike face-to-face exchanges, where consumers can challenge or ask questions of the producers, certification schemes offer no way of personally and immediately validating their claims – there simply is no feedback loop. In contrast, speaking to producers allows consumers to learn much about their food, and make assessments of trust. As Kathleen, one of the Moorland consumers who we interviewed put it:

> Yeah, I think they're really helpful ... And, you know, they're not gonna belittle you or make fun of you if you're asking about ... if you show an interest in what they're doing.

She felt that knowing the producers helped her to trust them, even when their labelling was not actually that good:

> ... because I've been going for such a long time now I know the producers, so I know where they're from and I know about their meat and I know about their kind of ethics towards their animals and I don't think that the food is, you know, maybe labelled as well as it could be and to be honest I do kind of go on trust, and I kind of think, you say this is free range, but it might not be ...

She also thought that the farmers' market had 'some kind of procedure' to ensure 'certain standards'; thus the arena of exchange in this case reinforces a sense of trust.

For many, the experience of using their scheme was all about trust: in the producer and in the way the food was produced, processed or retailed. This trust was rooted in knowing the person or people involved, with a critical dimension time and again being knowing the source, so that people felt linked in, and part of the food chain, closer to the land and the countryside. This was expressed through the experience of being involved, doing the weeding, helping with harvesting, being a 'member', using the shop, eating the produce, engaging with the producer:

> And you get an awful lot of trust in the setup because for instance ... Tish's got this eye for detail, she's got ... all the beautiful features that she's put into the café. You feel there's a person for you who wouldn't let anything else slide past her, so it's a very personal investment of trust ... and her staff, yes, it extends to her staff as well ... I think if they're over there doing it [cooking on the premises] if they're putting in ... um it comes back again to trusting the trader and here I feel they can. (Lilian, Farrington's customer)

> my impression is that it would be really difficult to fake it. You couldn't ... it would be very hard for somebody to farm the land and tend their livestock if they were completely uncaring and devoid of any environmental principles or

ethics and then come to a farmer's market and act like you were kind of, you know, a person that you wanted to do ... that I would want to do business with. (John, Moorland customer)

For many, the proximity and intimate relationships forged through participation, as well as knowing that the farmers and growers share the same food philosophy and hold similar outlooks to themselves, provide a significant sense of satisfaction and trust in the food:

> It's something to do with intimacy and that you can identify with the structure of it because you are close enough as a consumer to identify with the central concept and philosophy and that's attractive because so much now in everyday life is out of our hands. (EarthShare subscriber)

> It's as we said before, you know that the things are grown with love and respect. (EarthShare subscriber)

Sometimes the development of trust was such that people had radically changed practices: for example, one Moorland customer had abandoned being a vegetarian because, by getting to know the farmer, she had been able to develop sufficient trust in the integrity of their rearing and slaughtering system, as well as having access to what she knew was an accredited BSE-free herd. People valued the opportunity this close connection gave of restoring links and ties with the local community, feeling part of one's surroundings and making a contribution to supporting local life, including production:

> Another good thing is that it [Salop Drive Market Garden] involves the community, there's a lot of volunteers there and it does involve people ... and there will be a community garden there soon.

Schemes which do not offer people the chance to help on the farm, occasions to meet or engage during shopping opportunities, such as farmers' markets, nonetheless enable people to evaluate the source and quality of the produce through their being able to ask questions, and through the quality of the product and aesthetics of how it is presented. There were some differences in consumer experiences in this respect according to the scheme they were in, but the general story of trust, knowing the producer, knowing more about the food thus obtained, and about the food system in general (if only in contrast to the scheme) was similar across the board. It was even true of 'Adopt a sheep consumers', who had to rely almost entirely on web resources, unless they had had opportunity to visit the farm in Italy (which some had done). The relationship between producers and consumers in all the schemes was, by definition, two-way. Both sides contributed to building the confidence and trust in the other – 'creating' the other, as it were, as the 'ideal' partner or companion in the project.

Turning now to entanglement (Figure 5.1), consumers may not necessarily expect or desire this type of relationship, and it can engender a degree of moral obligation on the part of consumers to continue buying, to be consistent:

> … you actually feel kind of a little bit guilty, walking past them in the morning, 'They're such nice people. Oh, I should go and buy something from them'. [laughs] (John, Moorland customer)

Figure 5.1 Bristol farmers' market: 'reconnection' and entanglement. Photo by L. Venn.

Entanglement also entails changing routines and practices, and can require extra organization such as remembering to cancel a box delivery when away. Many schemes require a degree of commitment – signing up to be a 'member', paying by direct debit, or, as in the case of EarthShare, committing to working in production for a certain period and at certain seasons, as well as sharing the farmer's risks by not expecting produce if the season has been bad or a crop has failed. Those to whom we listened were largely very happy for this to have taken place, or had become so over time, as they got to know the producer (whether grower or rearer) and their relationship with them developed.

However, there was also a hint that involvement in schemes could require adjustments to behaviour which could become restrictive. As one EarthShare subscriber explained:

> ... I start with good intentions ... and then I'm thinking this is all too much, and I think to make that life change, particularly if you're working full-time, you're in mainstream, it just takes time.

Entanglement also means that consumers learn more about some of the difficulties entailed in actually growing fruit and vegetables, raising livestock and running a small business; as one person said, it 'puts food into perspective'. This knowledge seemed to result in an increase in tolerance for times of glut and scarcity, or for temporary blips in quality and consistency and also helped consumers take greater pleasure in seasonality. Finally, entanglement can sometimes, but not always, lead to a sense of belonging to a scheme. This is most evident in the case of EarthShare, which requires financial, and ideally, physical commitment.

EXPANDING THE SCOPE OF CAREFUL CONSUMPTION: A 'GRADUATION EFFECT'

In this section, we illustrate how identities and motivations can, for some consumers, change within the context of these direct relationships with producers. Several people spoke about a broadening view of 'consumption' as a result of engaging in different ways of buying food: acknowledging and questioning the production systems and context of one commodity (food), had led, in turn, to a realization of the impact of other consumption decisions. Hence, the data provide some evidence of a sort of 'graduation effect': as consumers pay more attention to their (food) consumption decisions (in relation to particular food commodities as a result of scheme participation) so they may also modify purchasing strategies within food more generally, and also then in other areas, partly through realizing their 'consumer' power. This was largely in relation to their own, individual perspectives and needs:

> food is obviously hugely important and a need rather than a want, but the extent to which just participation in something like this ... can alter how you think about other things ... It does and then you sort of think 'ok I've got these vegetables now and this is really working for me' and then you maybe sat there and think oh well maybe I should be thinking about what I put in ... if I'm

putting that *in* my body what am I putting *on* my body so then you think oh, well actually I'd quite like to live the simpler lifestyle and it just gets you thinking. (Julia, EarthShare subscriber)

Because of the scheme we now try and buy all our meat locally, at the local butchers and choose products with less packaging, we've also found that we are recycling more. (Waterland member)

People certainly talked about the change in their approaches to shopping in supermarkets as a result of experiencing both the different way of obtaining food through a scheme, and of consuming the food itself – its taste, quantity, quality, characteristics, etc.

But it was not always easy to achieve a balance between personal values and products available in the marketplace, and numerous interviewees spoke about their frustration over specific types of food products and/or supply chains that made procuring food that satisfied their personal principles increasingly difficult. This was true of both sourcing and production methods. For instance, some mentioned fish stocks, where it was not just a case of, for instance, avoiding purchasing cod (because of low stocks) but actually of eating less fish altogether, thereby contributing to reducing demand so as to allow wild stocks to regenerate and also to reduce reliance on intensively farmed production, which was seen as harmful in other ways:

Well that's the thing, I do eat fish and ... but I eat fish less and less now because of course it's the same problems with the farmed fish ... And then the fish stocks ... I mean, on and on ... I mean ... I mean I sometimes get so exasperated by you know, well humans but as consumers that em ... they think they can deplete all these stocks and that we're still going to be okay, but just ... it just seems, I don't want to really be part of it, so I'm endeavouring to do what I can. (Ruth, EarthShare subscriber)

It proved difficult to differentiate people clearly on the basis of their awareness and/or personal principles over consumption practices as prior motivations for joining a scheme, but it did seem that taking part made it easier to be self-aware – to account for and estimate one's consumption impact. Some had chosen proactively to consume in certain ways in other parts of their life too; for example, to use renewable energy sources, buy commodities with less packaging, and think about what happens to materials post-consumption, or had been managing their use of resources and were recycling before joining the scheme. Thus there seemed to be increasing self-actualization as 'ethical' consumers over time. Some specifically claimed they tried to 'do their bit', hoping their contribution would make a difference, perhaps by example. However, it was by no means the case that all involved in such schemes were trying to reduce their own 'consumption footprint' and also, very few in fact mentioned being part of organizations or movements. Even those active in trying to reduce their carbon footprint, such as John, a Moorland customer, felt that sometimes life was just 'too complicated':

> ... you kind of feel like, um, if you start questioning everything, you know, you don't get time to have a life. Spend all your time researching things ... Getting people to, you know, reliable tradespeople who can do things for a decent budget and actually turn up when they say they will and all that sort of thing and the thought of actually kind of putting another layer on it and starting to specify the materials that they use, just kind of fills me with dread and I think 'I can't cope doing this ethically as well!' 'It's bad enough to find a plumber!' [both laugh]. Let alone an ethical plumber! ... So, you know, there are things that you put off by feeling it just makes life too complicated.

However, despite this complexity, he felt he was not doing as much as he would like to, and that there were areas of living or decisions about consumption that probably demanded attention, with potential change to meet environmental, social or personal principles:

> I'm aware there are still sort of blind spots like, for instance, the clothing, I haven't really started to think about ethical and environmental dimensions very much about ... about the clothes side, I've just actually got my first pair of Hemp boots. [laughs] ... but that aside, you know in terms of transport and, well, all sorts of other things, you know, [I could] try and be quite environmentally focused ...

These conversations, which occurred both between interviewers and consumers in face-to-face encounters and during discussion of practices in workshops, all point to the implicit 'embeddedness' of consumption decisions both in everyday practices and in satisfaction with self. Thinking about consumption, actions and outcomes was underpinned by people's social and economic resources, their opportunities and the constraints they faced (both personal and practical, such as access to 'alternative' food schemes, or the nature of recycling provision by a local authority) and was driven by personal ethical frameworks and the sense of satisfaction derived from consumption practices, from getting to know 'producers' better, and from life itself. Knowledge, either of where and how to shop in certain ways, or, in relation to food, such as how to use unfamiliar products, also played a part, but was seldom mentioned explicitly as having been important in people choosing to take part in a scheme. (For instance, few said, 'I saw a TV programme/read an article/picked up a leaflet, and thought, "oh I must buy my food in a different way."') Rather, people said their practices reflected their personal values, which they saw as reinforced by information they acquired (for instance, about 'fair trade' or 'organic') and by meeting and engaging with the growers/rearers/shop managers. They were pleased to be able to put these personal values into practice, through the schemes or, if necessary, even through the mainstream industrialized food system – although many respondents expressed dissatisfaction with this option.

Several mentioned that they were now making more informed decisions, and were even learning about the elements of the food chain that they sometimes found hard to handle, such as what happens at the abattoir, although as Patricia, a Moorland customer was quick to assert, 'There are enough things to worry about ... Oh, oh, I can't ... I'm not going to think about that [how cattle are slaughtered]'. But respecting animals by going beyond a 'knowing denial' and coming to terms with the realities of production, potentially contributed to the emergence of a more transparent relationship between producer, food and consumer:

> People, all of the people, are sort of divorced from meat production because if you go to the supermarket you buy it and it's all wrapped in a bit of plastic you know and you don't know where it's come from or what it looked like of the bit of animal it is. (Farrington's customer)

> I don't mind eating anything if I feel ... you ought to be able to feel where it's come from, what sort of life it's had, it's just really primitive you know. (EarthShare subscriber)

Some of our research participants produced personal narratives that demonstrated a history of seeking out opportunities to 'live differently', including previous food consumption experiences which had been less than positive (the quality of box scheme produce had been unreliable, or farm shops had been unpleasant or unsatisfactory). For some, such negative encounters had led to people abandoning such ways of buying food and returning to more conventional, perhaps more consistent, sources, albeit satisfying a desire for produce which met personal standards such as being fairly traded or 'organic'. For several, however, poor quality or bad experiences had not discouraged them from their belief in the desirability of buying food from 'alternative' sources which enabled them to fulfil personal values, and actively to support such schemes and activities. In their narratives, people often mentioned their attempts to source directly from producers, and to obtain food produced in ways that 'respected the planet and people' and so would move from one source to another. For instance, a number of people had started off sourcing organic or local foods in mainstream supermarkets and then switched allegiances to local producers, box schemes or farm shops when they became aware of their existence – through word of mouth, chance encounter or, occasionally, looking in a local food directory.

People consistently described such switching in terms of *progress*: buying from smaller, local shops and independent retailers, or directly from or with/ as producers, was better than sourcing food which is local and/or organic through major supermarkets, because of the support for local economies and ecosystems, the intimacy engendered by knowing the producer, and the trust that built up about transparency and consistency in production systems.

SUMMARIZING REMARKS: INSIGHTS INTO IDENTITIES OF CARE

By examining in some detail the motivations described by the respondents in our research, this chapter casts light on the extent to which the framework of care can account for their actions and identities. We can summarize with two broad points: First, we suggest that the material presented here provides evidence that the majority of consumers we spoke to have a care-oriented sense of self, in that they are aware of the needs of others, human and non-human, close and distant. For many, the disposition to care is inseparable from their sense of identity, which is in turn fused with their perception of their own place and role in relationship to other people and the environment. We have already illustrated this in the discussion of the cares that motivated consumers. Second, the majority of respondents are prepared to act on their concerns, in order to repair and sustain theirs and others' life-worlds, thus fulfilling Tronto's definition.

Whilst an ethic of care therefore provides a framework for many of the consumption decisions of our respondents, there are other aspects which need to be considered too, particularly in terms of the sensual, material and also symbolic properties of the food made available through our cases. Consumers clearly expressed the pleasures and enjoyment they experienced in preparing and eating the food gained from the schemes, as illustrated in Box 5.1. In addition, an aspect which requires further consideration is the relationship between identities, motivations and actual practices. For instance, although consumers may talk about their consumption ideals, they may not put these into practice, for various reasons. In order to explore the ways in which consumers put their identities and motivations into action, the next chapter turns to the daily practices of consumption, and examines these within the context of choice and convenience.

CHAPTER 6

Locating Food in Everyday Life: Consumer Practices, Care, Convenience and Choice

INTRODUCTION

> I do think that there seems to be more interest now again in 'proper' food. Because I think it was a great big 'wa-hoo, how fabulous we don't have to cook' era somewhere back down the line, wasn't there? Where everything, you just shove it in the microwave, and that for a while was fantastic. And I think people now are beginning to think again and thinking 'There's more to life than this, isn't there?' (Fiona, Farrington's customer; retired professional, interviewed in 2004)

While the previous chapter focused on consumer identities and motives, this one explores in more depth the practices through which 'alternative' food relationships are built, and through which care for many people, places and things is enacted. The chapter examines the ways in which such relationships in turn influence everyday practices relating to food in general. It explores consumption within the context of consumers' feelings about, and interactions with, the natural environment, wider community, friend and family networks as well as the immediate family and household and routine practices. The focus here is on consumers and also on food itself, which we argue is central to understanding producer/consumer relationships and also the other relationships, motivations, feelings and identities that are brought to and taken from these schemes. The chapter draws on in-depth data gained from interviews with consumers in the five British-based schemes (interviews were not conducted with 'Adopt a sheep' parents) and the 'household study', which involved six households in keeping food diaries, taking photographs of their food and being visited by a researcher regularly over a three-week period.

The chapter highlights the ways in which people create their own practicalities within circumstances not of their own choosing. It examines notions of convenience and choice to argue that there is a complex array of factors (including identity, health, emotion, environment, knowledge, routine, love, etc.) that build the logic of quotidian consumption practices. It locates food shopping, growing, cooking and eating within relationships of care that create and constrain both practices and attitudes. The chapter argues that convenience and choice are not just located in anonymous 'big box' supermarkets on the edge of town. They are concepts and *experiences* that are socially created from the possibilities and priorities of life. The chapter is split broadly into two sections. The first uses the idea of 'convenience' in the food system to look at how the consumers we worked with got their food (through shopping, growing, gathering or sharing it). The second explores notions of 'choice' in the planning of meals, the preparation and eating of food. We focus on the notions of convenience and choice because of their prevalence in discourses surrounding the success of supermarkets. Our data allow for a rethinking of these notions and reveal the complex and nuanced ways in which practices are logical and meaningful to the people who carry them out. In each section we begin with a focus on practices but this quickly spirals outwards to look at the relationships these activities mediated and created with other household members, friends, the community and the natural environment.

PROCURING FOOD: CONVENIENCE, NORMALITY AND EVERYDAY LIFE

Accessing food through 'alternative' schemes can appear to mean giving up some of the convenience of conventional outlets such as supermarkets – to be tied to specific opening or pick-up times, to forgo choice with a box scheme, or easy parking at a city-centre farmers' market. However, the growing numbers of box schemes, farmers' markets and CSAs in the United Kingdom (see Chapter 1 for details) suggest that increasing numbers of people do not get – or do not only get – their food from conventionally convenient sources.

For our research participants accessing food could mean growing it themselves, swapping it with friends, taking part in a workshift, picking up their box or going to the shops. All of these activities were part of complex webs of meaning, practicality and social relations. By scrutinizing the practices of our participants we raise questions about the logic of the conventional supermarket trip, the notion of convenience and the concept of choice. This section looks at the various ways in which scheme members accessed food – both through the schemes they were members of, and in other ways. It begins by exploring the concept of convenience and then goes on to reflect on how our respondents talked about their food procurement practices and how these fitted with the logics of their daily lives and caring practices.

In order to understand the routine practices of food procurement and convenience as experienced by consumers it is necessary to examine what 'convenience' is and how it is produced within networks of social and technical behaviours, opportunities and objects. That is, we should not accept that certain places or practices are 'convenient' but should examine the behaviours, priorities and assumptions that appear to make them so. By doing this we can disturb the assumed efficiency of the conventional food system and re-centre the logics of care, pleasure and fulfilment within our understanding of people's food practices.

Elizabeth Shove (2003) has characterized convenience as defined within a world where scheduling is increasingly 'do-it-yourself'. The move to a service-based, post-industrial economy in much of the developed world has changed the nature of time for most people. Rather than being tied to externally imposed routines and collective modes of co-ordination, we are now involved increasingly in individual modes of co-ordination which appear to offer greater flexibility but actually demand increased work in terms of planning time and co-ordinating schedules with others. As we have become a society of list makers and diary keepers so there has been a decline in institutionally timed events, a spread of the 24/7 society and more flexible regimes of work and leisure. Yet the very increases in flexibility that are offered as a solution to problems of timing actually demand more careful scheduling themselves thus fuelling the spiral. Convenience is, therefore, socially produced in a self-reinforcing spiral whereby the practices and devices we use to achieve things 'conveniently' themselves fragment our time and make scheduling ever more complex (Shove 2003).

Convenience exists in a social context and is both constructed by and constructs notions of normality. We adjust our behaviours to fit with what is presumed to be normal and by doing so make some practices convenient while others become less so. In the United Kingdom, USA and much of Europe, 'convenience' in food procurement is increasingly seen to reside in the out-of-town, or edge-of-town, supermarket or hypermarket. The convenience of these shops is based on their accessibility by car, long opening hours, and the fact that they sell 'everything' under one roof, thus doing away with the need to visit separate specialist stores for meat, fish, vegetables, etc., as would have happened on the traditional High Street. As they are located at some distance from most people's homes and shoppers do not just 'pop in' when passing, supermarkets are then organized to make a single weekly shop more 'convenient'. They provide larger trolleys, wider aisles, larger packs of goods and products, such as bread, that have been specially processed to last seven days. When we adjust our behaviours to fit with this logic it becomes part of normality. The extent of our adjustment – the need for a car, the scheduling of special journeys and the purchase of larger fridges and freezers to store a week's worth of food – all become 'normal' and thus invisible (Shove and Southerton 2000). Alternative versions of convenience are also made invisible by these practices; we adjust so much to one way of doing things, and organize our lives to make that convenient, that other ways of accessing food are not often considered. In addition the social nature of normality – the fact that this way of getting food is seen as normal within wider society – means that structures: laws, planning guidelines, transport routes, employment schemes and many others, are put in place which support this way of shopping and undermine others (Simms 2007; Soper 2007b).

'Convenience' is also represented by processed and pre-prepared foods that supermarkets sell in large quantities and that can be put in a microwave, saucepan or oven and be ready to eat with the least amount of effort. These foods are often high in saturated fat, salt and sugar, can be much more expensive than raw ingredients and have more detrimental environmental effects through their use of packaging, inputs from the petrochemical industry and transport. However, they can also fit with the scheduling and time constraint problems that modern life creates. As Michelle Harrison states: 'It doesn't matter how much information you have, if you come home from work and you have to prepare a meal for three children. The provision of food on the table is more defined by people's energy and time than it is by many other things in their food cultures' (2007: 5). 'Convenience' foods have been designed and processed specifically to reduce the time and effort needed to prepare them and are marketed to people on this basis. However, there are many less processed, or more traditional, foods that are also quick and easy to prepare – cheese, eggs and fruit, for example – but these are neither celebrated by advertisers nor derided by commentators as 'convenience' foods. What is seen as convenient is not necessarily that which is quickest or easiest to use, but may often be that which has been produced and marketed specifically as 'convenient'.

Something is only convenient if it meets one's needs or fulfils the purpose that it has. Convenience means something more than being easy to get to by car or being suitable for the microwave. By looking in detail at how people procure food, select items, plan meals and learn new skills we examine how food has many purposes other than just delivering sustenance to a hungry body. Food is part of people's relationships with their families, friends, local communities and natural environment. It is a source of pleasure, fulfilment and learning. It is a focus for nostalgia about childhood and for worries about the future. Food from 'alternative' schemes can often meet people's desires to care about people and the planet much more effectively than food from supermarkets. It is more 'convenient', in these senses, in that it fits their understandings of their lives and their place in the world.

SHOPPING FOR FOOD

Shopping is a social activity that can be suffused with love and care, but it can also be stressful, a source of anxiety, tension and conflict. The choices we make about where to shop and what to buy position us in relationships with distant others and familiar loved ones. Our research shows that food shopping is not a simple process, even when it is not consciously examined. Consumers think carefully about their purchases and consume within personal ethical and practical frameworks that can appear to be inconvenient or contradictory but have a logic that is driven by complex webs of commitment, knowledge, time-constraint and technology (cf. Jackson et al. 2006).

All of the consumers we worked with accessed food from a number of sources. The amount purchased from 'alternative' schemes varied week to week, changed with the seasons and depended on circumstances. For the interviewees who were able to estimate, 10–25 per cent of their regular shop, be this weekly, fortnightly or monthly, was from the case study scheme. For almost all households, other sources of food included supermarkets at least sometimes; but also a very wide variety of local shops, markets, specialist retailers and Internet schemes. These sources were selected for an equally wide variety of reasons. This could be because of their location – near home or work, on a regular route or because they were out of the way and presented the chance for an 'outing'; or because they sold 'everything' or precisely because they specialized in just one type of food – cheese or fish for example. It could be because they were seen as being good value or good quality though expensive, because the staff were seen as friendly and/or knowledgeable or because the other customers were considered to be 'nice'. Most importantly consumers could choose one shop for one of these reasons and another for a very different or seemingly contradictory one. The shops fitted into their routines and lifestyles in different ways, and different relationships and priorities made their choices rational (cf. Gregson et al. 2002; Jackson et al. 2006).

For example, many of our participants used an 'alternative' food scheme for obtaining one type of food (normally good quality organic vegetables and/or meat) but used the cheapest supermarket for other items. One Farrington's customer, Victoria, explained the logic of her shopping practices:

> Well, I like to use [supermarket] for what I call groceries so it's sort of packets and jars, things like washing powder and that sort of thing. But we buy fruit and veg and cheese and things from here [Farrington's], and eggs, and a few other things. And we buy bread and cheese from the Fine Cheese Company in Bath and I buy fish from the fish shop in Bath and I buy meat from the Real Meat Company ... I suppose it probably does [take longer] although, because I've never done it the other way, I didn't really think about [it]. I've been buying from these shops in Bath for ten years so, you know, we used to live in Bath and so I've never got in to the habit of doing, just doing [supermarket]. And also it takes quite a long time to go round [supermarket] and, I mean, if I've, before I used to start working online, to get the stuff that I now order online, it would take more than an hour and so it's not, you know, that [much] quicker.

John, a Moorland customer explained that he found shopping at a number of outlets, cheaper, easier and more enjoyable:

> John: I find it cheaper than the supermarket ... Yeah absolutely.
> Interviewer: So, because that's one of the sort of criticisms, or people perceive it as being a compromise. To shop in these different places is going to take a long time and also the expense, but you don't find that at all?
> John: No I don't think that at all I think it's more of an enjoyable experience shopping in different places, meeting different people, talking to them about their different products and you know they're experts in their fields, they know their meat or their veg or whatever.

As these quotes reveal, there are many factors which influence how people shop and how they choose the sources of each of their food items. For Victoria, habit and familiarity are important but so are notions of convenience that reject a weekly shop – either online or in the store – as being too time consuming and John shows that shopping from a range of outlets can be cheap and enjoyable. Other participants made similar points. Many found large supermarkets oppressive or disorientating and would avoid them whenever possible. Some felt guilty for shopping there but had resigned themselves to the inevitability of supermarket supremacy: 'we don't like supermarkets but we have to use them, we have no choice' (Farrington's customer).

Consumers often adopted particular strategies when shopping at super-markets, such as only buying branded goods, only buying organic or only buying store cupboard goods. Some people deliberately used the smallest supermarket they could get to, both because this was quicker than walking around a large one and because they found it less confusing (cf. Jackson et al. 2006). Many reported dislike of supermarkets because of their environmental impacts, their effects on small shops, their excessive power within the food system and the nature of the food products sold in them. Supermarkets could also be rejected because the experience of using them was just plain unpleasant, as one Bristol farmers' market customer commented:

> I hated doing it [going to a supermarket], especially with a small child in tow. I just thought 'Why am I spending 70 odd pounds a week here when I could be going and getting something locally that's only round the corner from me.' I'm at work on a Wednesday [the day of the market] So it's like five minutes' walk for me. I can go there; I can buy really nice fruit and veg, nice meat, and um and it's from the local community I feel rather than it's from a great big supermarket.

This quote also highlights that when we shop we are not just meeting our need for food or a desire for good food, but also fulfilling ethical goals such as supporting the local community (cf. Enticott 2003a; 2003b). Other consumers commented that shopping from 'alternative' sources was a positively enjoyable experience. As the quotes below reveal, part of that pleasure comes from shopping in ways that are considered ethical or that allow consumers to 'do the right thing' (as outlined in Chapter 5).

> Well, because of the ethical things, that's going to sound very vague. But because of the ethical things and local shopping and ... well it's a nice experience and it's not like ... [the supermarket] is just not a pleasant experience (Laura, a Farrington's customer).

> Well I think the beauty of farmers' market is that it makes it ... it's not a chore. It's actually this is the whole, I think, reason why I'm so enthusiastic about that. [The] very thing I was saying at the beginning, like going there originally for the reason that it was, on paper, the right thing to do. In my mind the right thing to do. (John, a Moorland customer)

Mr and Mrs Staunton illustrate in Box 6.1 the complex ways in which shopping practices develop and show that what it means for shopping to be 'convenient' is not simple. Convenience is not just about numbers of car parking spaces or being able to buy everything under one roof. It can also be about the rhythm of routines and fitting in with multipurpose journeys as well as speed and the ease of finding the items that you do want within an ethical framework that is acceptable.

Box 6.1 MR AND MRS STAUNTON

Mr and Mrs Staunton, a couple in their sixties, live in Sandwell in the urban West Midlands. They are members of the Salop Drive bag scheme. Mrs Staunton works part-time, every morning, a couple of miles from their home. Mr Staunton is unable to work due to ill health. They have evolved a routine of shopping for food almost every day which suits their lifestyle and preferences. Mrs Staunton buys food for their evening meal on her way home from work. She particularly dislikes large supermarkets as she finds them too packed with people and she hates waiting in queues. She finds 'popping in' regularly to small shops to be much less hassle. Once a month, the couple go to their local farmers' market together, and buy homemade pies from a particular stall. The visit to the farmers' market is a pleasure rather than a chore with the added benefit that they come home with food that they both enjoy but would not make themselves.

Becoming involved in the Salop Drive scheme has made a difference to both their lives but particularly to Mr Staunton. Working at the market garden is his main activity and he goes there regularly both to tend his own plot and to help with the main section of the garden. He knows most of the people at the garden and describes it as having a sense of community. Getting food from the bag and the allotment has made a difference to their diet too, as they eat more vegetables now and have discovered new things. It has also changed how they cook; they are more adventurous and cook more meals from scratch. Mr Staunton now cooks more meals himself too, spurred by the recipe suggestions that come in the bag and his enthusiasm for the produce that comes from both his plot and the market garden as a whole.

Shopping from 'alternative' sources not only offered our interviewees a source of food, it provided opportunities to encounter like-minded shoppers and friends. Whether this is any different to supermarkets or other outlets is not clear but, considering the restricted opening times of the farmers' market or the collection time and organization of the EarthShare box and workshifts, it is highly likely that these schemes fostered these kinds of relationships more than conventional sources. Farrington's customers appeared to treat a visit to the farm shop as a social event, in part because of the café, where they could arrange to meet friends for lunch. EarthShare is organized in such a way that it particularly seems to bring people together and foster friendships: some members took it in turns to pick up the box from the collection point; others met at the collection point or shared workshifts on the farm. Many distributed surplus vegetables to friends and relations. A number of our interviewees clearly saw the project as a key actor in the local community, one describing it as 'a family of almost a thousand people'. Finding out that someone else was a member of EarthShare could also make new friendships possible as Ruth illustrated:

> … I met this guy, he was working at the Council, um, really lovely chap, but I didn't know him. I don't know what he's about. But I bumped into him collecting his box and, yeah, it was great, and suddenly there was this camaraderie and I saw him in a different light. Suddenly it's like, God! I've never been with that kind of guy.

For these consumers shopping from 'alternative' food schemes had purposes far beyond just accessing food. The schemes provide opportunities to socialize with existing friends and to meet new people.

Growing, Gathering and Sharing Food

As well as shopping for food from both 'conventional' and 'alternative' outlets, the consumers we worked with also accessed food by growing it for themselves, gathering it from the wild or exchanging it with friends and family. These methods of food provisioning were often linked to explicit philosophical positions about respect for the natural environment and care for loved ones.

Growing food was a popular activity among most of our interviewees. For many, self-provisioning was closely related to their participation in an 'alternative' food scheme. Experience of growing food could be a motivation for finding similar produce, or produce grown with a similar philosophy, when consumers could not provide for themselves. Alternatively, closer contact with food producers through schemes could be the inspiration to try growing food at home, even if this was just herbs on a window sill.

For participants in the Salop Drive and EarthShare schemes, growing food is an element of membership. EarthShare subscribers have to do three workshifts a year – unless they opt out of it by paying a higher subscription fee – and at Salop Drive members can both help on the main market garden and/or have their own allotment plots at the site. Active involvement in food growing through a scheme could be a source of fulfilment and a way to connect with like-minded people. For Ruth and Caroline, for example, who took part in the EarthShare workshifts, the toil on the soil provided a further source of pleasure, a real sense of achievement, which the other food sources could not grant, as their comments show:

> And also the day that I went and we picked the carrots and some broccoli ... after that day, I really felt the sense of kind of achievement when it were all packed and in the van and off it went and you really felt like you'd done some good. And just to sort of experience that again, of feeling that you've done a hard day's work, and they work really hard, no slacking [laughs].

> sometimes you go [to do workshifts] and it's a wonderful day and there's loads of people there and it's sort of really a bit of a jolly party except you have to do a little bit of work. But you know, you enjoy a bit of a chat you know there are ladies with their children around, and the children go and play in the mud and that's great.

At Salop Drive involvement in growing food can be a source of pleasure and social contacts too. As Box 6.1 shows, Mr Staunton's plot at the market garden has been important to him since he retired on grounds of ill health. He knows the other people involved in the scheme and can share knowledge and information with them. Growing food within the context of an organized scheme can have the multiple benefits of providing social contacts and a sense of community as well as fresh, healthy food.

Participants from all the case study schemes grew fruit or vegetables in their own gardens or in an allotment. Some of the vegetable growers were continuing a tradition carried out by preceding generations, be they parents or grandparents. Coming from a family where food had always been grown provided our participants with the knowledge and confidence to try growing food themselves and it could shape their tastes as one of the Salop Drive members said:

> [M]y dad always had an allotment ... So we've always had a certain amount of fresh veg which spoils you.

Whereas often the concept of 'spoiling' is associated with unhealthy foods, such as cakes or chocolate, this interviewee sees having access to fresh and tasty food as a child as having made her less tolerant of the lower quality foods that might be available in shops.

The scale of production varied among the households that grew their own food, but for most the garden provided some seasonal low-cost food. Julia (EarthShare) reflected on the convenience of having home-grown food in the garden and the pleasure that sourcing food this way can bring.

> I do enjoy going down and picking [vegetables] and it's just nice to have it fresh from the garden to the table as well. I mean, one place I used to live was out in the wilds and it was quite a long way to go to the shops, and [when] you're cooking for a lot of people, it was just lovely to be able to think 'Right, what am I going to cook today?', and you'd just go out into the allotment area and just think, that was your meal, and you sort of brought it back.

Growing food, perhaps the most labour-intensive way of procuring it of all, is seen by these consumers as convenient and enjoyable. Growing food ensures a supply that is as fresh as possible and often just outside the back door. Rather than a chore or a burden, these consumers portray both the act of growing food and the chance to eat home-grown food as a treat or indulgence.

All the households that grew fruit and vegetables expressed a desire to have fresh, good tasting produce, but some households also thought about growing organically and viewed food production as part of their attempt to live in a more sustainable or self-sufficient fashion. Growing food was also seen by at least some of our interviewees as spiritually fulfilling, giving them a closer connection to the natural world (see Box 6.2). Allotments were also seen as giving an escape from urban life where, as Kathleen (Moorland) put it 'we're all living on top of each other' and offering a 'nice lifestyle' in the open air and as part of a caring community. As Jon (Waterland) explained:

> It's the community that impresses me about it that it's really lovely how people help each other and look after each other's interests and look after each other's plots when, when you know when they're away and this kind of thing, I really like it.

While getting fresh local food from a box scheme, farm shop or CSA could be an inspiration to budding gardeners, there were also households which found that growing their own food made participation in a scheme less logical. For them, food from the garden or from an allotment site provided the family with enough food to last the summer months and so they would cut back on food from other sources:

Box 6.2 RUTH

Ruth is a subscriber to EarthShare who lives in a small village twelve miles from Elgin. She is in her forties, and is unemployed but while searching for jobs she does voluntary work with children and young people. During the past year she has cleared and planted a vegetable patch in her garden and she refers to it as 'a labour of love.' Despite her new vegetable garden, Ruth didn't think it would affect her EarthShare subscription, at least not immediately. The unfavourable weather conditions and lack of proper shelter for seedlings meant that Ruth could expect to lose part of her crop in the forthcoming year too. Distributing any surplus produce from the EarthShare box to friends and relatives helped Ruth make a success of her subscription, as she didn't like the idea of discarding vegetables she couldn't eat herself. She also exchanged home grown food, and food she had gathered from the wild with friends and made chutney to give away as presents. She was happy to keep growing her own food as well as subscribing to EarthShare as it gave her a sense of fulfilment and a greater connection to nature.

> We stopped it [delivery of a box] about the summer ... I think I stopped it some time beginning of August, and we've been getting it again since last Friday and the reason why we stopped it had nothing to do with quality, it we just that we had our own crop in the garden.

While Ruth (Box 6.2) started growing her own vegetables after becoming an EarthShare member, for others joining a scheme had the opposite effect and enabled them to reduce the amount of vegetables they were growing, freeing up time for other activities. In Julia's household, for example, subscribing to EarthShare had meant that they could invest more time in rearing their own animals for meat, sausages and eggs.

Some of our interviewees also engaged in gathering seasonal food from the wild (including one that collected road kill). These forms of food procurement were usually discussed by interviewees in terms of the pleasure that comes from finding things, and the quality of food that could be gathered. Collecting blackberries, chestnuts, wild mushrooms or elderflowers, for example, was also linked with other pleasurable outdoor pursuits such as walks in the country. This leisurely approach to food procurement is in stark contrast to the fastest possible dash around a supermarket and indicates yet another way in which food fits into routines and can be convenient and enjoyable without being 'quick'. Of course, these activities are easier for those who do not live in big urban areas, but even there these practices are not precluded.

Gathering wild food could also provide opportunities for gaining knowledge about a local area, for trying new recipes or for building relationships and caring for others. For example, Ian, one of the EarthShare subscribers ran workshops for other members to teach them about the wild harvest and to share his knowledge of the local environment. For other interviewees the collection of wild berries could be linked with the making of jams and preserves, which were consumed over the winter and/or given as gifts to family and friends.

Sharing food in this way was important to many of the consumers we talked to, and the harvesting of fruit and vegetables from the garden or allotment could also be a time for giving gifts. For some of our interviewees joining a scheme with a vegetable box or bag had also been an impetus to engage in food exchange with friends or family. Bag/box recipients were generally unhappy to waste any surplus food but as the box/bag sometimes delivered more food than they could eat themselves people would give food to friends. This might be as raw ingredients, in the form of prepared foods such as conserves, or by deliberately inviting friends to eat when they had a surplus. Passing on and exchanging food in this way enhances relationships that are built on care and reciprocity. The valuing of food when it is shared rather than wasted also expresses care for the wider environment and respect for the producers of the food (see Figure 6.1).

Box/bag schemes and CSA encourage sharing between friends because the amount delivered is fixed (normally calculated as suitable for two people or a family). A number of our interviewees shared their bag or box with a friend or had been introduced to a scheme by sharing with friends and had gone on to get their own bag or box. Sharing food can be a way to influence friends or family members who might have different philosophies or priorities when sourcing their food but it can also highlight differences and sometimes needs to be handled with care as Ruth illustrated:

> Although they have taken some cauliflower [EarthShare produce] because it's so huge, um this week from me, and my dad said 'oh that's, doesn't look like the kind of cauliflower we get'. It's like, but I don't mention organic to him because he's very, you know, mention the wrong kind of words and …

When her parents reciprocated in food exchange they bought her frozen convenience food or meals and drinks that she would have rather gone without and Ruth felt this undermined her chosen lifestyle and food choices (see also Box 6.2).

Figure 6.1 Consumers sharing EarthShare produce: 'reconnection' and pleasure. Photo courtesy of Barbara Taylor.

Food exchange appeared to be most important in the households that produced their own food and with relatives and friends who were also interested in food provenance and cooking. For example, for Julia (EarthShare), giving food to friends and family was part of their way of life and an important way in which care was expressed. From the harvest of fruit in their garden, she made jams and chutneys and other preserves, which she gave out in particular at Christmas time. They also gave close family and friends some of the sausages that her husband prepared. Food thus played a very important part in sustaining friendships and making new ones.

Although regular entertaining – another form of food exchange or food gift – was not on the agenda of all our informants, some hosted meals regularly and in several instances it was reciprocal in nature. Much of this was informal and sometimes involved taking surplus from a box or garden to a friend's house or inviting people to share. Sharing foods when entertaining friends and celebratory meals for family were the time for special effort and special ingredients, selecting foods carefully and putting effort into their preparation to express appreciation of and love for people who are cared about. However, the selection of special foods for important meals could mean changing or relaxing the normal rules that are used for shopping and buying out of season or exotic fruits. For example, Kathleen (Moorland) who usually steered clear of supermarkets would shop in one if she needed to produce a special meal and lacked an ingredient:

> It depends what it was and it depends what occasion. If I was like cooking dinner for lots of people and we needed tomatoes then I'd (get) tomatoes [in a supermarket] but I'd choose organic ones or you know ones that looked nice rather than just the bog standard ones.

Kathleen wanted to make sure that her guests enjoyed their meal, and for their sake she was happy to purchase ingredients she normally did not buy and to alter her rules regarding food. This raises the issue that caring is complicated and paradoxical. By choosing special foods to express care for friends and family, consumers may be relaxing rules they have established for themselves to care about their community or environment (if only buying local or organic food).

Detailed work with consumers reveals that the procurement of food needs to be understood within a context of practices, technologies, relationships and priorities. Diverse, and seemingly time-consuming, practices can become convenient when they meet consumers' needs, give them pleasure and allow them to care for the people, places and things that they feel responsible for. By using the concept of convenience to examine how consumers engage with 'alternative' food schemes we have highlighted the multifaceted logics that are used when accessing food. By doing this we have raised questions both about what forms of food procurement are convenient and what it is that make them so. We move now to look at activities surrounding the cooking and eating of food and use the concept of 'choice' to examine consumers' practices.

RETHINKING FOOD CHOICE

As discussed in Chapters 1 and 5, food choice is a complex issue and notoriously hard to study. However, the notion of 'choice' has become a mantra within food retailing, as well as being an important topic in academic debates around eating. Huge supermarkets with thousands of product lines all under one roof appear to offer the ultimate in choice for food consumers. A vegetable box scheme or CSA that predetermines which foods you will get and how much you will get of them appears to be the opposite. And a small stall in a farmers' market selling produce from a single source is hardly any different. But choice is not a simple thing and supermarkets only offer us one version of it (see Soper 2007b). As Simms argues 'supermarkets take away our choices about where and how to shop, by foreclosing on the possibility of local variety and by only stocking products that fit their fast-turnover model or come from suppliers prepared to accept their terms' (2007: 13). A small farm shop may stock more varieties of potato or apple in season than the largest superstore and a farmers' market stall may offer greater choice over cuts of meat and size of portions available. This section traces the ways in which our research participants chose food and how their choices interplayed with their daily practices, routines and relationships. This discussion is important because the lack of choice inherent in some 'alternative' food schemes (box/bag and CSA) may put some potential members off and the practicalities of accessing food this way need to be understood. Our findings show that lack of choice need not be problematic, that choice is not always welcome and that choice and variety in a diet are far from being the same thing.

Food Choices and Eating Patterns

The food schemes we worked with provided varying levels of choice in the foods they offered consumers. EarthShare allows subscribers to select either a large or small box, but after they have made that decision everyone gets exactly the same in their box each week. The only opportunity to vary the contents is by donating foods to, or taking things from, a 'gift box' which is left at each of the pick-up points. EarthShare also gives subscribers their 'fair share' in terms of quantity, so the volume of food a member receives can vary through the seasons – a factor that can have quite an impact on how people use produce from the scheme. Waterland allows customers to express a small number of preferences and buys in produce to keep variety up if necessary, thereby guaranteeing a consistent amount of food and the same number of items in the box throughout the year. Salop Drive does not offer members any choice officially but sometimes the delivery drivers will facilitate informal swaps of produce so people get more of what they like best. 'Adopt a sheep' allows parents to opt for vegetarian or non-vegetarian packages (includes salami) if they are adopting online, but parents who visit the farm can select goods from their shop (including cheeses, salamis, olive oil and wool products) to suit their tastes. Moorland's shop and stall at Bristol farmers' market offers an impressive range of cuts of meat and Farrington's farm shop stocks over 4,000 food products.

Although consumers access food from other sources as well, obtaining produce from 'alternative' schemes can greatly affect peoples' diets because of the ways in which foods are thought about and meals planned. Our research suggests that accessing food through these schemes encourages consumers to think about food in different ways, often to cook more, to eat more fruit and vegetables and to eat in more health-conscious ways.

Box or bag schemes, by nature, restrict the choice of foodstuffs provided to the subscribers. Instead of perceiving this as an impediment, the consumers in our study generally viewed it positively. Rather than seeing their box as foreclosing choices they viewed it as 'a surprise' or 'fun' and embraced the possibilities that getting food in this way offered. Choice in this case is not simple nor necessarily welcome. Vegetable boxes/bags were seen as convenient precisely because the items were pre-selected and delivered to the doorstep, or collected from the pick-up point. As Mrs Staunton (Salop Drive) put it:

> [I]t's quite good, plus the convenience, if you think about it, I mean you could be walking up and down Bearwood high street or West Bromwich thinking 'what am I going to get?'

She went on to comment:

> OK, you haven't really got a choice but you … you haven't got a choice but you get a choice of vegetables.

Thereby neatly revealing the difference between 'choice' in terms of the ability to select and 'choice' in terms of variety. Almost everyone we spoke to commented that accessing food through the scheme that they used meant trying new foods, new varieties of common foods and eating a wider variety of food (particularly fruit and vegetables). The Stauntons had been introduced to kohlrabi, pumpkin and callaloo through the Salop Drive bag, for example. Therefore, a reduction in choice, in terms of control over what could be selected, had in almost all cases increased the variety of foods consumed. Rather than hurrying down a supermarket aisle with a list of tried and tested ingredients, using an 'alternative' outlet meant that consumers were introduced to new foods regularly. A number of consumers had also used recipes that had been put in boxes to try new foods or to cook familiar foods in new ways. These consumers relied on information and support from producers (and other box scheme members who wrote recipes) to help them make a success of eating this way. Introducing consumers to new foods and ways of eating happens most obviously in box/bag schemes but is also true of farmers' markets and Farrington's farm shop. At Farrington's, while some produce is brought in, their own vegetables are prominently and attractively displayed, are seasonal and include unusual varieties, thereby tempting consumers to try new things. And, customers at the Moorland farmers' market stall would suggest new cuts to each other as well as getting advice from the producer, and broaden their experiences in that way.

Several people reported that they used the farm shop or farmers' market to buy only what is available and in season and would not then go to the supermarket to top up on exotics or unseasonable vegetables. As Frances, a Moorland customer, commented:

> There'll be a [shopping] list because sometimes I forget what I've bought before so I have to look in the fridge to see what I've got. But the purchases will be driven by what's there [at the farmers' market].

By shopping in this way, consumers are opting-out of choice and putting other priorities (for local or seasonal food, good relationships with producers, care for the self, others or the environment) above the ability to access whatever they want whenever they want it. However, this brought its own rewards, as one Waterland customer explained:

> I like being given something, I like the surprise of seeing what we've got this week, you know, because I know things change through the seasons. If I had to choose certain things it's a little bit of extra stress each week thinking 'Oh I've got to choose that' or whatever, but it would take some of the fun out of just getting something and I do like the idea of seasonal foods, things changing and not being able to get strawberries outside of say three or four weeks in the summer, you know. That's ... that makes me ... my enjoyment of strawberries all the better because I know I've only got a short period to eat them in, and the other thing is you know when you do eat them that they generally they've got a taste ...

This sentiment was echoed by Julie an EarthShare member:

> I was introduced to a lot of vegetables I'd never tried before, kohlrabi being one of them and Jerusalem artichoke and just various other things and I just get really excited on a Friday about [...] you think 'oh how sad', but no I just get so excited now, what is going to be in this box?

Many of our interviewees were clear about the benefits of eating seasonal food and the facets of seasonal produce that they most enjoyed, such as freshness, novelty and being able to look forward to things.

Consumers who did not pay much attention to seasonality or the origin of food were in the minority and were largely Farrington's customers, who viewed the shop as another supermarket, albeit a smaller and nicer one. However, even though the farm shop was clearly smaller in size than conventional supermarkets, in some instances it was able to provide a greater choice of foods. Liz (Farrington's) commended the large variety of meat products:

> What I do find with [supermarket] is there's not a lot of choice ... in their meat, they do have meat there but there's not a great deal of choice either, to be honest. We do have choice at Farrington's of different pork, even pork chops, you know, there's pork rib chops, there's chump chops, there's, so you've got a different choice. The same with the joints, with the pork or the lamb, you have the choice how you want to buy it. So that's a positive thing on the Farrington's side you do have a choice of how you want to buy it.

Having a specialist butcher on site with high quality fresh and frozen meat produce meant that Farrington's had been able to attract a number of customers who were normally quite happy to shop in supermarkets. Their wide range of convenience foods appealed to these consumers too. The farm shop stocks things such as preserves and chutneys, wholesome snacks, homemade ready-meals, as well as a self-service section of frozen berries and vegetable mixtures which customers can buy in the quantities they like.

Using 'alternative' sources of food gives consumers a new attitude towards choice. Rather than prioritizing access to the ranges of standardized foods that large supermarkets can offer, these consumers can enjoy the wide benefits that smaller food schemes give them. As Simms argues:

> [Supermarkets] give us choice paralysis, or choice fatigue. We get lost in aisles of endless jars, tins and ready meals – food remotely mass-produced and stripped of cultural context. All of this is for sale in big, impersonal, self interested supermarkets that have no concept of limits. In response, we understandably seek more authenticity, a sense of place, connection and human scale. (2007: 13)

Meal Planning and Cooking

As well as increasing the range of foods that people ate, we also found that having less choice about the foods available could mean expanding one's cooking repertoire. Box/bag schemes were frequently associated with the development of new knowledge about foods and new cooking skills. Accessing food in new and different ways could have an important effect on how people planned meals. Food from schemes, particularly fresh food, normally had to be eaten in a particular order so the most perishable items were not wasted. Subscribers to bag/box schemes therefore planned meals around the vegetables in the box, as an EarthShare member put it:

> I think it makes you think more because, prior to the box scheme if you were shopping you would have what ever you were having for your meal, 'oh we'll have that and that' ... but then it was like reversed, it was 'this is what you've got what are you going to do with it?' and so you look at it from a different angle. The veg is the important part of the meal now and you think 'well what can I have with the veg, what will go with this?'

Similarly customers of the farmers' market and farm shop were influenced by the availability of foodstuffs and special offers. For example, John explained that the whole weekly repertoire of dishes was clearly affected by the produce at the Bristol farmers' market:

> John: ... We usually have fish twice a week.
> Interviewer: On the day you've been to the farmers' market?
> John: And the day after. Yes. Two days. And then we get usually a big joint for the weekend which lasts us three days usually. And then we might have a couple of veggie meals ... We do try and keep things fresh and use things fresh and when it comes to what we've bought from the market, trying to schedule the way you use the vegetables so that the things that go off most quickly, say like a carrot you can keep in the fridge for a week or so and it's you know, take it out and don't really notice any difference from when you bought it, but it's some other things like purple sprouting broccoli, that quite quickly loses its appeal.

Mrs Staunton explained that she used up most of the vegetables from the Salop Drive bag as part of the Sunday dinner, and usually cooked a pot of soup with anything left over, which her husband heated up during the week for lunch. This was a new practice they had developed since they had started subscribing to the scheme. The idea of making a soup had been influenced by one of the recipes that were occasionally included in the vegetable bag. Mr Staunton had also started cooking after seeing a recipe in their bag for a curry which he now makes regularly when the ingredients for it are included. The contents of the bag have therefore driven both a change in eating patterns and, sometimes, in the gendered division of labour in the Staunton household.

By providing seasonal ingredients and/or the same ingredients week after week, and through the inclusion of recipes, weekly box/bag schemes appeared to increase the repertoire of dishes regularly prepared in the households we worked with. To eat seasonally successfully, people tended to have to experiment and try new recipes, and make an effort to find a variety of ways to prepare the same ingredient. Some consumers were also prepared to make up their own variations of classic dishes. For example a Waterland consumer explained:

> We had quite a lot of baby beets and [husband] had to work out what's he going to do with the beetroot, so we had, you know that toad in the hole ... we had beet in the hole.

While our interviewees generally liked experimenting with familiar ingredients, there were limits to what people were prepared to try. While two Waterland customers who had been overwhelmed with cucumber had discovered a recipe for cucumber soup that they described as delicious, and had used up lettuce in a lettuce risotto, Ruth (EarthShare) was having more trouble with her surplus of lettuce:

> Well with the lettuce, you know, I am now going 'oh no, I really don't want [more]' but, you know, it's there so I'll use it ... There are recipes for lettuce soup. But I just don't fancy it. I mean, you know, I should just use a lettuce, experiment, see what it's like and I might think ... I don't know, it just always sounded 'yuk'.

Our research suggests that accessing food through 'alternative' schemes does not replace food from more conventional sources in a simple way. It encourages people to think about food in new ways, to value food more highly and to gain skills and knowledge, often from scheme producers and other consumers, in order to make the process successful. One respondent suggested that the fulfilment that comes from supporting a local business could help overcome the problem of the extra effort needed to prepare fresh produce:

> *Respondent*: I mean, some evenings, yes, it can be a bit of a pain you know. You're home from work late, you're tired, but, if you are making a soup and you know the vegetables actually taste like vegetables.
> *Interviewer*: Do you like the fact then, I mean is local important to you?
> *Respondent*: Yes, very, yeah, ... It's about supporting your local community.

The qualities of food – both aspects such as taste and the meanings that it carries such as commitment to community – shape how foods will be treated; the care with which they will be cooked, whether they will be thoughtlessly wasted or whether they will be shared, lovingly, with others. While some of these qualities, such as taste, may be inherent to the food, other qualities are socially constructed and brought to foods by consumers because of their priorities and the relationships that they have with producers and others. Again this highlights the complexity of food choices and the contingent nature of convenience. Some foods are worth more effort, not just because of how they taste but because of the people and places that they come from.

Eating a meal with others, or commensality, signifies unity and sharing in most cultural contexts (Sobal and Nelson 2003). Much of the recent research on food habits and eating patterns has arisen from the concern about the fate of meals (Murcott 1997, Roos and Prättälä 1997, Kjaernes 2001; Moisio et al. 2004), especially *family meals* (Murcott 1997; Holm 2001) and, even when they do take place, research shows that organizing a shared family meal is not always straightforward and can be a source of tension and/or conflict (Charles and Kerr 1988; Valentine 1999). Living and eating as a family can mean negotiating priorities and tastes. Family members can express their care for each other by responding to preferences and taking trouble to provide foods that others liked. Negotiating meals within families can be difficult but was seen by many of our respondents as an important part of family life, as illustrated in Box 6.3.

Preparing meals around the tastes of family members reflects a sense of care in knowing and accommodating others' tastes (cf. Murcott 1983; DeVault 1991). However, this was not a simple capitulation to the priorities of others but rather an evolving negotiation. For some couples, tastes had developed together over time and were similar to each other, while in other households the cook's preferences dominated, so responsibility for providing meals could be a source of power or control as well as a pleasure or a burden. Thinking about the tastes and needs of others also provides a lens through which to view issues of choice. The constraints that come from catering to other people can limit choices that are available but also can be a reason to try new foods and to increase variety in a diet. By prioritizing the choices of other people over their own, consumers show that their desire to care is greater than their desire for ultimate choice.

Eating good food was important to all our interviewees, although exactly what good food was, or how much effort should be put into providing it was not necessarily something they would have agreed upon. Accessing food

---

Box 6.3 THE ROBINSON FAMILY

The Robinsons are a couple in their mid forties with four children aged eleven to twenty. They live in a former mining village south of Bath and shop at Farrington's regularly. Mr and Mrs Robinson run a business together and are now quite well off and able to spend much more on food than in the past. In the Robinson household sitting down for the evening meal together is the norm but family members do not always eat the same food. As one of the children is a vegetarian and another is very choosy about food, convenience foods enabled the family to have individualized eating habits. Mrs Robinson has devised various strategies to avoid using ready-meals for the whole family – either cooking the night before if she knew they were going to be busy or using homemade food from the freezer – yet for her vegetarian child, Mrs Robinson usually heats up a vegetarian ready-made meal or some other convenience food frequently bought from Farrington's. For the sake of family unity, Mrs Robinson would sometimes prepare vegetarian food from scratch. Cooking and eating as a family group was explicitly seen by the Robinsons as part of the socialization of children, and Mrs Robinson thought that routines around food preparation and eating were an important part of family life and preparation for the future.

---

from 'alternative' sources was both a cause and an effect of their commitment to eating well. For some consumers, 'alternative' schemes had been sought out deliberately because of the perceived quality or variety of their produce. For others, the food they got from the schemes had been an inspiration to cook more, or to eat more adventurously. For nearly everyone we spoke to, these processes went hand in hand with membership of the schemes providing knowledge and inspiration that then affected attitudes to food and eating in general. This could be through introducing them to unusual foods or new recipes or just by enabling them and encouraging them to eat more healthfully.

SUMMARIZING REMARKS: RECONNECTED CONSUMERS

The consumers we worked with are clearly revealed in this chapter to be knowledgeable, thoughtful and caring on many levels. They are far from the model of the alienated, economic rationalizer searching out cheap, convenient food and knowing little of the implications. Rather they are rational on their own terms, participating in practices that have an emotional, or moral, logic as well as an economic one. 'Reconnection' with the production of their food has had wide-ranging implications for most of these consumers. Involvement in these schemes went beyond relationships with individuals and, for some participants, encompassed much broader notions of community, education and support for a way of life they believed in. Participation in the 'alternative' food sector allowed for and encouraged practices that embraced caring at many levels.

Detailed analysis of 'alternative' consumption practices reveals how problematic the 'common-sense' notions of choice and convenience that are normally associated with the food system can be. Our analysis shows these concepts can only be understood within consumers' wider practices of everyday life and their ethical frameworks. 'Alternative' food schemes may appear to be limited in the choice of foods they offer, or inconvenient and time consuming in their access arrangements, but clearly, for some consumers at least, they meet needs for good food, valued relationships, sense of community, and care for the wider environment in a way no large food retailer can. This chapter, and these consumers, show the pleasures that are possible from doing things differently, the practical ways that different forms of food procurement can fit into busy lives, and the simple contentment of eating food that you like from sources that you care about.

CHAPTER 7

Conclusions: 'Reconnection' through Care

INTRODUCTION

> ... if you can do a little thing in some little way that does help either the environment or your community then you know ... you're making a small contribution. It doesn't mean you're going to change the world or social policy in general, but your little bit, and if a lot of people adopted that attitude then social policy and community welfare *would* change ... (Helen, Waterland consumer; office worker, interviewed in 2005)

In this book, we have argued that diverse 'alternative' food schemes, businesses or initiatives have the potential to 'reconnect' producers, consumers and food. This 'reconnection' can foster a recognition of the value of 'good' food, in terms of health, social justice and the environment, and it can meet people's desires to care for both human and non-human, and close and distant 'others'. While the socio-economic and environmental problems with the industrial food system are increasingly high profile, and anxieties about food are common (see Chapter 1), there is also growing evidence in support of the social, economic and environmental benefits of 'alternative' food supply arrangements. The New Economics Foundation (2001), for example, conducted research which found that every £10 spent with a local food initiative like a box scheme was worth £25 to the local area; but the same amount spent in a supermarket was only worth £14. Pretty and colleagues (2005) have calculated that if the average food basket were all organic, subsidies were all used for agri-environmental purposes, and food was locally sourced or predominantly transported by rail and then brought home by walking/cycling/bus/home delivery, then each person in the United Kingdom could be saved around £2.50 per week. There is also evidence to suggest that 'alternative' food initiatives may be able to address social issues, such as supplying food to disadvantaged minority ethnic groups and bringing diverse people together in their local area (see, for example, details of United Kingdom projects on the Food Access Network, Sustain website). In addition to the work on food poverty in the United Kingdom (Dowler et al. 2001a, 2001b), research in the USA in particular has begun to examine the ways in which food projects, notably CSAs, can address issues of social inequality (Allen 1999; Guthman, Morris and Allen 2006; Guthman 2007; Trauger 2007).

Within this context, our research represents one of the first sustained and detailed engagements with producers and consumers involved in trying to construct 'alternative', and 'better', ways of provisioning food. Over a period of three years we collected detailed qualitative data through interviews with producers and consumers, consumer workshops and an in-depth 'household' study that involved consumers in recording, discussing and photographing their food purchase and eating habits. Crucially, in listening simultaneously to producers and consumers in the same schemes, we have been able to examine how the identities, motives and practices of each are co-constituted. Thus, we have shown the ways in which producers try to make sense of consumer behaviour and make efforts not only to adapt their own practices in accordance with their understandings of consumer motives and identities, but also to influence consumer subjectivities in line with their own ethical frameworks and business requirements (Chapter 4). We have also cast light on the ways in which consumers perceive producers, often in terms of trust and respect, but also with feelings of obligation and loyalty. The material and symbolic properties of food, such as its taste, healthiness, appearance, and the way in which it has been produced and then sold to the consumer, are all important. In seeking agreement on what these properties should be, consumers and producers can be regarded as being engaged in collaborative projects to improve their own and others' worlds at different scales, including the body, home, farm, community, region, nation and international community.

In this chapter, we draw some conclusions from our encounters with producers and consumers involved in 'alternative' food endeavours. We reflect on what our empirical investigations have revealed about the nature of 'reconnection' within the context of the complex lives and daily decision-making processes of our respondents. Finally, we consider the implications of our findings for the futures of 'alternative' food schemes and the food system more widely.

CARING TO 'RECONNECT'

The people who took part in our research are actively involved in building food production and consumption arrangements which are better suited to meeting their practical needs, sustaining their lifestyles, addressing their anxieties and satisfying their daily ethical dilemmas. In other words, we have engaged with people who have found solutions, even if only partial, to the practical and ethical problems they are confronted with in the course of their daily lives.

For us, perhaps the most striking aspect of the research is the utility of the notion of care ethics for making sense of the identities, motives and practices of the respondents we listened to. As discussed in Chapter 2, the theoretical literature on care has resonated strongly with our empirical data, in which consumers and producers spoke to us about the cares that motivated them to do things differently. The different manifestations of 'reconnection' outlined in Chapter 2 relate in varied ways to an ethic of care and this enables us to make critical distinctions between them. So for example, the idea of 'reconnecting' people with nature is the most obviously related to an ethic of care because it is concerned with repairing and maintaining our world (to paraphrase Tronto 1993) so that humans and non-humans can live in it as well as possible. The 'reconnection' of people with product, process and place can also be located within an ethic of care about food, the people who produce it, and the environment. Yet it is also prone to appropriation by commercial interests who want to use the notion to market 'speciality' or regional products without embarking on any fundamental changes to the relations of production or consumption. Of the three different strands, or styles, of 'reconnection', that of 'reconnecting' producers with their market, however, appears to be most bound up with ideas about increasing profitability and enabling businesses to prosper, without necessarily paying direct attention to the needs of others, nor to ideas of maintenance and repair. Yet our research shows that while producers trying to 'reconnect' with their market may well be motivated primarily by a profit-seeking agenda, this does not rule out behaviours that are also caring. So for example, and as detailed in Chapter 4, the producers or growers in our research cared about food production, in terms of the food itself (the ways it is produced and marketed), the environmental and social conditions in which it is produced, the possibilities that certain modes of food production might contribute to ethically 'better' ecological and social relationships, and the relationships that they, as producers, have with consumers.

The consumers in our research demonstrated a great complexity of motivations and desires, which, combined with circumstances, had prompted or enabled them to engage in some form of 'reconnection'. A number of common themes emerged as being important in encouraging people either to start a scheme in the first place, or to continue using it, perhaps after starting it through chance or out of interest. These motivations can be thought of as interlocking 'cares' operating across different scales, from the home through to the local neighbourhood, and the wider community of humankind, and encompassing concerns for people, food, animals, soil and ecosystems. As detailed in Chapter 5, we identified three key sets of motives: first, care for local economies, environments and future generations; second, care for health and wholeness of self and loved others; and finally, care *about*, rather than *for* transparency and integrity in food systems, including issues relating to science and governance. The distinction between 'care for' and 'care about' is important in this last set of motivations, for it distinguishes between actions which can be, and are, taken in order to benefit others in some way, and concerns, worries or anxieties about a particular situation. We can summarize with two broad points: First, we suggest that the majority of consumers we spoke to have a care-oriented sense of self – or disposition – in that they are aware of the needs of others, human and non-human, close and distant. Second, the majority of respondents are prepared to act on this awareness, in order to repair and sustain theirs and others' life-worlds, thus fulfilling Tronto's definition.

At this point, and in order to further refine our interpretation of the nature of care expressed by the respondents in our different cases, we turn again to Tronto's work, this time in relation to the different phases of caring. Tronto (1993) identifies four analytically separate, but interconnected phases. The first is 'caring about', which involves the recognition in the first place that care is necessary. In other words, 'it involves noting the existence of a need and making an assessment that this need should be met' (Tronto 1993: 106). This recognition can occur at individual and societal levels. We have argued in this book that our respondents – both producers and consumers – have recognized the existence of needs that, in their view, should be met. These include the need for producers to make a fair and 'decent' living, the need for consumers and their families to have access to safe, fresh food, and the need for community and environmental resources to be protected, enhanced and sustained. The second phase of caring identified by Tronto is 'taking care of', whereby responsibility is assumed for the identified need and for deciding how to respond to it. To cite Tronto (1993: 106) again: '[R]ather than simply focusing on the need of the other person, taking care of involves the recognition that one can act to address these unmet needs. If one believes that nothing can be done about a problem, then there is no appropriate "taking care of". Again, we argue that the people we encountered in our research all exhibited a preparedness to act to meet the needs that they had recognized, whether these be the needs of their children, spouse or partner, or the needs of the producer or the wider community and environment, or the needs of all of these recipients simultaneously. Tronto's third phase of caring is 'care-giving', which involves the direct meeting of needs for care: 'it involves physical work, and almost always requires that care-givers come into contact with the objects of care' (1993: 107). Examples of care-giving cited by Tronto include the nurse administering medication to the sick, the repair person fixing a broken thing, the mother talking to her child about the day's events, or neighbours helping one another. In our research, care-giving is most obviously expressed through the preparation of food for loved ones – the physical work of growing, buying, carrying, peeling, cleaning, scraping, cooking, washing up, freezing, and disposing or recycling of food are part and parcel of the care work relating to food. The kinds of foods produced and consumed in our cases – such as fresh fruit, salad, or vegetables straight from the soil – tend to require more of this work than say, 'convenience' foods provided in oven or microwave-ready forms, or ready washed and chopped in plastic bags. Yet this work is undertaken because the care-giver believes that the end result will be of benefit to those people, or environments that s/he cares about. In the case of EarthShare care-giving extends to include working on the land – weeding, harvesting and digging, on order to care for the soil, the community and the growers. Of course the care-giver receives a share of the harvest in return for this labour, but our evidence suggests that this is only one element in the motivational mix; equally important are notions of connection with the soil, providing a secure and fair income for growers, and caring for the soil for future generations. The one case where care-giving is perhaps problematic is 'Adopt a sheep' because the relationship between producer and consumers is spatially extended, and as Tronto and others have agreed, care-giving *usually* requires spatial proximity. In some instances, this spatial proximity is achieved, when 'parents' go to visit the farm in Abruzzo and can volunteer to help with the work. However, whilst it is true that this particular scheme does not facilitate care-giving so easily, it does involve meeting the needs for care, albeit through virtually-mediated relationships between producer and consumers; relationships which enable the producers to continue a threatened way of life which sustains traditional products and practices, an endangered sheep breed to persist, and a particular mountain ecosystem to be reproduced. Moreover, the motives for joining the scheme are often expressed in terms of caring about and taking care of all of these elements. Relations of care then, are still being played out through this scheme, maybe even between the giver and receiver of an adoption certificate as a gift.

The final phase of care is 'care-receiving', which recognizes that the object of care will respond to the care it receives: 'the tuned piano sounds good again, the patient feels better, or the starving children seem healthier after being fed' (Tronto 1993: 107). This recognition provides the only means of knowing whether caring needs have actually been met. In our research, we have seen many examples of objects and subjects responding to care: gardens, vegetable plots and animals flourishing; producers sustaining their livelihoods; consumers enjoying healthier, more varied and tasty foods. Consumers clearly expressed the pleasure and sense of fulfilment they experienced in eating and sharing food that is 'good' in every sense of the word. Consumers found pleasure in their participation in 'alternative' food schemes in many ways, be this through their interactions with producers, the experience of procuring food in new ways, the taste of the food, the surprise of discovering new foods or in the feeling that they were 'doing the right thing'. Here, 'pleasure' is an effect of both the sensual characteristics of the food and the social relations in which its consumption is situated, combined with a knowledge that the food is ethically 'good.' As shown in Chapter 4, producers also clearly gained a sense of satisfaction from creating direct relationships with consumers and providing good quality products, which in turn enabled them to maintain their farms or business. In these cases economic imperatives become entangled with a range of 'goods' associated with intersubjective relationships, making it difficult to discern whether the economic, the social or the ethical is most important to the particular producer–consumer relationships involved.

In addition to the pleasures identified by consumer and producers, deciding to care through 'reconnection' can have uncomfortable consequences for consumers, and Tronto also emphasizes that care is often fraught with conflict. So for instance, the need to care for oneself can come into conflict with the care that must be given to others. The consumer may want to give care by joining a CSA, but may not be able to do so because a spouse, partner or other family members do not recognize a need for that particular care, or because limited financial resources have to be used carefully and for agreed ends. Care-receivers may have different ideas about their needs than do care-givers; think of the young child stubbornly refusing to eat their 'greens' – care recipients are not always passive. As shown in our discussion of the idea of 'entanglement' in Chapter 5, caring through 'reconnection' can be practically difficult (or impossible if there are no schemes nearby) and it can be emotionally demanding and raise new anxieties: As Ruth, one of the consumers from EarthShare put it '[This] really opened it up, probably too far you know, at the early stages, because you then felt that you're swimming in it.' Entanglement sums up the senses of loyalty, guilt and obligation that can arise from closer connection. It is precisely these emotional entanglements which mean that 'reconnection' can be difficult and can make considerable demands on consumers and producers alike. For the latter, particularly those working on a small scale, it can create heavy physical and emotional workloads. On the other hand, the emotional dimensions of entanglement also mean that large supermarkets and indeed larger 'alternatives' will find 'reconnection' through care difficult to replicate, although they are obviously adept at appropriating the discourses of 'reconnection' which we identified in Chapter 2 (especially in terms of 'reconnections' with product, process and place).

Sticking with Tronto's (1993, 2006) definition, we maintain that care necessitates actions and these actions are embedded within a disposition of being concerned about the needs of human and non-human others. We argue, therefore, that it is important to examine the mutually constituted identities, motives and practices of those involved. We stress that this book is not about suggesting that some people do not care, or that those participating in 'alternative' food practices must care more, or in a better way, than those who are not involved. People may have different ways of caring, and different emotions, motivations and practices may be involved depending on who is caring for who, what and where. Moreover, practices and choices are always constrained by circumstances and care may also become an effect of the relationships played out in 'alternative' food arrangements, rather than simply a preceding motivation which leads to engagement with them.

We are not suggesting that the people we talked to in our research are selfless, in the sense of sacrificing their own needs completely in order to meet the needs of others. The relational sense of self suggested by the ethic of care is one which is aware of the needs of others, not one which is consumed by those needs (although we acknowledge that there are many caring roles in which sense of self can be eroded through constant attention to the needs of others). In the context of our research, thinking of the needs of others has many positive effects, enabling producers to sustain livelihoods, and consumers to live lives with less ethical conflict, less anxiety, more pleasure and joy. In many ways then, the ethic of care may have possibilities for producers and consumers to construct 'reconnected' subjectivities; senses of self which are less fragmented by anxieties, unhappiness and stress.

Care, Choice and Convenience

Care is not simply about being concerned or anxious about the welfare of others but it involves taking steps to address those concerns (Tronto 1993, 2006) by accepting the burden of responsibility. In the case of consumption, this can mean modifying one's own expectations and requirements. Evidence that consumers are prepared to embrace these modifications is perhaps most clearly shown in our findings relating to notions of choice and convenience, as discussed in Chapter 6. Our work with consumers allowed us to look at food procurement in relation to their daily lives, routines, household structures and priorities. This approach enabled us to take a new look at the issue of choice in the food system and to suggest ways in which choice can be thought about differently. Large retailers portray the choice of goods that they offer as a huge benefit to consumers, but their notion of choice can be illusory. Supermarkets have contributed to the standardization of the agri-food system and this has actually reduced choice in many ways: shrinking the number of farmers, the number of stores in local neighbourhoods, the breeds of animals reared and the varieties of crops grown. Where supermarkets have increased choice most, it is to customers who can afford it, and is in the provision of out of season fruit and vegetables. This has been at great cost to the natural environment and to some people in the poorest countries of the world, who see land that was once used to grow subsistence crops for local consumption turned over to the provision of high cost horticultural foods (mangetout, baby sweetcorn) or flowers for export (Barrett et al. 1999; Hughes 2000). As well as offering consumers choice based on something other than cost or appearance (Soper 2007b), our research shows that procuring food from 'alternative' sources can make people question whether 'choice' is really welcome when it depends on degrading ecosystems and perpetuating exploitative trade relationships.

It is also important to distinguish between choice and variety. In our research, the interviewees who were given the least choice in their food schemes were often the people who ate the widest varieties of food, ate the most fresh foods and cooked healthy meals from scratch. Often, lack of choice had encouraged them to learn new recipes and sometimes new cooking skills. It had also put people in closer contact with the natural environment through their ability to appreciate the changing seasons and by seeing food as it comes out of the ground – misshapen or with mud on.

Our approach has also enabled us to ask questions about the nature of convenience in food procurement. Inspired by Shove's work (2003), we have looked at consumers' activities within the contexts of their daily lives and ethical priorities, and have been able to take a broad and imaginative view of what convenience can mean. First, we would argue that the most convenient way to access food is not necessarily in car-based trips to large supermarkets. The consumers we interviewed were clear that having a box delivered, collecting a box from a pick-up point, shopping daily at local shops and markets, or harvesting food from a garden could all be quick and easy ways to get food. Second, not all consumers wanted to get food in the fastest possible way, rather they wanted to enjoy the experience. Sources of food that were less busy, that were run by more knowledgeable and less stressed staff, that enabled people to meet existing friends or make new ones, could meet their needs better than those which were more alienating. Last, for the consumers we worked with, procuring food was not just about getting food quickly and cheaply, it was a process that had to meet their ethical and caring concerns too. Ways of sourcing food which address peoples' concerns for the environment, for near and distant others, for producers and their own health, were all more 'convenient' than sources that precluded this. Simms (2007: 321) has written that we need to find new ways to measure the success of actors in the food system: '[W]ho is to say that the "consumer interest" is better embodied in a four-pack of baked beans that costs less than £1 than by having a small, independent shopkeeper who saves you from depression by smiling, remembering your name and having the time to chat each morning and evening?' The concept of 'convenience' should be similarly interrogated. Something is only convenient when it fills its purpose, and as we have shown throughout this book, the purposes embodied in shopping for, cooking and eating food are much broader than physical sustenance with the least possible effort.

We hope that by bringing ideas about care to our understanding of producer and consumer relationships and identities, we contribute to current debates about why and how 'alternative' food practices occur. Moreover, our analytical approach to describing food arrangements (see Chapter 3) casts light on the range of spaces, relationships, identities and practices which can be knitted together in unique ways to create individual solutions to the problems of where to source 'good' food and how to care. We theorize food networks as relational and spatialized processes of 'becoming', rooted in the materiality of food production–consumption, rather than static representations in time. We have also argued (in Chapter 2) that the use of the binary concepts 'alternative' and 'conventional' is problematic in the analysis of food systems, mainly because it tends to simplify and gloss over the differences between a whole range of practices, spaces, ethical frameworks and agendas which currently shape food production and consumption relationships. The label of 'alternative' is not always helpful to those who are active in trying to improve food supply arrangements, in terms of health, social justice and the environment. Not many of our respondents saw themselves as 'alternative', although some did see themselves as trying to be 'more ethical' and some felt that they thought differently from most people, notably in terms of having an 'open mind', as illustrated by the following comment from an EarthShare subscriber:

> I think you've got to be interested in it to take that initial step ... Yes, I think you have to have an open mind and there's people that we know when they hear about the box they're just; they're quite closed to things. I would like to think I would have an open mind and maybe that's why I'm interested in it.

Furthermore, our respondents were not uncritical of others whom they came across, or knew about in general, even though they sometimes had to refrain from speaking up for fear of offending or upsetting friends and family. The need for people as shoppers and consumers to be informed, to engage and take responsibility for, and care about the quality and provenance of the food they eat, was referred to several times by different people in different schemes, both in interview and in workshops. Some of our interviewees were quite irritated by those who had no such desire for knowledge and engagement:

> This food, is ... is a sort of, um ... it's a manifestation of ... of personality ... and taking responsibility as well. Um, it permeates everything. Um, and that is an irritation that people seem to ... some seem to divorce from life, you know, you just shovel it in, and it keeps you going or it makes you fat, whatever choices you make ... I can feel a sort of irritation ... and I feel it a lot with my [*family member*] (laughs) ... She doesn't want her meat to look like meat. And I think that's such a cop out because somebody has had to be faced with a dead animal.

Interestingly, this lack of engagement, or interest, was sometimes expressed in terms of peoples' ability or desire to 'care' about food and related issues, as highlighted in the following comments from Moorland and Salop Drive customers respectively:

> ... people are not interested, they don't care. You won't ... you can't educate people who don't want to know

I mean, you'll always get the folks who couldn't care less, won't you? Who are not bothered that it's fresher than what you get from the shops and they're not bothered that it's organic, you know, but you'll always get folks like that, won't you?

Even where respondents were critical of other consumers' actions, however, they often remained sensitive to the contexts of other peoples' lives and the reasons why other people may not want to think about their food or to change the consumption practices. Thus, for example, an EarthShare subscriber, Ruth felt that consumers do not 'question enough' but at the same time recognized that 'when you do start to question things of course, it's very unsettling.' Not only this, but for families with parents working and children at school, 'it's not easy' to do things differently, especially when the family's clothes and other items could all be purchased at the supermarket. Strong feelings of mistrust and frustration were often directed at supermarkets, as the frontline or manifestation of the opacity of the food system, but were couched in terms which took account of the realities of peoples' lives. Even the more overtly critical respondents, such as David, a Moorland customer, were careful to recognize these aspects. He argued that

> ... people have got material wealth and possessions to worry about. They don't question what's going on with the politics. No, they're too busy having a big wide screen TV. They don't care how it's been produced, they just want the cheapest one ... and it's kind of linked in with as long as they're kept happy and quiet, and being kept happy and quiet is having enough money and cheap products to buy.

Later in the conversation, he acknowledged that he was 'middle class' in the way he looked at things and in a 'luxurious position'.

IMPLICATIONS AND POSSIBILITIES

Despite our desire to emphasize the range and complexity of motives driving people to participate in schemes such as those we examined, the question nevertheless arises as to the potential for some sort of broader political project which seeks to change the overall food supply system for the better, without reverting to a story of 'alternatives' positioned against a monolithic 'conventional' food system. Authors such as Allen et al. (2003) and Grey (2000) have argued that 'alternative' food schemes can have the potential to challenge social and economic inequality and to support an agenda of radical social change. This might seem like a tall order for a bit of grocery shopping! However, in the practices of the consumers and producers we worked with, we can perhaps see the seeds of such a process. Simms has argued that:

> In human life, along with shelter, little is more important than how we meet our basic needs for food, drink and a few other essentials … The way they are controlled carries with it a sort of DNA for society. It determines how we relate to our neighbourhoods, and whether communities thrive or decline. It sets out how towns and cities relate to the countryside. To an extent, it determines how we think about ourselves, either as passive consumers or active citizens. (2007: 5)

While we do not completely accept Simms's posit of 'passive consumer' versus 'active citizen' (as discussed in Chapter 2, people are probably more nuanced than such a potential binary implies), the point to emphasize is that because it is important to us, food has an effect on how we structure our society and how we behave in other areas of our lives. For many of the consumers we worked with, it has also shaped their attitudes to other areas of their lives through the 'graduation effect' discussed in Chapter 5.

Indeed, we would echo DuPuis and Goodman's (2005: 369) call for 'an inclusive and reflexive politics in place [that] would understand local food systems not as local "resistance" against a global capitalist "logic" but as a mutually constitutive, imperfect, political process.' In this 'imperfect' system they argue actors are 'allowed to be reflexive about both their own norms and about the structural economic logics of production'. The plurality of motivations and the openness to new ideas that we have found among producers and consumers perhaps suggest what such a reflexive politics might be like, and again challenges the 'either/or' notion of 'good citizen: bad consumer'. Our analytical approach helps us to understand our case studies as continual practices of partial resistance, against what are experienced as monolithic power relations. In many instances actors do not set out to challenge structures of power in food supply, but nevertheless contribute to a practical critique of those structures through their actions and discourse. The value of our analytical fields approach is that it enables us not only to examine the discursive construction of scheme activities (through looking at the fields of motives and identities) but also to detail the practices occurring. For any particular project, even though within some of the fields the evidence is for practices which are not counter to dominant power relations (so, for example, 'Adopt a sheep' air freights products all over the globe to generally wealthy and privileged consumers), in other fields things may be happening which do resist or challenge the status quo ('Adopt a sheep' enables endangered small-scale cultural practices and a rare breed to continue to exist and adapt to changing circumstances). This is apparent for all of our case studies, even if they might ordinarily be seen as being located towards the more 'alternative' (like EarthShare) or 'conventional' (like Farrington's) ends of a spectrum. The approach we have taken shows that such a spectrum or dichotomy is problematic, and instead that a more complex and multidimensional analysis of the specific arrangements of projects across a diverse range of analytical fields opens up opportunities for assessing the plurality of relationships between schemes and power relations in an overall food supply system. We can thus locate where, in specific projects, in which fields and in what relationships between fields, is the capacity to effect change and challenge established power relations, while retaining an essential sense of the diversity and specificity of activities. In addition, the recognition of the multidimensionality of such schemes also enables us to move beyond the emphasis on economic imperatives for farmers to connect with the market and to examine ethical, emotional and reflexive spaces of 'reconnection' which are constructed through the interrelationships of producers and consumers involved in 'alternative' food endeavours.

CHALLENGES FOR 'ALTERNATIVE' FOOD INITIATIVES

> That's what the farmer's markets mustn't do. They mustn't be on the corner of every street because then they're nothing special and then they'll never compete against the supermarkets and they'll get wiped out. You know because they're no longer of any real value ... (Joan, a Moorland customer, 2004)

We asked the growers and consumers in our case studies to consider the challenges facing their own scheme and 'alternative' food initiatives more widely. Two major threats were identified. The first, as suggested by the quote above, was the major supermarkets, which are expanding the range of locally sourced and organic products, have already moved into home delivery and have extensive advertising budgets with which to create a sense of 'reconnection' with product, process and place. Having said this, the presence of supermarkets is not always and necessarily a threat to 'alternative' food schemes because people use the two in complementary ways. The success of 'alternatives' depends in no small part on their ability to differentiate themselves, notably through their relative temporal and spatial marginality, and crucially, through the types of 'reconnections' they are able to forge between producers and consumers. Another issue which many respondents raised as a potential challenge to the kind of scheme they were using, or were managing, supplying or members of, is the relatively recent appearance (in the United Kingdom at least) of larger scale operations, which deliver from regional distribution centres (such as Abel and Cole, or River Nene box delivery schemes). These operations deliver 'locality' foods, that is, foods with distinct provenance as opposed to foods from the immediate location, many of which are produced under certified 'organic' labels (Commission on the Future of Farming and Food 2002; Morris and Buller 2003). These were seen as different by our research respondents because of their size and thus the relationships engendered between 'producers' and 'consumers'. One of the key aspects which the consumers in our research enjoyed and valued was having some sense of knowing the producer and being able to relate to them on a personal level. It is this aspect, we argue, that gives 'alternatives' their potential to transform production–consumption relationships and can help them to endure and thrive. However, this reliance on producer identities, motives and presence can also be a weakness because it can place heavy personal demands on those producers. As discussed in Chapter 4, producer roles are extended beyond that of simply growing food, and can reach into the realms of educator and entertainer. For publicly funded schemes, which usually have a health promotion or therapeutic dimension, the key threat lies in the continued possibility that funding will not be renewed and that the scheme will not be able to become self-sustaining.

It should be stressed that the consumers in our research expressed very high levels of satisfaction and every one of our respondents would recommend the scheme they used to others. Nevertheless, they were very clear about the aspects that could prevent or hinder participation in 'alternative' food practices at different stages. One factor that consumers suggested would limit use is the perception that little in the way of store cupboard goods and general domestic products is sold (although in fact the larger operations usually do offer these goods). Second, in terms of encouraging consumers to try 'alternative' food schemes in the first place, several respondents from our different case studies identified the terminology associated with them as a potential barrier to participation. In particular, the term 'CSA (or Community Supported Agriculture)' was seen as too 'theoretical' for some people. Particular terminology was also seen as possibly leading people to associate schemes with fringe, radical or spiritual groups, which could prevent people joining, either because they feel they would not 'fit in', or because they do not want to be associated with these explicit value systems. 'Alternative' is itself a word which consumers found difficult to associate with, creating visions of certain types of people and practices which they did not necessarily relate to. So for example, Paul, who buys a Waterland vegetable box commented:

> I don't feel I'm that different 'cos I still go to supermarkets, that is, the Co-Op. I still go to conventional shops and buy things in packets, you know, and everything in my cupboard there is, you know, it's jars, it's in packets. Okay I get the veggie box scheme but it's easy, it's delivered to the door. I don't feel I'm very 'alternative' [although] I'm very adventurous with food, but when I've said that in the past to Andrea who moved in the house six months ago, she thinks I'm batty, she says 'You're about as 'alternative' as you get!' ...

Many of those we talked to were keen to stress their own 'normality': as well as rejecting the notion of themselves as 'alternative', they did not perceive themselves as part of a cohesive social movement in any sense. We met very few individuals with a campaigning agenda or any sense of mission to convert others to their way of thinking. So, for example, Mary, an EarthShare subscriber, clearly located food purchase in the private sphere, seeing it as very much a personal issue:

> *Interviewer*: You don't think then that it (ie the scheme) would suit everybody?
> *Respondent*: No, not at all. Why should it? You know, some people love to go to [supermarket], and others have their own funny little private reasons for the way they live, just like I do.

For Mary, consumption is about choosing how to spend her money but at the same time she recognizes that even though she is not on a very big income, she is relatively well off compared to others. She is not interested in judging the actions of others, because she herself has lived 'on the dole ... and I know what it's like and I know it's not funny, and I know about judgement'. She thus empathizes with unknown others who may be living in difficult situations and positions her own participation in EarthShare as a luxury. Like most of our respondents she represented herself as someone who acted on her own beliefs as consistently as she could, within circumstances which, in many ways, are beyond her control and which can change.

Relative cost could also sometimes be an issue, and farm shops were perceived by some people as expensive and as stocking only a limited range of goods. Respondents also expressed awareness of potential constraints on other peoples' ability to choose where to source their food, which they supposed might affect their practices. So Jon, for instance, who buys a Waterland box, recognized that 'my ethos causes me to put up with the prices, which obviously a lot of people wouldn't, you know, if you're trying to feed a family on a shoestring, you know £6.50 a week on organic vegetables is a luxury.' Another Waterland consumer, Helen, made a similar point:

Helen: … I think that's when you'll find that box schemes appeal to, I'm sorry to say this but—

Interviewer: No, go on.

Helen: white, middle-class professional. That's the group that box schemes appeal to … They have the time and the money to take, what's the word, um, to take an interest in their community. They have the ability to do it. When you are on a very tight budget, you know if you are a single parent family, then your consideration is how can I feed my child and for how little? You know, what money do I have? So, you know, whether it's organic … where it came from in the world, people don't care.

Pauline, a Farrington's customer also commented that 'people are much busier … younger people with families … the woman is quite often doing a part-time job and you know there just isn't the time and certainly you get fed up of washing lettuces all year round'. These expressions/commentaries on others' behaviours and motivations were more in a spirit of understanding than condemnation or mistrust. Many of the consumers we spoke to were realistic about the demands schemes make on practice, such as pick-up times, market times, restrictions of eating seasonal food; it was acknowledged that changing peoples' consumption practices can be difficult. For those who had left box schemes or the CSA, the most common reason given was their inability to cope with the quantity or type of produce.

SOME CLOSING THOUGHTS

All the schemes which we have researched are robust and have flourished during the research period. While we have outlined some of the challenges facing these initiatives, we also want to stress that their successes should not be measured on the basis of economic indicators alone. Rather, it is necessary to examine their benefits in terms of environmental and consumer health, quality of life and well-being, community relations, happiness and ethical fulfilment enabled through the ability to express care.

Critics may argue that our book deals only with a minority of consumers, and relatively wealthy and privileged ones at that. We counter this with two points. First, our study included consumers who do not necessarily conform to the usual stereotype of the middle-class 'beard and sandals' brigade parodied by those who wish to diminish the potential of 'alternatives' to challenge dominant power relations within the food system and society more broadly. It is often claimed that those who take part in schemes such as those we worked with in this research, are more likely to be higher income consumers, and older. However (and as detailed in Appendix 2), over half of the consumers who completed our questionnaires had household incomes of less than £30,000 p.a., and 35 per cent were below £20,000 p.a., which is modest for the UK at the time of the survey (average household incomes in the UK in 2005–6 were *c.* £26,700 (Jones 2007)). Those enjoying an income of over £50,000 were mostly, but not exclusively, 'Adopt a sheep' consumers, which supports the idea that 'Adopt a sheep' is largely a form of luxury or conspicuous consumption – and as shown by our questionnaire data, a subscription is often given as a gift. Across the case studies, those in work tended to be professionals in the public or private sectors, but there was quite a range of occupations, including engineers, company directors and senior project managers as well as therapists, writers, gardeners and 'home-makers'. At least six were registered unemployed and claiming state benefits of some kind. It seemed both from the questionnaires people had completed, and also from comments and circumstances revealed in discussions, that there was more of a diversity of household situations, family arrangements, employment experiences, household income and other social factors among those using 'alternative' sources and schemes than we had expected from the literature.

The important point is that consumer interest in sourcing fresh and good quality food direct from the grower, or in becoming involved in the growing of their food, is not simply related to socio-economic class or income. The Soil Association's 2006 Market Report, for example, suggests that the numbers of people buying organic food have also risen, with two out of three consumers now knowingly buying organic food (65.4 per cent) and over half of people in the most disadvantaged social groups (C2, D and E) now buying organic food and drink. It is a simplification to argue that consumers (especially those on low incomes) are 'only' interested in getting food as cheaply as possible. It is also worth pointing out that the perception that 'alternative' sources of food are more expensive is also not necessarily accurate. Table 7.1 shows a comparison of a typical large Waterland vegetable box with similar products from Tesco and Sainsbury's (two of the leading

UK supermarkets at the time of writing). Our second point is that, whilst it may be the case that only a minority of the population consistently buy their food from sources other than supermarkets, this is not a reason to dismiss that minority as unimportant and merely 'fringe'. One obvious reason why more people do not access food through 'alternatives' is simply that not enough of them exist. Indeed, in the case of the provision of local foods, there is evidence to suggest a distinct 'geography of re-localization' weighted towards the south and south-west of England (Ricketts Hein et al. 2006). Moreover, the environment within which 'alternatives' have to try and grow is extremely competitive and potentially hostile, given the abilities of mainstream retailers to establish control over supply chains, offer a huge range of products and services, and achieve economies of scale which allow

Table 7.1 Price Comparison of Waterland Box with Vegetables Available at Tesco and Sainsbury's

Produce in Waterland Box	Tesco	Sainsbury
550g fresh beetroot	Not available	£1.98 (cooked and vacuum packed not fresh)
400g Carrots	23p	46p
600g onions	70p	76p
1.5kg new potatoes	£2.97	£3.73
100g chard	Not available	Not available
350g courgettes (with flowers still on from Waterland)	£1.15	£1.27
1 lettuce (Oak leaf)	99p (2 little gems)	99p (2 little gems)
1 head of garlic	28p	43p
6 organic eggs	£1.59	£1.59
Total cost £11.75	£7. 91 (with two items less than the Waterland box)	£11.21 (with one item less than the Waterland box)

Prices correct on 31 July 2007.
All Waterland produce is organic, locally produced and delivered. The box costs £10.50 and eggs are £1.25 extra. The supermarket products are organic and prices are taken from the supermarket websites (Tesco have a note that 'prices at your local store may vary'). Only the origin of some produce is listed and none of the products on this list were flagged as being British. Sainsbury's have recently introduced an organic 'seasonal vegetable box' of eight items delivered for £10.99. The products are guaranteed organic and details of the growers are supplied with the box but are not available on the website.

them to offer products at discounted prices. Their influence is also firmly entrenched because of the way in which supermarket shopping has become so 'normalized' within the routines of the United Kingdom's 'work–life' balance, to the extent that the supermarket has come to be seen as the ultimate symbol of 'convenience'.

Yet as our research shows, not everyone agrees that supermarkets are convenient, and 'choice' can be a double-edged sword. Many of the consumers we spoke to were highly aware of the environmental impacts of supermarkets and mistrusted their trading and labelling practices. Having said which, it is also important to note that not everyone we spoke to was 'anti-supermarket'. As we have shown/argued, it would be a mistake to try and characterize the consumers and producers we spoke to as purely 'alternative' in any clear sense because their practices are always situated within complex and individualized frameworks built upon a mixture of practically and ethically bound decisions, which can, in turn, be modified as life events occur (e.g. birth of children, marriage/divorce, moving house). Moreover, it is highly unlikely that consumers will be able to operate exclusively through 'reconnected' sorts of relationships. Thus, there is no evidence in our research for a coherent or collective oppositional movement, despite the political potential through 'reconnection' we discuss above.

In keeping with our relational approach to understanding 'alternative' food practices, the evidence shows that these practices are co-constituted with conventional practices in complicated ways. This does not dilute their significance. Rather, we argue that the practices we have examined suggest that producers and consumers are prepared to think carefully about their relationships with others, human and non-human, close and distant. They are also prepared to act in ways which not only meet their own needs but also address the needs of those others. Participation in 'alternative' food schemes might not save the world, at least not in the short term, but it might help to build the knowledge, and positive relationships that create the capacity for change. As such, we believe that the evidence presented in this book should lend support to all those who want to build more equitable, more sustainable, and more closely connected relationships between consumers and the producers of their food.

Researching 'Alternative' Food Schemes

INTRODUCTION

This appendix tells the story of how we defined the subject of our research and 'brought into being' the 'alternative' food relationships that form the focus of this book. It explains how the food schemes were chosen, how we engaged with producers and consumers and how we started to make sense of the rich data that emerged from these encounters.

STAGE ONE: CHOOSING THE SCHEMES

Before schemes could be chosen for detailed research, it was necessary to construct a database from which potential cases could be selected. In order to devise criteria for inclusion in the database, we undertook an extensive review of academic and 'grey' literature (as described in Chapter 3) and we also consulted a specially convened panel of experts representing institutions active in the 'alternative' food sector. The agencies represented are listed in Box AI.I.

The panel was invited to review, scrutinize and challenge our work at the outset, halfway point and end of the project. By combining insights from the panel with concepts from the literature review we developed a selection framework consisting of four parameters. Each food project, scheme or initiative identified during the scoping exercise had to encompass at least one of the following to be included in the project database:

I.   an attempt to connect consumers, producers and food;
2.   use of non-conventional supply/distribution channels – detached from industrial supply and demand distribution and corporately controlled food chains;

Box A1.1 INSTITUTIONS REPRESENTED ON THE CONSULTATION PANEL

- Henry Doubleday Research Foundation
- Foundation for Local Food Initiatives
- Food Ethics Council
- Co-operatives UK
- Soil Association
- National Consumer Council
- Sustainable Development Commission
- Arthur Rank Centre
- Womens' Institute
- Food Links UK / Somerset Foodlinks
- Coventry City Council
- DEFRA food and farming team

3. adoption of principles of social embeddedness – in other words, founded on the principles of trust, community and local ownership of resources;
4. be based around a notion of 'quality' – defined in relation to place-specific traditions, heritage and environmental features.

Using these parameters, schemes, initiatives and projects were identified from the Internet, industry journals, the media (newspapers and radio programmes), academic journals and previous research. The aim was to attain a representative breadth of operational examples rather than an exhaustive list (for more details, see Venn et al. 2006).

Database construction stopped once a point had been reached when no new arrangements of production–consumption were being found. Having collected in excess of 140 entries in the database we conducted a content analysis of the promotional materials produced by schemes in order to better understand the ways in which they represented themselves and their aims. We were then faced with the challenge of choosing six cases for detailed study and so it was necessary to develop criteria for selecting these. Given our focus on the nature of producer–consumer relationships, we created a typology of relationships into which our database entries could be fitted. This typology is reproduced in Chapter 1, and a full description of the case studies which were eventually settled on is provided in Chapter 3.

STAGE 2: INCREMENTAL QUALITATIVE RESEARCH

The methods used were incremental, in that each stage of research built on, and was informed by the previous stage, the aim being to build depth and detail over time. Our general aim in using these methods was to try to facilitate people in reflecting and articulating their reasons for getting involved, and their experiences of having done so. It is often hard for people to make explicit why they do things which are broadly everyday activities, and to speculate on the difference such practices have, or might have, made to their thinking and behaviour in other spheres. However, by using different approaches and repeating questions over periods of several months, as well as making the participation as pleasurable as we could, we feel we enabled people to express their views and understandings. Through detailed empirical work we were in touch with a cross section of consumers at different times and places, who were inevitably largely self-selected. The sample size is reasonable for qualitative work (see Appendix 2 for further details) and, while not intended to be representative, the material provides several, quite diverse, sets of reflections on motivations, beliefs and trajectories of connection, 'reconnection' and entanglement by consumers and producers of different types, socio-economic position and places.

Scheme Manager Interviews

Plans to organize an initial producer workshop proved impossible, as managers could not afford time away from the business. This is indicative of the limited human capital on which our case studies survive and testament to the centrality of the producer to running the schemes on a daily basis. As such, the workshop was substituted with individual scheme visits. The interviews, lasting up to two hours, were recorded, transcribed and coded using Nvivo software. In an effort to make the research mutually beneficial, producers were given the opportunity to suggest information of organizational interest which could be incorporated into the consumer research. Approximately one year after the initial interview, follow-up interviews were held, with the aim of exploring what changes had occurred to the scheme. Feedback from the consumer workshops which had been held in the period following the first interview was also given to producers.

Consumer Workshops

Two rounds of workshops were held involving eighty-nine consumers participating in the five UK-based schemes. The first round aimed mainly at finding out more about consumers' perceptions of food in general and the case study project they were involved with in particular. The second round explored consumers' ideas about factors of success and future scenarios both for the scheme they were involved in and the 'alternative sector' more broadly. Scheme managers assisted in recruiting consumers by displaying flyers or putting them into the vegetable bags/boxes. Vouchers were offered as an incentive for participation. The sample was thus largely self-selecting. The workshops were each attended by two members of the research team and were recorded, transcribed, summarized and coded. Summaries were sent to all participants. Given the international membership of the 'Adopt a sheep' scheme, the research team hosted an online focus group for the consumers involved.

Consumer Interviews

Forty-four interviewees were recruited predominantly from the pool of consumer workshop participants. The interviews, lasting up to two hours, were semi-structured but included discussion of the following key points:

- involvement and experience with the specific scheme;
- the evolution of food consumption practices;
- use of technology in relation to food shopping;
- discursive understandings of food and its production;
- relationships with food from different sources.

Two hundred questionnaires were sent to 'Adopt a sheep' consumers and fifty-eight were completed and returned. Approximately one year after the initial interview, thirty-two consumers from all six case studies were interviewed by telephone, the main aim being to find out whether there had been any significant changes to their shopping practices during the previous twelve months or so.

Household Research

Information provided during the workshops and interviews was used to select six households with different socio-economic and demographic characteristics as well as different attitudes towards food. Each household was visited up to three times, with intervals of at least two weeks between visits. As well as participating in in-depth interviews, the households collected food purchase receipts over a four-week period, and took photographs of meals or eating events using cameras provided by the researchers. The reason a camera was provided, rather than a food diary, the traditional instrument in nutrition research, is that taking pictures is quicker, more fun and provides qualitative information about the contents and contexts of eating. Furthermore, younger members of the household were also encouraged to take part by taking pictures. Participants were also encouraged to write accompanying notes in a diary. This facilitated detailed discussions about consumers' food knowledges, practices and ethical frameworks. All interviews were recorded, with permission from the participants, and field notes were written after each session. As a gesture of thanks, participants were given vouchers to spend at the case study schemes. In order to comply with data protection requirements and ensure that participants were fully aware of, and happy with, the ways in which information would be used, consent forms were provided. Participants signed these and were given copies to keep.

Figure AI.I summarizes the research stages.

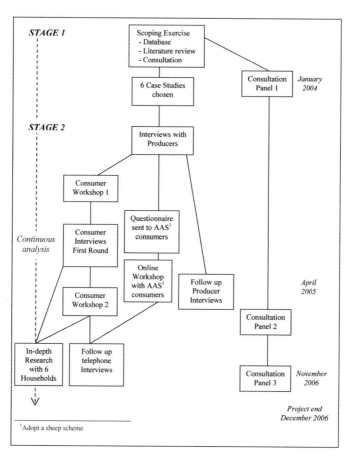

Figure AI.I Research methods.

Consumer Profile

In each of the consumer workshops we used a short socio-demographic questionnaire to collect simple quantitative data from those taking part. There were a total of 89 participants in the two rounds of consumer workshops, and 58 returned questionnaires of the 200 sent to members of ' Adopt a sheep'. A variety of questionnaire formats was used over two years; not all participants completed them or answered all questions, so that the sample base in the figures below varies, but the questionnaires nonetheless furnished us with basic information about who took part in the consumer interviews, surveys and workshops. A summary of these data is briefly presented here; of course, the patterns shown reflect the circumstances of those who engaged with us, who may not in fact be typical scheme consumers, but we had no reason to suppose those whom we met were markedly different from other members or customers, from what we observed or from what the producers themselves knew.

CONSUMER SOCIO-DEMOGRAPHIC CHARACTERISTICS

It is often claimed that those who take part in schemes such as those we worked with in this research, are more likely to be higher income consumers, and older. As shown in Table A2.1, however, over half of the consumers who completed the questionnaire had household incomes of less than £30,000 p.a., and 35 per cent were below £20,000 p.a., which is modest for the UK at the time of the survey (average household incomes in the UK in 2005–6 were c. £26,500; Jones 2007). Those enjoying an income of over £50,000 were mostly, but not exclusively, 'Adopt a sheep' consumers, which supports the idea that 'Adopt a sheep' is largely a form of luxury or conspicuous consumption – and as shown by our questionnaire data, a subscription is often given as a gift.

Table A2.1 Household Income per Annum (£)

Income (£)	Percent of Consumers
<10,000	6
11,000–20,000	29
21,000–30,000	20
31,000–40,000	11
41,000–50,000	5
>50,000	29

Sample size: 65.

Sixty-two per cent of our respondents were female; over half of the sample were over the age of 55 as shown in Table A2.2, 30 per cent were under 45 years (and at least one participant was under 25 years old).

Only about a fifth had dependent children living at home, which was not surprising given the age range, and almost a quarter were retired. Those in work tended to be professionals in the public or private sectors, but there was quite a range of occupations, including engineers, company directors and senior project managers as well as therapists, writers, gardeners and 'home-makers'. At least six were registered unemployed and claiming state benefits of some kind. It seemed both from the questionnaires people had completed, and also from comments and circumstances revealed in discussions, that there was more of a diversity of household situations, family arrangements, employment experiences, household income and other social factors among those using 'alternative' sources and schemes than we had expected from the literature.

Table A2.2 Age Profile of Consumers in Workshops

Age (years)	Percent of Consumers
15–24	1
25–34	13
35–44	17
45–54	14
55–64	28
65+	27

Notes

1 CONTEXTUALIZING 'ALTERNATIVE' FOOD RELATIONSHIPS

1. Our research was mainly with consumers and producers in the United Kingdom, with some reference to other developed market economies in the global North; hence most of our discussion refers to this context but we acknowledge that there is much scope for research that investigates the implications of 'alternative' food relationships for the global South.
2. There are also major environmental implications but it is beyond the scope of this book to deal with these in any depth. See, for example, Pretty (2002); Pretty et al. (2005).

2 CONCEPTUALIZING 'ALTERNATIVES' WITHIN A FRAMEWORK OF CARE

1. The remit of Policy Commission on the Future of Farming and Food, which produced the Curry Report of the same name, in 2001, covered only England. Similar concerns have been expressed in other nations in the United Kingdom.
2. Later in their paper, Barnett et al. do recognize that the ability to engage in the performative practices associated with ethical consumption may be unevenly distributed along lines of class, gender, race and ethnicity (2005b: 41).

3 ANALYTICAL DESCRIPTION OF SIX 'ALTERNATIVE' FOOD SCHEMES

1. Note, these analytical fields were first introduced in Holloway et al. (2007).
2. LETS are Local Exchange Trading Systems or Schemes. They are usually community-based mutual aid networks in which people exchange all kinds of goods and services with one another, without the need for money. See www.letslinkuk.net.
3. For other accounts of the scheme, see Holloway (2002), Holloway and Kneafsey (2004), and Holloway et al. (2006).

5 BUYING AND EATING FOOD: CONSUMERS AND CONSUMPTION

1. Consumers who took part in the in-depth interviews and household research are referenced by alias in the text. Consumers whose comments were recorded during workshops are reported as unnamed research participants.

References

Acheson, D. (1998) *Independent Inquiry into Inequalities in Health*. London: The Stationery Office.

Allen, P. (1999) 'Connecting the Social and the Ecological in Sustainable Agriculture', in P. Allen (ed.) *Food for the Future: Conditions and Contradictions of Sustainability*, New York: John Wiley and Sons, pp. 1–16.

Allen, P., FitzSimmons, M., Goodman, M. and Warner, K. (2003) 'Shifting Plates in the Agrifood Landscape: The Tectonics of Alternative Agrifood Initiatives in California', *Journal of Rural Studies* 19: 61–75.

Balfour, E. B. (1943) *The Living Soil*, London: Faber and Faber.

Barham, E. (2003) 'Translating Terroir: The Global Challenge of French AOC Labelling', *Journal of Rural Studies* 19: 127–38.

Barnett, C., Cloke, P., Clarke, N. and Malpass, A. (2005a) 'The Political Ethics of Consumerism', *Consumer Policy Review* 15: 2–8.

Barnett, C., Cloke, P., Clarke, N. and Malpass, A. (2005b) 'Consuming Ethics: Articulating the Subjects and Spaces of Ethical Consumption', *Antipode* 37: 23–45.

Barnett, C., Clarke, M., Cloke, P. and Malpass, A. (2006) 'Politics in an Ethical Register', http://www.open2.net/interdependenceday/ethicalregister. html, accessed 31 January 2008

Barrett, H., Ilbery, B., Browne, A. and Binns, T. (1999) 'Globalisation and the Changing Networks of Food Supply: The Importation of Fresh Horticultural Produce from Kenya into the UK', *Transactions of the Institute of British Geographers* 24: 159–74.

Beardsworth, A. and Keil, T. (1997) *Sociology on the Menu: An Invitation to the Study of Food and Society*, London: Routledge.

Beck, U. (1992) *Risk and Society: Towards a New Modernity*, London: Sage.

Bondi, L. (2005) 'Making Connections and Thinking through Emotions: Between Geography and Psychotherapy', *Transactions of the Institute of British Geographers* 30: 433–48.

Bové, J. and Dufour, F. (2005) *Food for the Future*, Cambridge: Polity Press.

Burchardt, T., Le Grand, J. and Piachaud, D. (2002) 'Introduction', in J. Hills, J. Le Grand and D. Piachaud (eds) *Understanding Social Exclusion*, Oxford: Oxford University Press, pp. 1–12.

Burnett, J. (1989) *Plenty and Want: A Social History of Diet in England from 1815 to the Present Day*, 3rd edition, London: Routledge

Castree, N. (2001) 'Editorial: Commodity Fetishism, Geographical Imaginations and Imaginative Geographies', *Environment and Planning A* 33: 1519–25.

Charles, N. and Kerr, M. (1988) *Women, Food and Families*, Manchester: Manchester University Press.

Clarke, N., Barnett, C., Cloke, P. and Malpass, A. (2007) 'Globalizing the Consumer: Doing Politics in an Ethical Register', *Political Geography* 26: 231–49.

Cobbett, W. (1979 [1822]) *Cottage Economy*, Oxford: Oxford University Press.

Collet, E. and Mormont, M. (2003) 'Managing Pests, Consumers and Commitments: The Case of Apple Growers and Pear Growers in the Lower Meuse Region', *Environment and Planning A* 35: 413–27.

Commission on the Future of Farming and Food (2002) 'Farming & Food: a sustainable future, Report of the Policy Commission on the Future of Farming and Food', available at: http://archive.cabinetoffice.gov.uk/farming/.

Cook, I. and Crang, P. (1996) 'The World on a Plate: Culinary Culture, Displacement and Geographical Knowledges', *Journal of Material Culture* 1: 131–53.

Cook, I., Crang, P. and Thorpe, M. (1998) 'Biographies and Geographies: Consumer Understandings of the Origins of Food', *British Food Journal* 100: 162–7.

Council for the Protection of Rural England (2001) *Sustainable Local Foods*, London: CPRE.

Countryside Agency (2002) *Eat the View: Promoting Sustainable Local Products*, Wetherby: Countryside Agency Publications.

Cousin, G. (2005) 'Case Study Research', *Journal of Geography in Higher Education* 29: 421–7.

Defra (2002a) *Farming and Food's Contribution to Sustainable Development Economic and Statistical Analyses*, available online at www.defra.gov.uk/farm/sustain/newstrategy/index.htm.

Defra (2002b) *The Strategy for Sustainable Farming and Food: Facing the Future*, available online at http://www.defra.gov.uk/farm/policy/sustain/pdf/sffs.pdf.

Defra (2006) *Agriculture in the United Kingdom 2006*, available online at http://statistics.defra.gov.uk/esg/publications/auk/2006/default.asp.

Defra (2007) Sustainable Farming and Food Strategy – indicator data sheet: Social outcome: Public health in particular through improved nutrition and workplace health and safety: Core indicator 7.04: Farmer suicide rates, available online at http://statistics.defra.gov.uk/esg/indicators/d704_data.htm, accessed 29 July 2007.

DeLind, L. and Ferguson, A. E. (1999) 'Is This a Women's Movement? The Relationship of Gender to Community-Supported Agriculture in Michigan', *Human Organization* 58: 190–200.

Department of Health (2004) *Choosing Health: Making Healthier Choices Easier*, London: Department of Health.

DeVault, M. L. (1991) *Feeding the Family: The Social Organization of Caring as Gendered Work*, Chicago: The University of Chicago Press.

Dowler, E. and Caraher, M. (2003) 'Local Food Projects: The New Philanthropy?', *The Political Quarterly* 74: 57–65.

Dowler, E., Blair, A., Rex, D., Donkin, A. and Grundy, C. (2001a) *Measuring Access to Healthy Food in Sandwell: Final Report June 2001*, Coventry: University of Warwick. Available online at http://www.chdf.org.au/i-cms_file?page=128/Sandwell.pdf.

Dowler, E., Turner, S. and Dobson, B. (2001b) *Poverty Bites: Food Health and Poor Families*, London: Child Poverty Action Group.

Dowler, E., Caraher, M. and Lincoln, P. (2007) 'Inequalities in Food and Nutrition: Challenging "Lifestyles"', in E. Dowler and N. Spencer (eds) *Challenging Health Inequalities: from Acheson to 'Choosing Health'*, Bristol: Policy Press, pp. 127–55.

Draper, A. and Green, J. (2003) 'Food Safety and Consumers: Constructions of Choice and Risk', in E. Dowler and C. Jones Finer (eds) *The Welfare of Food: Rights and Responsibilities in a Changing World*, Oxford: Blackwell Publishing, pp. 54–69.

Duffy, R., Fearne, A. and Healing, V. (2005) 'Reconnection in the UK Food Chain – Bridging the Communication Gap Between Food Producers and Consumers', *British Food Journal* 107: 17–33.

Dunant, S. and Porter, R. (1996) 'Introducing Anxiety', in S. Dunant and R. Porter (eds) *The Age of Anxiety*, London: Virago, pp. ix–xviii.

DuPuis, E. and Goodman, D. (2005) 'Shall We Go "Home" to Eat?: Towards a Reflexive Politics of Localism', *Journal of Rural Studies* 21: 259–371.

EarthShare (2005) www.earthshare.org.

Enticott, G. (2003a) 'Risking the Rural: Nature, Morality and the Consumption of Unpasteurised Milk', *Journal of Rural Studies* 19: 411–24.

Enticott, G. (2003b) 'Lay Immunology, Local Foods and Rural Identity: Defending Unpasteurised Milk in England', *Sociologia Ruralis* 43: 257–70.

Eostre Organics, www.eostreorganics.co.uk/growers_waterland.htm, accessed 14 June 2007.

European Commission (2004) Eurostat: Portrait of the Regions Italy: Abruzzo, available online at http://circa.europa.eu/irc/dsis/regportraits/info/data/en/index.htm, accessed 31 July 2007.

Fairtrade Foundation: Fairtade in the UK: Sales, available online at http://www.fairtrade.org.uk, accessed 17 July 07.

Farm Crisis Network, www.farmcrisisnetwork.org.uk.

Farmers' Weekly (2007) 13 July 2007, p. 26.

Farrington's Farm shop, www.farringtons.co.uk.

Fischler, C. (1980) 'Food Habits, Social Change and the Nature/Culture Dilemma', *Social Science Information,* 19: 937–53.

Fischler, C. (1988) 'Food, Self and Identity', *Social Science Information* 27: 275–92.

Fisher, B. and Tronto, J. V. (1991) 'Toward a Feminist Theory of Care', in E. Abel and M. Nelson (eds) *Circles of care: Work and Identity in Women's Lives,* Albany: State University of New York Press.

Food and Agriculture Organization of the United Nations (2001) Ethical Issues in Food and Agriculture, Rome: Food and Agriculture Organization

Foundation for Local Food Initiatives (2003) *Flair Report 2003: The Development of the Local Food Sector 2000 to 2003,* Bristol: Foundation for Local Food Initiatives.

Friedberg, S. (2004) 'The Ethical Complex of Corporate Food Power', *Environment and Planning D: Society and Space* 22:513–31.

Gabriel, Y. and Lang, T. (2006) *The Unmanageable Consumer,* 2nd edition, London: Sage.

Galbraith, J. K. (1974) *Economics and the Public Purpose,* London: Andre Deutsch.

General Register Office for Scotland: 2001 Census Report to the Scottish Parliament, available online at www.gro-scotland.gov.uk, accessed 19 July 2007.

Gibson-Graham, J. K. (1996) *The End of Capitalism (As We Knew It): A Feminist Critique of Political Economy,* Oxford: Blackwell.

Gilligan, C. (1982) *In a Different Voice: Psychological Theory and Women's Development,* Cambridge, MA: Harvard University Press.

Gilligan, C. (1993) 'Reply to critics', in M. J. Larrabee (ed.) *An Ethic of Care: Feminist and Interdisciplinary Perspectives,* London: Routledge, pp. 207–14.

Goodman, D. (1999) 'Agro-Food Studies in the "Age of Ecology": Nature, Corporeality, Bio-Politics', *Sociologia Ruralis* 39: 17–38.

Goodman, D. (2003) 'The Quality "Turn" and Alternative Food Practices: Reflections and Agenda', *Journal of Rural Studies* 19: 1–7.

Gregson, N., Crewe, L. and Brooks, K. (2002) 'Shopping, Space, and Practice', *Environment and Planning D: Society and Space* 20: 597–617.

Grey, M. (2000) 'The Industrial Food Stream and Its Alternatives in the United States: An Introduction', *Human Organization* 59: 143–50.

Guthman, J. (2004) *Agrarian Dreams: The Paradox of Organic Farming in California,* California: University of California Press.

Guthman, J. (2007) 'Race, Subjectivity, and the Politics of Conversion in Alternative Food Movements', Paper presented at the Association of American Geographers Annual Meeting, San Francisco, April 2007.

Guthman, J., Morris, A. W. and Allen, P. (2006) 'Squaring Farm Security and Food Security in Two Types of Alternative Food Institutions', *Rural Sociology* 71: 662–84.

Guy, C. M. (1996) 'Corporate Strategies in Food Retailing and their Local Impacts: A Case Study of Cardiff', *Environment and Planning A* 28: 1575–602.

Halfacree, K. (1999) 'A New Space or Spatial Effacement? Alternative Futures for the Post-Productivist Countryside', in N. Walford, J. Everitt, and D. Napton (eds) *Reshaping the Countryside: Perceptions and Processes of Rural Change,* Wallingford: CAB International, pp. 67–76.

Harrison, M. (2007) in *Rural Economy and Land Use Programme Briefing Series No 5,* The Rural economy and Land Use Debates 2007. Newcastle upon Tyne: Rural Economy and Land Use Programme.

Harrison, R., Newholm, T. and Shaw, D. (eds) (2005) *The Ethical Consumer,* London: Sage.

Hartwick, E. (1998) 'Geographies of Consumption: A Commodity-Chain Approach', *Environment and Planning D: Society & Space* 16: 423–37.

Harvey, G. (2006) *We Want Real Food,* London: Constable and Robinson.

Hassanein, N. (2003) 'Practicing Food Democracy: A Pragmatic Politics of Transformation', *Journal of Rural Studies* 19: 77–86.

Hendrickson, M. and Heffernan, W. (2002) 'Opening Spaces through Relocalization: Locating Potential Resistance in the Weaknesses of the Global Food System', *Sociologia Ruralis* 42: 347–68.

Hines, C. (2000) *Localization: A Global Manifesto,* London: Earthscan.

Hinrichs, C. (2000) 'Embeddedness and Local Food Systems: Notes on Two Types of Direct Agricultural Markets', *Journal of Rural Sociology* 16: 295–303.

Hinrichs, C. (2003) 'The Practice and Politics of Food System Localization', *Journal of Rural Studies* 20: 33–45.

Holloway, L. (2002) 'Virtual Vegetables and Adopted Sheep: Ethical Relation, Authenticity and Internet-Mediated Food Production Technologies', *Area* 34: 70–81.

Holloway, L. (2004) 'Showing and Telling Farming: Agricultural Shows and Re-Imaging British Agriculture', *Journal of Rural Studies* 20: 319–30.

Holloway, L. (2005) 'Aesthetics, Genetics and Evaluating Animal Bodies: Locating and Displacing Cattle on Show and in Figures', *Environment and Planning D: Society and Space* 23: 883–902.

Holloway, L. and Kneafsey, M. (2000) 'Reading the Space of the Farmers Market: A Case Study from the United Kingdom', *Sociologia Ruralis* 4: 285–99.

Holloway, L. and Kneafsey, M. (2004) 'Producing-Consuming Food: Closeness, Connectedness and Rurality in Four "Alternative" Food Networks', in L. Holloway and M. Kneafsey (eds) *Geographies of Rural Cultures and Societies*, Aldershot: Ashgate.

Holloway, L. Cox, R., Venn, L., Kneafsey, M., Dowler, E. and Tuomainen, H. (2006) 'Managing Sustainable Farmed Landscape through "Alternative" Food Networks: A Case Study from Italy', *Geographical Journal* 172: 219–29.

Holloway, L., Kneafsey, M., Venn, L., Cox, R., Dowler, E. and Tuomainen, H. (2007) 'Possible Food Economies: a Methodological framework for Exploring Food Production-Consumption Relationships', *Sociologia Ruralis* 47: 1–19.

Holm, L. (2001) 'Family Meals', in U. Kjaernes (ed.) *Eating patterns: a day in the lives of Nordic Peoples*, Lysaker: National Institute for Consumer Research, pp. 199–212.

Hughes, A. (2000) 'Retailers, Knowledges and Changing Commodity Networks: The Case of the Cut Flower Trade', *Geoforum* 31: 175–90.

Hunter, D. J. (2005) 'Choosing or Losing Health?' *Journal Epidemiology and Community Health* 59: 1010–13.

Ideal for All, www.idealforall.co.uk.

Ilbery, B. (2005) 'Changing Geographies of Global Food Production', in P. Daniels, M. Bradshaw, D. Shaw and J. Sidaway (eds) *An introduction to Human Geography: Issues for the 21st Century*, 2nd edition, Harlow: Pearson Education Ltd, pp. 168–84.

Ilbery, B. and Kneafsey, M. (1998) 'Product and Place: Promoting Quality Products and Services in the Lagging Rural Regions of the European Union', *European Urban and Regional Studies* 5: 329–41.

Ilbery, B. and Kneafsey, M. (2000) 'Registering Regional Speciality Food and Drink Products in the United Kingdom: The Case of PDOs and PGIs', *Area* 32: 317–25.

Ilbery, B. and Maye, D. (2005) 'Alternative (Shorter) Food Supply Chains and Specialist Livestock Products in the Scottish-English Borders', *Environment and Planning A* 37: 823–44.

Ilbery, B., Kneafsey, M. and Bamford, M. (2000) 'Protecting and Promoting Regional Speciality Food and Drink Products in the UK: The Case of PDOs and PGIs', *Outlook on Agriculture* 29: 31–7.

Ilbery, B., Maye, D., Kneafsey, M., Jenkins, T. and Walkley, C. (2004) 'Forecasting Food Supply Chain Developments in Lagging Rural Regions: Evidence from the UK', *Journal of Rural Studies* 20: 331–44.

Ilbery, B., Morris, C., Buller, H., Maye, D. and Kneafsey, M. (2005) 'Product, Process and Place: An Examination of Marketing and Labelling Schemes in Europe and North America', *European Urban and Regional Studies* 12: 116–32.

Institute of Grocery Distribution (2005a) *The Local and Regional Food Opportunity.* Available online at www.igd.com/consumer.

Institute of Grocery Distribution (2005b) *Connecting Consumers with Farming and Farm Produce: report to the Sustainable Farming and Food Strategy Implementation Group,* available onine at www.igd.com, accessed 25 November 2005.

Institute of Grocery Distribution (2006) *Shopper trends in 2006.* Available online at www.igd.com, accessed 25 July 2007.

Jackson, P., Perez del Aguila, R., Clarke, I., Hallsworth, A., de Kervenoael, R. and Kirkup, M. (2006) 'Retail Restructuring and Consumer Choice 2: Understanding Consumer Choice at the Household Level', *Environment and Planning A* 38: 47–67.

Jackson, P., Russell, P. and Ward, N. (2007) 'The Appropriation of "Alternative" Discourses by "Mainstream" Food Retailers', in D. Maye, L. Holloway and M. Kneafsey (eds) *Alternative Food Geographies: Representation and Practice,* Oxford: Elsevier, pp. 309–30.

Jarvis, H. (2007) 'Home Truths About Care-Less Competitiveness', *International Journal of Urban and Regional Research* 31: 207–14.

Jones, F. (2007) 'The Effects of Taxes and Benefits on Household Income, 2005–6', ONS web publication: http://www.statistics.gov.uk/cci/article.asp?id=1804, posted 17 May 2007.

Kirwan, J. (2004) 'Alternative Strategies in the UK Agro-Food System: Interrogating the Alterity of Farmers Markets', *Sociologia Ruralis* 44: 395–415.

Kjaernes, U. (ed.) (2001) *Eating Patterns: a Day in the Lives of Nordic Peoples*, Lysaker: The National Institute for Consumer Research.

Kloppenberg, J. (1991) 'Social Theory and the De/Reconstruction of Agricultural Science: A New Agenda for Rural Sociology', *Sociologia Ruralis* 32: 519–48.

Kloppenberg, J., Hendrickson, J. and Stenvenson, G. (1996) 'Coming into the Foodshed', *Agriculture and Human Values* 13: 33–42.

Kneafsey, M. and Ilbery, B. (2001) 'Regional Images and the Promotion of Speciality Food and Drink in the West Country', *Geography* 86: 131–40.

Lamine, C. (2005) 'Settling Shared Uncertainties: Local Partnerships Between Producers and Consumers', *Sociologia Ruralis* 45: 324–45.

Lang, T. and Heasman, M. (2004) *Food Wars: The Global Battle for Mouths, Minds and Markets*, London: Earthscan.

Larrabee, M. J. (ed.) (1993) *An Ethic of Care. Feminist and Interdisciplinary Perspectives*, London: Routledge.

Lawrence, F. (2004) *Not on the Label: What Really Goes into the Food on Your Plate*, London: Penguin Group.

Lawson, V. (2007) 'Geographies of Care and Responsibility', Presidential Address, *Annals of the Association of American Geographers* 97: 1–11.

Levitt, E. (1980) *The Psychology of Anxiety*, 2nd edition, Mahwal, NJ: Lawrence Erlbaum Associates.

Leyshon, A. and Lee, R. (2003) 'Introduction: Alternative Economic Geographies', in A. Leyshon, R. Lee and C. Williams (eds) *Alternative Economic Spaces*, London: Sage.

Marsden, T. and Smith, E. (2005) 'Ecological Entrepreneurship: Sustainable Development in Local Communities through Quality Food Production and Local Branding', *Geoforum* 36: 441–51.

Marsden, T., Banks, J. and Bristow, G. (2000a) 'Food Supply Chain Approaches: Exploring Their Role in Rural Development', *Sociologia Ruralis* 40: 424–38.

Marsden, T., Flynn, A. and Harrison, M. (2000b) *Consuming Interests: The Social Provision of Foods*, London: UCL Press.

Marsden, T., Banks, J., Renting, H. and van der Ploeg, J. D. (2001) 'The Road Towards Sustainable Rural Development: Issues of Theory, Policy and Research Practice', *Journal of Environmental Policy and Planning* 3: 75–84.

Marsden, T., Banks, J. and Bristow, G. (2002) 'The Social Management of Rural Nature: Understanding Agrarian Based Rural Development', *Environment and Planning A* 34: 809–25.

Massey, D. (2000) 'Entanglements of Power: Reflections', in J. Sharp, P. Routledge, C. Philo and R. Paddison (eds) *Entanglements of Power: Geographies of Domination/Resistance*, London: Routledge, pp. 279–86.

Massey, D. (2005) *For Space*, London: Sage Publications Ltd.

Maxey, L. (2007) 'From 'Alternative' to 'Sustainable' Food', in D. Maye, L Holloway and M. Kneafsey, (eds) *Alternative Food Geographies: Representation and Place*, London: Elsevier, pp. 55–76.

May, M. (1996) 'Earth Matters: Thinking About the Environment', in S. Dunant and R. Porter (eds) *The Age of Anxiety*, London: Virago, pp. 41–62.

May, R. (1950) *The Meaning of Anxiety*, New York: The Ronald Press Company.

McDowell, L. (2004) 'Work, Workfare, Work/Life Balance and an Ethic of Care', *Progress in Human Geography* 28: 145–63.

Midgley, M (1996) 'Earth Matters: Thinking About the Environment', in S. Dunant and R. Porter (eds) *The Age of Anxiety*, London: Virago, pp. 41–62

Miller, D. (2001) 'The Poverty of Morality', *Journal of Consumer Culture* I: 225–43.

Milligan, C., Atkinson, S., Skinner, M. and Wiles, J. (2007) 'Geographies of Care: A Commentary', *New Zealand Geographer* 63: 135–40.

Millstone, E. and Lang, T. (2006) *The Atlas of Food: Who Eats What, Where and Why*, London: Earthscan.

Mintel, (2003) *Attitudes Towards Buying Local Produce – UK – January 2003*, London: Mintel market research organisation.

Moisio, R., Arnould, E. J. and Price, L. (2004) 'Between Mothers and Markets: Constructing Family Identity through Homemade Food', *Journal of Consumer Culture* 4: 361–84.

Morgan, K., Marsden, T. and Murdoch, J. (2006) *Worlds of Food: Place, Power and Provenance in the Food Chain*, Oxford: University Press.

Morris, C. and Buller, H. (2003) 'The Local Food Sector: A Preliminary Assessment of Its Form and Impact in Gloucestershire', *British Food Journal* 105: 559–66.

Mulgan, G. (1996) 'High Tech and High Angst', in S. Dunant and R. Porter (eds) *The Age of Anxiety*, London: Virago, pp. I–19.

Murcott, A. (1983) '"It's a pleasure to cook for him": Food, Mealtimes and Gender in Some South Wales Households', in E. Gamarnikow, D. H. J. Morgann, J. Purvis and D. Taylorson (eds) *The Public and the Private*, London: Heinemann, pp. 62–77.

Murcott, A. (1997) 'Family meals – a thing of the past?', in P. Caplan (ed.) *Food, health and identity*, London: Routledge, pp. 55–76.

Murcott, A (ed.) (1998a) *The Nation's Diet: The Social Science of Food Choice*, London: Longman.

Murcott, A. (1998b) 'Food Choice, the Social Sciences and the 'Nation's Diet' Research Programme', in A. Murcott (ed.) *The Nation's Diet: The Social Science of Food Choice*, London: Longman, pp. 1–22.

Murdoch, J., Marsden, T. and Banks, J. (2000) 'Quality, Nature and Embeddedness: Some Theoretical Considerations in the Context of the Local Food Sector', *Economic Geography* 76: 107–25.

National Consumer Council (2006) *Short-changed on health?*

National Farmers' Union *Plan, November 2006–2007.*

National Farmers' Retail & Markets Association, www.farma.org, accessed 29 May 2007 and 6 June 2007.

National Farmers' Retail & Markets Association (2006) *Sector Briefing: Farmers' Markets in the UK. Nine Years and Counting*, available online at www.farma.org. uk, accessed 26 July 2007.

National Statistics Online: Neighbourhood Statistics, www.statistics.gov. uk, accessed 19 July 2007.

New Economics Foundation (2001) *Local Food Better for Rural Economy than Supermarket Shopping*, 7 August 2001, available online at www.nef.org.

New Policy Institute (2007) Monitoring Poverty and Social Exclusion 2007. Available at www.poverty.org.uk., accessed 29 January 2008.

NCH, The Children's Charity (2004) *Going Hungry: the Struggle to Eat Healthily*, available online at http://www.nch.org.uk/uploads/documents/going_ hungrymainreport2.pdf.

O'Rourke, K. (2003) '"Long-distance" Trade: Long-Distance Trade between 1750 and 1914', in J. Mokyr (ed) *Oxford Encyclopedia of Economic History*, volume 3, Oxford University Press, pp. 365–70

O'Neill, M. (2005) *Putting Food Access on the Radar: How to Target and Prioritise Communities at Risk*, London: National Consumer Council.

Popke, J. (2006) 'Geography and Ethics: Everyday Mediations through Care and Consumption', *Progress in Human Geography* 30: 504–12.

Popkin, B. M. (1999) 'Urbanization, Lifestyle Changes and the Nutrition Transition', *World Development* 27: 11.

Pretty, J. (2002) *Agri-Culture: Reconnecting People, Land and Nature*, London: Earthscan.

Pretty, J. N., Ball, A. S., Lang, T. and Morison, J. I. L. (2005) 'Farm Costs and Food Miles: An Assessment of the Full Cost of the UK Weekly Food Basket', *Food Policy* 30: 1–19.

Rappaport, E. (2006) 'Packaging China: Foreign Articles and Dangerous Tastes in the Mid-Victorian Tea Party', in F. Trentmann (ed.) *The Making of the Consumer: Knowledge, Power and Identity in the Modern World*, Oxford: Berg, pp. 125–46.

Renting, H., Marsden, T. and Banks, J. (2003) 'Understanding Alternative Food Networks: Exploring the Role of Short Food Supply Chains in Rural Development', *Environment and Planning A* 35: 393–411.

Renton, A. (2007) 'Ripe Target', *The Guardian*, 27 March 2007.

Ricketts Hein, J., Ilbery, B. and Kneafsey, M. (2006) 'Distribution of Local Food Activity in England and Wales: An Index of Food Relocalization', *Regional Studies* 40: 289–301.

Roos, E. and Prättälä, R. (1997) 'Meal Pattern and Nutrient Intake Among Adult Finns', *Appetite* 29: 11–27.

Sage, C. (2003) 'Social Embeddedness and Relations of Regard: Alternative "Good Food" Networks in South-West Ireland', *Journal of Rural Studies* 19: 47–60.

Sassatelli, R. (2004) 'The Political Morality of Food. Discourses, Contestation and Alternative Consumption', in M. Harvey, A. McMeeckin, and A. Warde (eds) *Qualities of Food. Alternative Theoretical and Empirical Approaches*, Manchester: Manchester University Press, pp. 176–91.

Scientific Advisory Committee on Nutrition (2003) *Salt and Health*, Norwich: The Stationery Office.

Scottish Executive: Health Statistics, www.clearingtheair.gov.uk, accessed 19 July 2007.

Scottish Neighbourhood Statistics: Quick Profile Report, www.sns.gov.uk, accessed 19 July 2007.

Seyfang, G. (2006) 'Ecological Citizenship and Sustainable Consumption: Examining Local Organic Food Networks', *Journal of Rural Studies* 22: 383–95.

Seymour, S., Lowe, P., Ward, N. and Clark, J. (1997) 'Environmental "Others" and "Elites": Rural Pollution and Changing Power Relations in the Countryside', in P. Milbourne (ed.) *Revealing Rural Others: Representation, Power and Identity in the British Countryside*, London: Pinter, pp. 57–74.

Shove, E. (2003) *Comfort, Cleanliness and Convenience: The Social Organization of Normality*, Oxford: Berg.

Shove, E. and Southerton, D. (2000) 'Defrosting the Freezer: from Novelty to Convenience – a Narrative of Normalization', *Journal of Material Culture* 5: 301–19.

Silk, J. (2000) 'Caring at a Distance: (Im)partiality, Moral Motivation and the Ethics of Representation', *Ethics, Place and Environment* 3: 303–22.

Simms, A. (2007), *Tescopoly: How One Shop Came Out on Top and Why It Matters*, London: Constable.

Slee, B. and Kirwan, J. (2007) 'Exploring Hybridity in Food Supply Chains', Paper presented to the 105th EAAE Seminar on International Marketing and International Trade of Quality Food Products, Bologna, March 2007.

Slow Food, http://www.slowfood.com/ accessed 25 July 2007.

Smith, D. (1998) 'How Far Should We Care? on the Spatial Scope of Beneficence', *Progress in Human Geography* 22: 15–38.

Smith, D. (2000) *Moral Geographies: Ethics in a World of Difference*, Edinburgh: Edinburgh University Press.

Sobal, J. and Nelson, M. K. (2003) 'Commensal Eating Patterns: A Community Study', *Appetite* 41: 181–90.

Soil Association, www.soilassociation.org.

Soil Association (2005a) *Organic Food: Facts and Figures 2005*, available online at www.soilassociation.org.

Soil Association (2005b) *Toxic Shock: The Link between Pesticides and Cancer* (Information Sheet, 15 November 2005), available online at www. soilassociation.org.

Soil Association (2006) *Organic Market Report.* Summary available online at www.soilassociation.org.

Soil Association (2007) *Organic Works*, policy report, available online at www.soilassociation.org.

Soper, K. (2007a) 'Re-thinking the "Good Life": The Citizenship Dimension of Consumer Dissatisfaction with Consumerism', *Journal of Consumer Culture* 7(2): 205–29.

Soper, K. (2007b) 'What Does Choice Mean When It Comes to Shopping?', *Food Ethics*, magazine of the Food Ethics Council, 2(2): 10–11.

Stake, R. E. (1995) *The Art of Case Study Research,* Thousand Oaks, CA: Sage.

Stassart, P. and Whatmore, S. (2003) 'Metabolising Risk: Food Scares and the Un/Remaking of Belgian Beef', *Environment and Planning A* 35: 449–62.

Stock, P. V. (2007) '"Good Farmers" as reflexive Producers: An Examination of Family Organic Farmers in the US Midwest', *Sociologia Ruralis* 47: 83–102.

Strategy Unit of the Cabinet Office (2008) *Food an Analysis of the Issues*.

Sustain (2001) *Eating Oil – Food in a Changing Climate*, London: Sustain: The alliance for better farming and food.

Sustain (2002) *Local Food: Benefits, Obstacles and Opportunities*, London: Sustain: The alliance for better farming and food.

Tansey, G. and Worsley, T. (1995) *The Food System: A Guide*, London: Earthscan.

The Highland Council: Ward Statistics, www.highland.gov.uk, accessed 19 July 2007.

Trauger, A. (2007) 'Connecting Social Justice to Sustainabilty: Discourse and Practice in Sustainable Agriculture in Pennsylvania', in D. Maye, L. Holloway and M. Kneafsey (eds) *Alternative Food Geographies: Representation and Practice,* Oxford: Elsevier, pp. 39–54.

Trentmann, F. (2006) 'The Modern Genealogy of the Consumer: Meanings, Knowledge and Identities', in J. Brewer and F. Trentmann (eds) *Consumer Cultures, Global Perspectives: Historical Trajectories, Transnational Exchanges,* Oxford: Berg, pp. 19–69.

Trentmann, F. (2007) 'Before "Fair Trade": Empire, Free Trade and the Moral Economies of Food in the Modern World', *Environment and Planning D: Society and Space* 25: 1079–102.

Tronto, J. C. (1993) *Moral Boundaries: A Political Argument for an Ethic of Care,* London: Routledge.

Tronto, J. C. (2006) 'Vicious Circles of Privatized Caring', in M. Hamington and D. Miller (eds) *Socializing Care: Feminist Ethics and Public Issues,* Lanham, MD: Rowman and Littlefield, pp. 3–26.

Valentine, G. (1999) 'Eating in: Home, consumption and identity,' *Sociological Review* 47: 491–524.

Venn, L., Kneafsey, M., Holloway, L., Cox, R., Dowler, E. and Tuomainen, H. (2006) 'Researching European "Alternative" Food Networks: Some Methodological Considerations', *Area* 38: 248–58.

Waterland Organics, www.waterlandorganics.co.uk, accessed 14 June 2007.

Watts, D, Ilbery, B. and Maye, D. (2005) 'Making Reconnections in Agro-Food Geography: Alternative Systems of Food Provision', *Progress in Human Geography* 29: 22–40.

Weatherell, C., Tregear, A. and Allinson, J. (2003) 'In Search of Concerned Consumer: UK Public Perceptions of Food, Farming and Buying Local', *Journal of Rural Studies* 19: 233–44.

Wells, B. and Gradwell, S. (2001) 'Gender and Resource Management: Community Supported Agriculture As Caring-Practice', *Agriculture and Human Values* 18: 107–19.

Welsh Assembly Government: Quality of Food Strategy, Task and Finish Report Group. Undated, available at http://new.wales.gov.uk/dphhp/publication/improvement/food/quality/full-report-e.pdf?lang=en, accessed 27 January 2008.

Westlake, T. (1993) 'The Disadvantaged Consumer: Problems and Policies', in R. D. F. Bromley and C. J. Thomas (eds) *Retail Change: Contemporary Issues,* London: UCL Press, pp. 172–91.

Whatmore, S. (1997) 'Dissecting the Autonomous Self: Hybrid Carto-graphies for a Relational Ethics', *Environment and Planning D: Society and Space* 15: 37–53.

Winter, M. (2003a) 'Embeddedness, the New Food Economy and Defensive Localism', *Journal of Rural Studies* 19: 23–32.

Winter, M. (2003b) 'Responding to the Crisis: The Policy Impact of the Foot-and-Mouth Epidemic', *The Political Quarterly* 74: 47–56.

Wiskerke, J. S. C. (2003) 'On Promising Niches and Constraining Socio-Technical Regimes: The Case of Dutch Wheat and Bread', *Environment and Planning A* 35: 429–48.

Working Group on Local Food (2003) *Local Food – A Snapshot of the Sector Report of the Working Group on Local Food*, Cheltenham: FSA.

World Health Organization/Food and Agriculture Organization (2003) *Diet, Nutrition and the Prevention of Chronic Diseases: Report of a Joint WHO/FAO Expert Consultation*, WHO Technical Report Series: Technical Report 916, Geneva: WHO/Rome: FAO.

World Health Organization: Recommendations for preventing cancer, available online at http://www.who.int/en/, accessed 25 July 2007.

Wrigley, N. (1998) 'How British Retailers Have Shaped Food Choice', in A. Murcott (ed.) *The Nation's Diet: The Social Science of Food Choice*, London: Longman, pp. 112–28.

Wrigley, N. (2002) '"Food Deserts" in British Cities: Policy Context and Research Priorities', *Urban Studies* 39: 2029–40.

Index